Praise for *Friendgevity*:

"I was blown away by this book. Dr. Jan Yager's *Friendgevity* is an astoundingly provocative read on a topic that remains so important to all of us. This book is filled with information and research in a format that is relatable and resonating. She covers it all, including research and advice on the latest impact social media and technology have on friendship today. This is a book that provokes self-awareness, and at the same time provides a usable road map to understanding the questions, fears and celebration we experience around the friendships we value so much in our lives. Bravo Dr. Yager and thank you."

—Liz Pryor, author, What Did I Do Wrong?

"Great book! In a very practical way, Dr. Jan Yager explores the benefits of having friends as well as how we can improve our relationships and the problems we encounter. Love the mini- assessments, including how well do you know your best friend. Wish I had read Chapter 8, "14 Tough Friendship Situations and How to Deal with Each One," so I would have known what to do when my best friend of years 'ghosted' me. It would have helped to know that others experience the same thing. "

—Linda Swindling, JD, CSP, author
of *Ask Outrageously*

"Dr. Jan Yager's latest book on friendship, *Friendgevity*, is a tour de force! She has packed this fast read with solid up-to-date research, tons of practical examples, and lots of easy-to-follow advice on how even one good friend can make you a happier and healthier person. When you read this book, you'll have all the building blocks you need to initiate, nurture, and maintain the friendships that can last you a lifetime. "

—Don Gabor, author of *How to Start a Conversation and Make Friends*

Selected Books by Jan Yager, Ph.D.

Nonfiction
Friendshifts
When Friendship Hurts
365 Daily Affirmations for Friendship
365 Daily Affirmations for Healthy and Nurturing Relationships
Who's That Sitting at My Desk? Workship, Friendship, or Foe?
Productive Relationships
Business Protocol
Grow Global
Effective Business and Nonfiction Writing
Help Yourself Now
How to Self-Publish Your Book
Foreign Rights and Wrongs
How to Finish Everything You Start
Work Less, Do More: The 7-Day Productivity Makeover
Creative Time Management for the New Millennium
365 Daily Affirmations for Time Management
The Fast Track Guide to Speaking in Public
21 Ways to Financial Freedom
The Fast Track Guide to Losing Weight and Keeping It Off
365 Daily Affirmations for Happiness
125 Ways to Meet the Love of Your Life
Road Signs on Life's Journey
Victims

Fiction
On the Run
The Pretty One
Untimely Death (with Fred Yager)
Just Your Everyday People (with Fred Yager)

Children's Books (Illustrated by Mitzi Lyman)
The Cantaloupe Cat
The Quiet Dog
The Reading Rabbit

Journals
Friendship Thoughts, Famous Quotes, and a Journal
So, What's Your Favorite Color?
Birthday Tracker and a Journal

Friendgevity

Making and Keeping the Friends Who Enhance and Even Extend Your Life

Jan Yager, Ph.D.

Hannacroix Creek Books, Inc.
Stamford, Connecticut

Published by:
Hannacroix Creek Books, Inc.
1127 High Ridge Road, #110
Stamford, CT 06905 USA
https://www.hannacroixcreekbooks.com
e-mail: hannacroix@aol.com

This publication contains the opinions and ideas of its author and is designed to provide useful advice regarding the subject matter covered. It is sold with the understanding that the author and publisher are not engaged in rendering legal, psychological, or professional services in this publication. Laws vary from state to state, country to country, and if the reader requires expert assistance or legal advice, a competent professional should be consulted.

In some cases, to preserve the identity of those interviewed who requested anonymity, a fictitious name is used.

The complete citations for books or articles mentioned in the body of this book appear in the Bibliography.

The author and publisher specifically disclaim any responsibility for any liability, loss or risk, personal or otherwise, which is incurred as a consequence, directly or indirectly, of the use and application of any of the contents of this book.

Library of Congress Control Number: 2019905057

ISBN: 978-1-938998-11-9 (trade paperback)

**For my loving and devoted family
and friends**

Contents

Introduction

"... I was hospitalized at 2 a.m. after a diagnosis of diabetes. The next morning, at around 10 a.m., a friend [who had seen] my Instagram picture, stood next to my bed with a balloon."

—24-year-old Dutch woman

I coined the word *friendgevity* to emphasize what most of us know instinctively, what the scientific research has been telling us since as far back as 1979, and what more recent research is reconfirming. Namely, that even one close friend can extend your life. *Friendgevity* is meant to be a wake-up call that who our friends are, and even whether we have any friends, can determine how long we live and even the recovery rates for a heart attack or cancer, among other diseases. But it also sounds the alarm that the wrong friends can wreak havoc on your life, as you will see in Chapter 6, "Fatal Friends and Frenemies."

It is my goal that *Friendgevity* will help you to make better choices about who your friends are as well as to motivate you to put more time and effort into the positive friendships you already have. Because your life just might depend on it.

One of my missions since I started writing about friendship more than four decades ago, including when it was the focus of my sociology dissertation, was to get the word out that friendship should be more than an "extra" relationship that you get around to after you have dealt with all the other more compelling relationships and demands in your life. I have been spreading the word that friends can enhance your life and even extend it and, on the other hand, that choosing the wrong friends can cause conflicts that can make you emotionally ill, physically sick, or even kill you. More recent research reinforces just how critical these ideas are, as we are learning that friends can also slow down, or even halt, the onset of dementia.

Sometimes we take our friendships for granted until there is a dramatic change in our everyday lives. Later in this chapter you will read a discussion about The Impact of the Pandemic on Friendship. Prior to that major event, I had a *friendshifts* experience when, on December

12th, 2012, my husband Fred and I arrived in Nashville, excited about starting what we thought would be our new life in that unique Southern metropolis known as Music City. I happen to remember the exact date because it was also the day of the tragic Sandy Hook Elementary School massacre which rocked the entire nation and the world, although not as much in Tennessee as in my adopted state of Connecticut, where Newtown is located.

Fred and I had lived in Connecticut for the previous 24 years, having relocated from Manhattan around 50 minutes away. We raised our two sons there, and now that they were grown, we were free to relocate for a new career opportunity, which is what we did.

During the week, Fred went to his job while I worked from home. Despite having freelance work to occupy me, I soon started feeling isolated, so I tried to make new friends. It had been 24 years since I had to create a network from scratch, and I had forgotten just how hard it could be to find kindred spirits. I did connect with an executive administrator at Fred's job, Elizabeth Loving, and the three of us would go out to dinner or dancing at one of the popular downtown country music spots. But Elizabeth soon left for a new position in Florida, so I was back to square one.

After a few months, I befriended Linda, the wife of another executive at Fred's new job. She was commuting from Florida to Nashville, so we only got together every couple of months for lunch. But I cherished those get-togethers. Then, after a year and a half, Fred's job ended and we moved back to our home in Connecticut. I was relieved to return to the friends that I had left behind in my hometown and in relatively nearby New Jersey and New York City. The powerful depression and deep sadness I had been feeling in Nashville cleared up almost instantly when I could interact on a regular basis with my old friends. That Nashville experience was a firsthand reminder of the power of friendship and how we can sometimes underemphasize its value until it is missing.

Like so many that I interviewed for *Friendgevity*, I had found that keeping in touch with old friends via social media was not enough for me. I needed to be able to get together with a friend in person. In fact, it seemed that the more time I spent on Facebook reading about everyone else's exciting trips or joyful interactions, the more depressed I began to feel. It seems I am not alone in this reaction. As reported in *Science Daily*, researchers at the University of Pittsburgh Schools of the Health Sciences, funded by the National Institutes of Health, found that for certain populations, such as 19- to 32-year-olds, the more time someone spent on social media, the greater the likelihood—to the tune of 1.7 times—that they would be depressed.

Although I have written three previous books on friendship that have been translated into more than 30 languages—a scholarly, selectively, annotated bibliography, *Friendship,* and the popular books *Friendshifts* and *When Friendship Hurts*—I knew I had to write this new book about the impact social media is having on our friendships as well as to issue a fresh wake-up call about the pluses and potential downsides of friendship. Yes, there can sometimes be a downside although, over the years, I have found that few want to publicly admit to that. This became so clear to me when I was doing the author tour for *When Friendship Hurts.*

Occasionally I was asked if I could bring someone with a problematical friendship on the show with me to share his or her personal experiences. Even those I interviewed who had shared with me about a harmful or disappointing friendship suddenly declared that they had *only* positive friendships. Yes, there seemed to be a stigma to openly admitting that a friendship had conflicts or even that a friendship had actually failed, because practically everyone wants to believe in just having a perfect long-lasting BFF (best friends forever).

I have been working on *Friendgevity* for more than a decade, looking at friendship in light of the more recent scientific research on friendship and longevity as well as the positive and negative impact of social media on our friendships. Hence, *Friendgevity: Making and Keeping the Friends Who Enhance and Even Extend Your Life,* is the result of all that primary and secondary research as well as my own soul searching about my own friends and our friendships.

For *Friendgevity,* I conducted six separate 10-question surveys through Survey Monkey Audience that were answered by 873 men and women from throughout the U.S., Australia, and the United Kingdom. I also did a more extensive snowball sample whereby I asked men and women that I knew to fill out my confidential survey and invited them to forward the link to their network of acquaintances, friends, or relatives.

In that way, the snowball survey, which began with 50 questions but ended up asking 100, was completed by 178 men and women from throughout the U.S. and 18 countries around the world, including the Netherlands, the U.K., Japan, South Africa, Australia, New Zealand, Belgium, Sweden, France, Japan, Germany, Russia, India, Spain, Austria, Ireland, and Canada. In addition to the 1,051 who were surveyed—582 women and 452 men with 17 skipping the question about gender—I interviewed 50 men and women about their friendships including several pairs of friends. (See Appendix V for a detailed list of the seven surveys.)

Friendgevity also benefited from the 1,000+ previous friendship surveys and 250+ interviews dating back decades, including the original research for my previous friendship books, *Friendshifts* and *When Friendship Hurts,* my related books on work relationships, such as *Productive Relationships, Who's That Sitting at My Desk? Workship, Friendship, or Foe?, Grow Global,* and *Business Protocol,* my other relationship books, including *Single in America, 365 Daily Affirmations for Healthy and Nurturing Relationships,* and *365 Daily Affirmations for Friendship,* and my 1983 sociology dissertation, "Friendship Patterns Among Young Urban Single Women" [City University of New York (CUNY) Graduate Center].

In addition to exploring friendship and longevity, and the impact of social media on friendship, there was another reason I felt compelled to research and write *Friendgevity.* Although I certainly dealt with problematical friendships in both *Friendshifts* and *When Friendship Hurts,* the anecdotes and examples that I shared, especially in *When Friendship Hurts,* were mostly of the relatively familiar emotional betrayal, broken promises, or drifting- apart types.

But over the years I have learned that, unfortunately, horrific friendship situations do happen.

They are antithetical to *friendgevity,* in which friendship increases one's life expectancy, since they can cause a friend's death. This type of situation became all too real for me in January 2017 when my husband's 25-year-old great-nephew, Billy "Webb" Yager, was tragically killed when Webb's friend crashed his car into a tree. Webb, a passenger in the back seat, was killed instantly. What had started out as a fun evening for three friends ended with one friend dead, another sustaining non-life-threatening injuries, and the driver eventually being sentenced to 6 to 12 years in prison for second degree vehicular manslaughter because he was driving under the influence and speeding, among other unlawful acts.

Since I returned to college teaching in 2014, I have been teaching victimology, the scientific study of victims, especially victims of crime, as well as criminology and penology, the study of criminal behavior and of prisons, introductory sociology, race and ethnicity, and international victimology, at John Jay College of Criminal Justice, one of the senior colleges at the City University of New York (CUNY). In addition to my extended family's personal tragedy described above, I have researched and learned about numerous other negative friendship-related situations. Like that of Julio Briones, a New Jersey man who, when he was 19, went to the movies with his friend. His friend's friends soon showed up, and Julio found himself swept up in their criminal activities.

The rest, as they say, is history—an unfortunate history that ended up landing Julio in prison with an initial sentence of 39 years. He was eventually able to get his sentence for robbery, carjacking, and weapons possession reduced to 12 years. He was released after serving 10 years and has been a model citizen, businessman, husband, and father ever since.

For me, those are only two of the dramatic situations that are cautionary tales about just how pivotal friendship choices are. You will read about many others in *Friendgevity*.

Some of you may be familiar with the research that is telling us how much friendship really matters. For others, this information may be eye-opening. Friendship is the subject of interdisciplinary research, with studies being carried out in the fields of medicine, neuroscience, neurology, psychology, anthropology, and sociology. Philosophers as far back as Plato and Aristotle have waxed eloquently on this relationship as, later on, did essayists Michel de Montaigne and Ralph Waldo Emerson. More recently, friendship has become the focus of cutting-edge studies in laboratories and universities around the world.

I salute the epic work of research psychologists Julianne Holt-Lunstad, Timothy B. Smith, and J. Bradley Layton. In their study, "Social Relationships and Mortality Risk: A Meta-Analytic Review," published in 2010 in *PLOS Medicine,* they share the results of their analysis of 148 studies "that provided quantitative data regarding individuals' mortality as a function of social relationships" representing 308,849 male and female participants who were followed, on average, for 7.5 years. Their conclusion: there was a "50% increased likelihood of survival for participants with stronger social relationships."

In their conclusion to the study, the authors remind us of the groundbreaking 1945 study by Dr. René Spitz, published in the *Psychoanalytic Study of the Child*, which helped to explain that the high rate of infant mortality in orphanages was due to lack of adequate human contact. Dr. Spitz's association between those two factors, which we take for granted now but was revolutionary at the time, transformed the way orphanages cared for infants. With the implementation of greater physical and emotional contact between caregivers and infants, the infant mortality rate dramatically declined.

Holt-Lunstad, Smith, and Layton assert that the indisputable conclusion from their voluminous research should dramatically increase public awareness of the importance of social relationships to longevity.

They suggest adding inadequate social relationships to the list of risk factors for mortality that doctors use to caution their patients. As they state in their article's conclusion, "The magnitude of this effect is comparable with quitting smoking and it exceeds many well-known risk factors for mortality (e.g. obesity, physical inactivity)."

There needs to be heightened public awareness about the dramatic negative impact that inadequate social relationships have on longevity and, conversely, the indisputable positive effect that having even one positive friendship can have. As people age, and the chance that they will be alone—due to the death of a spouse, divorce, or even the death or relocation of friends or family members—increases, the need for a strong social network, and knowing how to create one if other long-standing relationships have ended or are unreachable, is even more important.

Most everyone knows that obesity, smoking, and inactivity can kill you. But so can loneliness, which, fortunately, is completely preventable or reversible.

Facebook Makes Friend a Verb

A secondary theme to this new book is the impact of social media on friendship. It is hard to believe Facebook has only been with us for 14 years. Launched in 2004 by Mark Zuckerberg and his Harvard College roommates and classmates to college students, becoming available to the public in 2006, the site's impact was to turn the noun *friend* into a verb, "to friend."

As for the concept of friendship, which in my research I had always divided into three categories—best, close, and casual—*friend* now became a generic term for anyone that you connected with through Facebook. There had been other social media sites that helped friends, family, and even coworkers to connect, or even new friendships to form, like Myspace, founded in 2003. But it is Facebook that has made a difference in a big way, to the tune of more than two billion subscribers worldwide today. On Facebook, it's not unusual for users to have hundreds or even thousands of "Facebook friends," which I call FBFs.

A key question I explore in this book is whether Facebook or any other social media site like Instagram, Snapchat, Twitter, Pinterest, or LinkedIn have actually changed the original concept of friendship in a positive, negative, or any meaningful way. For example, if someone has 500 friends on Facebook, why might he or she still be lonely? Is sitting in front of the computer screen connecting to Facebook friends (FBFs) near and far as fulfilling as spending time in person with people you care about and who care about you? As noted before, some studies show that spending an inordinately large amount of time on Facebook can actually contribute to feelings of loneliness or depression.

The Impact of the Pandemic on Friendship

*Original art by Andres Alvez showing friends
videoconferencing because of pandemic*

Starting in March 2020 in the United States, and even earlier in other parts of the world especially China and Europe, a new infectious disease called COVID-19 impacted everyday life causing businesses to shut down, families to "shelter in place," and hundreds of thousands of deaths. As unemployment rates rose, and businesses closed, downsized, or changed how they did their business, largely moving to online, the pandemic influenced friendship as well.

For some, the pandemic, and its aftermath, caused a close friendship to dissolve to the point of almost ending. For others, the way they went about their friendship, especially when it was impossible to visit in person, dramatically changed. For many, instead of the pandemic ending friendships, it was the catalyst to forming new ones. As indicated in the original art work by Andres Alvez at the beginning of this discussion, the way that friends communicated changed as they resorted to videoconferencing via such services as Zoom, on their computers or their mobile phones.

Based on interviews related to the pandemic, here are some real life stories that reflect pandemic-related friendship phenomena. Following those stories, I will share some additional insights I have about friendship and the pandemic that you might find useful.

The Pandemic Highlighted Disparities In Friends

Malika Bowling considers herself an incredibly lucky woman, and rightly so. She is happily married, her husband's doing well enough in his job that she is able to do all the activities she loves to do including blogging (Roamilicious), traveling (pandemic permitting!), and working as a marketing consultant. She works hard but she does not have to worry about money, especially since she and her husband have saved enough that they could deal with a rainy day or two.

Unfortunately, the situation is quite different for Malika's formerly close friend Lola (not her real name). They met six years ago after Lola moved from a country in Central America to be with her then husband. Lola became part of Malika's circle of friends in Atlanta. They had lots of fun together as they went together to wine tasting parties, going on hikes, having tea, and taking yoga classes.

Fast forward a few years, Lola divorced her husband and her managerial job has become uncertain. She is living paycheck to pay check as she faces having to lay off her staff and her job might even end unexpectedly.

The way the pandemic unraveled their friendship was that Lola called Malika a month ago and they did not have a good connection. It seems that Lola was sharing about her economic plight and her despair but Malika did not get to hear much of what she was saying. What was supposed to be a call from a caring friend (Malika) to her upset friend (Lola) turned into an interaction that unraveled their friendship, at least for now. As Malika explains, "A simple check-in conversation resulted in a nasty text exchange as she felt I wasn't sympathetic to her plight." Malika adds, "On the defensive, my savings have come from sacrifice and a lack of lusting after shiny new toys."

Recently Lola sent Malika a message through Facebook asking her how she was doing. Malika replied that she was okay but she did not pursue the friendship further.

Malika has advice from this experience, even if she is not yet able to take it herself. She says, "If you have issues with somebody, let them know. If you feel like it's salvageable, talk it out."

Developing A Friendship Routine

To deal with the pandemic, especially for those who were single and living alone, developing friendship routines, particularly during the "sheltering in place" or lockdown days, weeks, and even months, became a necessity. Whether it was calling a friend on a particular day and time, or setting up a movie night or a game night with friends throughout the U.S. and even internationally, what used to be more casual became a routine for many. Based on my interviews related to friendship and the pandemic, as well as my observations, a return to the telephone as the preferred way of communicate, in addition to social media posts, texts, or e-mails, plus videoconferencing via Zoom, or using FaceTime on the iPhone, had to replace in-person meetings. Friends with romantic partners or spouses as well as family members living at home reported regularly checking in on their single friends in a much more concerted way than they might have been doing prior to the pandemic. Rather than seeing those new routines as a burden, the more regular communication with friends, even those nearby with whom in-person get together were temporarily put on hold, were a welcome antidote to the reported isolation from working from home, if at all, and the restrictions on in-person get togethers.

Finding A New Family of Friends Because of the Pandemic

Dana Humphrey is a 37-year-old life coach and "death doula," which is someone who helps with the process of dying, much like a midwife assists with a birth. She lives in Rockaway Beach, Queens, New York. On March

14th, 2020, she flew to Guatemala to attend a leadership retreat, the day before they closed the border to Americans and Canadians because of the pandemic. She went to the retreat only to find that it was not going to take place. She, and 11 other attendees from around the world—from other parts of the U.S., the UK, Belgium, Spain, Australia, Israel, and Mexico—all found themselves stuck in Guatemala unable to return home because of the pandemic.

They decided to all go to a small town of 500 where they rented a house together. For the next three months, until travel opened up again, they lived, ate, worked, and developed friendships together.

Not only did Dana, who grew up in California, outside of San Francisco, develop new friends during her Guatemala pandemic adventure, but it caused her to re-evaluate her old ones. "There's a kind of before and after. I think of the motto, 'Make new friends, but keep the old,' and some of the old ones, it's okay to let them go. She continues, "I'm actually really am happy spending time by myself. She's not searching for more friends right now in the way she might have been before. "I have this beautiful net of friends that I know really have my back. I'm not in need of other friendships."

Only a few months before the pandemic and sheltering in place rules were put in place, James Ryan relocated from Manhattan to Albany with just his dog to start a new business, Time For Homes, a national non-profit concerned with eliminating chronic homelessness. "I was able to make a few local friends before the lockdown," James explains. He is now living with a partner he met at a board game café before the pandemic. They decided to quarantine together. But their only contact with friends since the lockdown is having "socially distant dinners with a neighbor in our building."

Friendship Rules That the Pandemic Changed or Emphasized

There are some who find themselves eager to give their friends advice whenever they have a problem that needs to be solved. Whether it's by phone, text, e-mail, or videoconferencing, these friends—and you may be one of them—find it easier to give opinions than to just listen.

Stop yourself! More than ever, your friends, especially those who are living alone and not even going out of their apartments or homes for work, need a sounding board. They need someone to listen, and listen attentively, and with compassion and empathy. They do not need instant suggestions which may not even be the right ones.

Is it possible to get a little burnt out on empathy during the pandemic when every day the death toll may be rising and news about an effective vaccine is still in the future? Empathy, ideally, should know no limits. If your friend needs your empathy and you are feeling burned out by their demands, give them what they need and want, and then get yourself replenished by someone else, whether that is another friend, a romantic partner, or a family member. It is like an empathy tree with the strong trunk of the tree, you, being the one who gives out empathy and all the branches from that tree leading to those who need the empathy. You could be the trunk but also be one of the branches simultaneously.

For some, the consistency of setting up a routine of talking at a specific time every day during the pandemic is comfortable for them. For others, that would be too much of a commitment or too confining a strategy.

What has been working for me is to call my friends, especially my single ones, when I'm sitting in the parking lot while my husband is in a store purchasing essentials for us. I know how fortunate I am to have my husband's company since we are both able to work from home for now. The ways that single people avoid isolation, like going out to events or parties, the pandemic made impossible for months. So, staying in touch by phone, text, or videoconferencing became for so many their lifeline.

One of my single friends, who lost her husband to COVID-19, ventured into New York City to have lunch with a friend as they dined outside and were social distancing. But another widowed friend has been too worried about getting COVID due to her underlying asthma to venture out of her house since March, except to walk her dog. She stays in touch through videoconferencing and we talk regularly on the phone.

For some, however, like Nance L. Schick, the pandemic has not altered the way she communicates with her best friend. They have lived far apart for many of the nearly forty years they have been friends. Nance is in Manhattan, and her best friend is currently in California. They initially met when they were eleven and both living in Kentucky. Wendi moves many times after they met, but they have always kept in touch with letters, phone calls, and visits. When they were in in the same city in their teens and 20s, they were together several times per week and even lived together briefly. Yet they have often talked about the fact that even if they lived closer to each other now, they would probably get together in person infrequently. Nance, who is 51, explains: "We laugh about it now because there's no one in our lives that we spend that kind of time with.

We're both professional women and we are very busy and independent." Regular phone calls keep them connected, through the pandemic and in non-pandemic times.

For long distance friendships, like Nance and her best friend Wendi, staying in touch by phone, texts, e-mails, and even posts on Facebook had already become second nature to them. The pandemic has just been a continuation of those modes of communication. Since the pandemic, if one or both friends found themselves alone and isolated, there might have been an increase in the frequency of the communications. In-person visits had always been only on an occasional basis for so many friends. In those cases, the pandemic did not dramatically change a particular friendship or even a view of friendship.

But for others, the pandemic of 2020 forced them to sort out their friendships and even their family networks and relationships. Who is there for you? Who can weather the storms of the kind of disparity in circumstances that led Malika and Lola to wind down their friendship? Who can even find that despite the unexpected demands on time, relationships, work, and routines caused by the pandemic that it might even be possible to make new friends like Dana Humphrey's new family of 12 from her forced three month sojourn in Guatemala or James Ryan's new friends and partner that he met in his new hometown of Albany, New York.

For some, the pandemic forced taking a definite stand about what their limitations were in certain friendships. For example, Ed Rule, a career management consultant who is "single with grandkids" is working from home in Melbourne, Australia. He found that the pandemic compelled him to take a break for a few days from certain friends that he had developed through work who went on and on for more than an hour on the telephone about their problems. "The controlled distancing I spoke of is at the professional friendship level."

Mary Potter Kenyon, co-author of *Mary & Me: A Lasting Link Through Ink*, continues to write letters to her friend Mary, but they "resorted to Zoom meetings or the phone a few times." Mary Potter Kenyon, a widow who lives with her 17-year-old daughter, has found that the pandemic has heightened her sense of aloneness. In August 2020, five months after she began working from home on March 18, Mary shared about what she misses most: "I sure miss the hugs and personal conversations with friends," she explains. A sentiment that so many throughout the world would share!

In Chapter 1, "Friendship, Dementia, and Longevity: Research

Findings and Reflections," one of the core themes of this book is addressed, namely, the way that friendship research is confirming for us that friendship can affect our longevity and even our ability to withstand pain.

My best friend

My second-best friend

Some of my close friends

My absolute-worst-best friend

Chapter 1
Friendship, Longevity, and Dementia

"By differentiating between friends, children, and other relatives, we were able to show that it is friends, rather than children or relatives, which confer most benefit to survival in later life."

—Australian study by Lynne C. Giles, et al., reported in the *Journal of Epidemiology and Community Health*

Research Findings and Reflections

If you want to live longer, have at least one close friend. I would also add, as you will see in this chapter, ensure it is a *positive* friend, not someone with whom you have a lot of conflict.

Friends Extend Your Life

To put it in simple terms, having friends = *friendgevity*.

Since the late 1970s, because of the results of the Lisa Berkman and Leonard Syme groundbreaking study of 6,928 randomly- selected adults in Alameda County, California, published in the February 1979 issue of the *American Journal of Epidemiology*, we have known that friendship, or having a marriage partner, can extend your life. Conversely, lacking friendship or other social or community ties, may mean you could die sooner. What made the results of the Berkman/Syme 1979 study so pivotal was that it highlighted a factor in longevity that everyone could do something about—making sure you were either married or had at least one close friend. The study showed that regardless of such personal habits as smoking, drinking, obesity, inactivity, income level, or even the use of preventive health services, having one close friend or a significant other prolonged your life.

But the groundbreaking Berkman/Syme study combined significant others/married partners with friends. The longitudinal study conducted by Lynne C. Giles, et al., "Effect of Social Networks on 10 Year Survival in

Very Old Australians: The Australian Longitudinal Study of Aging," was especially important because it isolated friends from spouses or children, as few studies before had done. Instead of looking at more generic "social ties" or "social relationships," it looked specifically at friendship's impact on longevity. As noted in the introductory quote to this chapter, *"it is friends, rather than children or relatives,* which confer most benefit to survival in later life" (emphasis mine).

Since the benefit of friendship to longevity is one of the central themes of this book, here is a sample of some of the key interdisciplinary global research studies, drawn from epidemiology, sociology, psychology, neuroscience, and medicine. It begins with the 1979 Berkman and Syme study that is credited with stimulating modern-day research in the area of friends, health, and longevity. (You will find full citations in the Bibliography at the back of *Friendgevity*.)

> 1979 – Lisa F. Berkman and Leonard S. Syme, "Social Network, Host Resistance and Mortality: A Nine-Year Follow-Up Study of Alameda County Residents." Published in the *American Journal of Epidemiology*.
> 1987 – James S. House, "Social Support and Social Structure." Published in the *Sociological Forum*.
> 2004 – Shelden Cohen, "Social Relationships and Health." Published in the *American Psychologist* and Lynne C. Giles, et al., "Effect of Social Networks on 10 Year Survival in Very Old Australians: The Australian Longitudinal Study of Aging." Published in the *Journal of Epidemiology and Community Health*.2
> 2005 – Edith Guilley, et al, "Association Between Social Relationships and Survival of Swiss Octogenarians: A Five-Year Prospective, Population-Based Study." Published in *Aging Clinical and Experimental Research*.
> 2010 – Julianne Holt-Lundstad, Timothy B. Smith, and J. Bradley Layton, "Social Relationships and Mortality Risk: A Meta-Analytic Review." Published in *PLOS Medicine*.
> 2012 – Carla M. Perissinotto, et al., "Loneliness in Older Persons: A Predictor of Functional Decline and Death." Published in the *Archives of Internal Medicine*.
> 2016 – Claire Yang, et. al., "Social Relationships and Physiological Determinants of Longevity Across the Human Life Span." Published in the *Proceedings of the National Academy of Sciences of the United States of America*.

Do not Argue Constantly with Your Friends If You Want to Live Longer

The key to life extension when it comes to friends goes a little deeper than just having them. According to a study of 10,000 men and women between the ages of 36 and 52 conducted by researchers at the University of Copenhagen in Denmark, an occasional argument with a friend is okay. But if you argue all the time, it could actually shorten your life.

Constant arguing with a partner or children was also a heightened risk factor for increasing the chances of dying. As Bahar Gholipour reports in her article about the study in Live Science, "People who had reported frequent conflict with someone in their social circle had two to three times higher risk of dying during the study period" when compared to those who did not get into such continual conflicts.

Friendship Can Help Reduce the 10th Leading Cause of Death: Suicide

According to the nonprofit resource Suicide Awareness Voices of Education (SAVE), in 2014 in the United States there were 42,773 suicide deaths. Add to that the more than 38,000 deaths from automobile accidents and the more than 12,000 homicides (with an estimated 45% caused by friends or acquaintances), and you can see the staggering number of potentially preventable deaths.

In many of those situations, especially suicide, there is often a connection to friendship, including how having one or more positive friends might have reduced depression, a leading cause of suicide.

I am not saying that social media is a cause of suicide, or that it is directly linked to suicide. But if suicide is related to depression, and the evidence is now telling us that spending too much time on social media can increase depression, then perhaps you and those you care about who are experiencing depression might want to reduce the amount of time you spend on social media and increase the time you spend with people face to face or even on the phone, as well as getting professional help, if needed.

Mai-Ly N. Steers and her colleagues at the University of Houston researched the connection between Facebook and depression in their journal article, "Seeing Everyone Else's Highlight Reels: How Facebook Usage Is Linked to Depressive Symptoms." They posited that it was the tendency to make "social comparisons"—seeing other people as happier, living more fun lives, having better relationships—that exacerbated symptoms in those already depressed or who were heading in that direction.

Friendship Lowers the Risk of Dementia

There is even more news about friendship and its impact on health and especially aging- related health issues, such as dementia, that we should take to heart. Namely, research in the last decade has discovered that friendship lowers your risk of getting dementia, one of the most feared physical and mental changes related to aging. Previously we thought dementia was pretty much a question of heredity with some physical conditions, like obesity, being added risk factors. But it was supposedly something that you just had to accept as a condition you might get. Who would have thought that having a friend could lower your risk of getting dementia, a disease that not only robs the mind of some or all of its memories, but a disease that can eventually kill you?

The idea that having at least one friend could lower your risk of getting dementia seems like an oversimplification of a very complex area of medicine and neuroscience. Yet this research- supported concept empowers all of us because now there is something we can do to lower our risk of dementia.

A study by Bryan D. James, Robert S. Wilson, Lisa L. Barnes, and David A. Bennett, as reported in 2011 in the *Journal of the International Neurological Society (JINS)*, followed 1,138 men and women with a mean age of 79.6 for up to 12 years. to explore the relationship between social activity with cognitive decline. Their findings are quite startling. Just a one-point increase in someone's social activity score led to a 47% decrease in the rate of decline of cognitive functioning. If someone was deemed "frequently socially active," their rate of decline was reduced by an astounding 70%. The scientists conclude: "These results confirm that more socially active older adults experience less cognitive decline in old age."

But it is also important to note that in a study by Jan Holwerda Tjalling, et al, at the Amsterdam Study of the Elderly (AMSTEL), as reported by *Science Daily* on December 10, 2011 from the *British Medical Journal*, it was "feeling lonely" that was associated with an elevated risk of dementia in the senior years. The report makes a clear distinction between *being/living* alone and *feeling* alone. They point out that, ". . . it is not the objective situation, but, rather the perceived absence of social attachments that increased the risk of cognitive decline."

Only you can decide how many people, and what type of people, it will take to help you to avoid feeling lonely. Just like Durkheim's discovery at the end of the 19th century that suicide rates were lower among those who were married, these new studies find that you are less likely to develop dementia if you are socially connected. For those who are single and living alone, especially for those who are suddenly single, avoiding the "feeling lonely" that contributes to dementia might require more socializing with friends or even considering getting a roommate. The data from the Amsterdam Study of the Elderly (AMSTEL) is very strong in this regard: ". . . those who lived alone or who were no longer married were between 70% and 80% more likely to develop dementia than those who lived with others or who were married."

Good Friends Reduce Our Stress Level

In "Friends with Benefits: Being Highly Social Cuts Dementia Risk by 70%," Maia Szalavitz refers to a study by Bryan James which points out the relationship between a lowered stress level and a reduction in the risk of dementia. Says James: "Socializing relieves stress, and there's a huge connection between stress and problems with the brain as we get older."

An intriguing Japanese study of rats, reported on in 2005 by Rachel Adelson on the American Psychological Association (APA) website, found that the presence of another rat lowered the measurable stress levels of the first rat. But what was especially interesting is that there were even better stress-lowering benefits if the second rat had not been through what the first rat had experienced. Extrapolating this study's findings to human beings, Jim Winslow of the National Institute of Mental Health (NIMH) is quoted as saying: "It's best to get reinforcement from someone who's not in the same lifeboat after you've gone over the side."

These findings should be kept in mind by those seeking out support groups so they can be around individuals going through similar experiences to them. Those groups may be very helpful, but leaning on the shoulder of someone who is *not* in the same or a similar situation seems to have its benefits as well.

Laughing with a Friend Improves Your Ability to Withstand Pain

There's a fascinating finding from the anthropology and primate studies of Oxford University anthropologist and psychologist Robin Dunbar (explored in more again in Chapter 3, "Assessing Your Friendship Skills and Current Network"). As reported by Maria Konnikova in "The Limits of Friendship," published in *The New Yorker*, Dunbar found that laughter helped his subjects keep their hands in ice water or hold an uncomfortable chair position much longer than they were able to before. Their laughter was the result of a face-to-face experience, which is why we all must seriously consider the downside of a preponderance of computer-based connections.

What does being able to better withstand pain have to do with longevity? As we age, most of us will be exposed to more and more types of pain, both physical and emotional. According to the research, having friends should help us to better endure both types of pain.

Pick the Right Friends if You Want to Live a Longer and Healthier Life

In Chapter 6, "Frenemies and Fatal Friends," I discuss how the wrong friends can put you in harm's way, such as in the potentially lethal combination of being the passenger in the car of a friend who is drinking and driving, texting and driving, or just being a careless driver. Another example is being assaulted or even the worst possible situation, being permanently maimed or killed by a friend. Exactly how many friends kill friends is hard to determine since in cases where the relationship between victim and offender is known, most statistics lump friends/acquaintances into one category.

A Friend Can Make You Feel Emotionally Upset or Physically Ill

Far less dramatic than being physically assaulted or killed by a friend or former friend, but still worth noting, is the way some friends can make you physically or emotionally ill, which can adversely impact the quality of your life as well as your longevity. Just as positive or good friends can lower your stress level, negative friends can make you sick. Of the 73 men and women in my snowball confidential international friendship survey who answered the question "Have you ever had a friendship that made you physically or emotionally ill?" Nearly four in ten (39.73%) wrote *yes*.

Interestingly, there was a distinct gender disparity in the answer to this question: 55% of those who answered *yes* were women, but only 21.21% of the men had that experience.

For the women, here are the ways their friends caused physical or emotional problems:

- Four friends let their other friend down
- Led to a nervous breakdown
- Headaches, stress, tightness in my neck
- Anxiety

- Led to mental illness & substance abuse in teens and 20s
- Made me physically and emotionally ill
- Anger
- Lost weight
- Depression, knocked self-esteem
- Depression and sadness

For men, here are the ways they stipulated a friend had emotionally or physically made them ill:

- Anger
- Emotionally draining
- Stress, distress

Loneliness Increases Your Chance of Functional Decline or Dying

John Cacioppo, a neuroscientist who is credited with creating a new subdiscipline known as social neuroscience, has been quoted as saying that "Chronic loneliness increases the odds of an early death by 20 percent." Physician and gerontologist Carla M. Perissinotto and her team conducted a 6-year longitudinal study with a nationally representative sample of 1,604 people with a mean age of 70.9 years.

This cohort study was part of the Health and Retirement Study. In addition to a greater likelihood of dying, the researchers found four measures of functional decline, which was determined by interviews with family members, including an increased difficulty in climbing stairs; a decline in walking; an increased difficulty in upper extremity tasks; and difficulty in ADL (activities of daily living) functions, including bathing, dressing, transferring, using the toilet, and eating. Their conclusion: "Loneliness was associated with [an] increased risk of death over the 6-year follow-up period (22.8% versus 14.2%) . . ." and "Loneliness was associated with all measures of functional decline..." (Unfortunately the research does not specifically address friendship although it does define loneliness as the "subjective feeling of isolation, not belong, or lacking companionship." Research and self- reports affirm that having at least one positive friend contributes feeling connected, belonging, and having companionship.

"Weak Ties" Can Help Your Health as Well

As Jennifer Breheny Wallace points out in her *Washington Post* article, "Even Casual Ties to Others Can Better Your Health," the benefits of friendship are not bestowed only by the so- called "strong" ties which we associate with close or best friends. Sheldon Cohen, professor of psychology and director of the Laboratory for the Study of Stress, Immunity, and Disease at Carnegie Mellon University, did a study of 4,000 people ages 52 to 94 on lung function, a good predictor of longevity. He assessed lung function at the beginning of the study and four years later. The results were that social connections—"weak ties," or what tend to be thought of or categorized as casual friends—had as much of a positive effect on lung function as "strong ties" such as spouses or children.

Friends Can Improve the Survival Rate after a Cancer Diagnosis

As discussed in their scholarly article, published in the *Journal of Clinical Oncology*, "Social Networks, Social Support, and Survival After Breast Cancer Diagnosis," researchers Candyce H. Kroenke, et. al. analyzed 2,835 women from the Nurses' Health Study who had been diagnosed with stages 1 to 4 breast cancer between 1992 and 2002. (The total sample of the Nurses' Health Study (NHS) was 121,700 American female nurses.) In 2004, out of the 2,835 research sample, 224 had passed away; 107 related to breast cancer. Based on several social support assessments at different points in time, the researchers determined that "women who were social isolated before diagnosis had a subsequent 66% increased risk of all-cause mortality...and a two-fold increased risk of breast cancer mortality...compared with women who were socially integrated." (Please note, however, that this study grouped contact with close friends, close relatives, and children into one category that they labeled "sociability." Using the Berkman-Syme Social Networks Index (SNI), they grouped the respondents into four categories: social isolated; moderately isolated; moderately integrated; and socially integrated.

A Supportive Network Decreases the Chance of Dying in the First Six Months Following a Heart Attack

Lisa F. Berkman, Ph.D. et. al. studied 195 men and women who were hospitalized for acute myocardial infarction (a heart attack) between

1982 and 1988. Reporting in 1992 in the *Annals of Internal Medicine* on the results of their analysis of mortality during the first 6 months after the heart attack, the researchers concluded: "Patients who had no one on whom to rely for emotional support also had twice the risk for death compared with those who had two or more sources of support…."

Other studies confirm the positive impact of social support after a heart attack, such as the study of 887 patients reported on in 1999 by Nancy Frasure-Smith, Ph.D. et. al, "Social Support, Depression, and Mortality During the First Year After Myocardial Infarction," Frasure-Smith et. al. concluded: "We observed that as previously reported, depressed patients were at significantly increased risk of post-MI mortality. However, this was not true for those who perceived very high levels of social support. Not only were depressed individuals with high support at baseline not at increased risk for cardiac mortality, but also their depression symptoms were more likely to improve than those of the depressed with low to moderate support."

The 2014 study by Emily M. Bucholz, et. al. also looked at the health, depression, and quality of life one year after a heart attack on 3,432 patients under the age of 55. Bucholz et. al.'s conclusions were consistent with other studies about the impact of social networks after a heart attack; a year after the heart attack, those patients—male and female—who were categorized as having a low perceived social support (LPSS) "had a worse health status and more depressive symptoms."

Social Isolation and Loneliness are Risk Factors for Stroke, Coronary Heart Disease, and High Blood Pressure

Additional studies have found a link between loneliness and social isolation and increased blood pressure, which is associated with cardiovascular disease, as well as an greater risk for stroke or coronary heart disease and premature death. Those are the findings in the studies carried out by Louise C. Hawkley, et. al, published in *Psycho. Aging*, and by Nicole K. Valtorta, et. al, in *Heart*.

***

Still wondering if friendship has healing powers? Take this True or False test that follows to assess your knowledge of just how pivotal friendship really is. Mark your answer *True* or *False* and then check your responses against the correct answers that follow. (No looking ahead, now! This is a test.)

True or False Test: Just How Vital is the Friendship Bond?

1. Friends can lower your chances of getting a cold. *True or False?*
2. Good friends make you happier. *True or False?*
3. Intrusive or over-controlling friendships are one of the risk factors for dementia. *True or False?*
4. Having even one friend can increase your longevity by at least ten years. *True or False?*
5. The best predictor of whether or not there are additional attacks after myocardial infarction (heart attack) is not depression but lacking a close confidant. *True or False?*
6. You will live longer after being diagnosed with Stages II and III breast cancer if you have "dependable, non-household relationships" (friends). *True or False?*
7. The hormone oxytocin, which is released in response to stress, stimulates the seeking of health- affirming "tend and befriend" connections, not just "fight or flight." By reducing stress, friendship improves health and longevity. *True or False?*

The correct answer to *all* of the above questions is "True." Pat yourself on the back if you got 100%, especially is you wrote "true" to question five, which might have surprised many of you, if you've been thrust into the caregiving role for a parent, family member, or if you are wondering if you should take the time, even monthly, to visit a friend who has had a heart attack. As Dickens, et. al. conclude in their study of further cardiac events following myocardial infarction (MI), "We did find that having a close confidant approximately halved the risk of having a subsequent cardiac event, even after controlling for demographic and coronary risk factors, severity of MI, and discharge medication." This study defined a close confident in the following way: "someone with whom the patient had regular contact (at least once a month) and with whom he or she could share sensitive personal information and gain support."

Here are the sources for the above questions/answers; complete citations are in the Bibliography at the back of this book:

Susan Gilbert, "Social Ties Reduce Risk of a Cold." *New York Times*
Mayo Clinic. "Friendships: Enrich your life and improve your health."

Jing Liao, et al., "Negative Aspects of Close Relationships as Risk Factors for Cognitive Aging,"
American Journal of Epidemiology.

Lisa F. Berkman and Leonard Syme. "Social Networks, Host Resistance and Morality: A Nine- Year Follow-up Study of Alameda County Residents." *American Journal of Epidemiology.*

C. M. Dickens, et al., "Lack of a close confidant, but not depression, predicts further cardiac events after myocardial infarction," *Heart.*

K. L. Weihs, M.D., et. al. "Dependable Social Relationships Predict Overall Survival in Stages II and III Breast Carcinoma Patients." *Journal of Psychosomatic Research.*

Shelley E. Taylor. "Tend and Befriend: Biobehavioral Bases of Affiliation under Stress." *Current Directions in Psychological Science.*

Dissenting Opinion: Is it Family or Friends that Increased Longevity?

As a friendship coach, researcher, and author, I would like to say, unequivocally, that friendship is the key factor in improving longevity. As noted throughout this chapter, there is a preponderance of scientific evidence supporting the idea that friendship is critical to increasing longevity. But there is a dissenting opinion as voiced in a study shared at the 111th Annual Meeting of the American Sociological Association. The co-authors, James Iveniuk, a post- doctoral researcher at the University of Toronto Dalla Lana School of Public Health, and L. Philip Schumm, a senior bio-statistician at the University of Chicago, found that upon a reanalysis of data collected on 57–85-year-olds from the 2005/2006 and 2010/2011 survey waves by the National Social Life, Health, and Aging Project (NSHAP), those who reported being extremely close to non-spousal family members had a 6% risk of mortality compared to a higher rate of 14% for those who did not.

The press release related to the findings of the paper, "Social Relationships and Mortality in Older Adulthood," and popular write-ups about the press release, including "Study Reveals That Family is Key to Longevity Not Friends," published in *Pulse*, need to be evaluated with caution and additional research. Longitudinal studies are especially needed to see if the overwhelming evidence that friendship has a dramatic impact on longevity holds up.

Reconfirming friendship's place in improving longevity is especially important since, as the population ages and marriage partners die, for the majority of seniors, it will be to friends, or even to family, not romantic partners, that they will be turning for companionship. That will hopefully help to offset the negative impact of singleness that sociologist Emile Durkheim discovered in his late 19th century empirical surveys linking marital status to suicide rates. (Marrieds had lower suicide rates than singles especially single adult males who had the highest rates.)

If it is true that family is a key factor for longevity, but if family, and a spouse, are no longer around, the benefit of friendship as a substitute for those relationships could be the longevity booster that hypothetically is available to everyone. Family are those you are related to and a marriage partner, especially in the senior years, may no longer be an option. In theory, friendship is continually available. You do not have to be related. There are no legal or even financial ties or complications. It should be a relatively easy connection to make, or maintain. Unfortunately, many fall short in this regard, especially in their older years as declining health, more limited mobility, and other emotional and physical challenges make starting new friendships more difficult than previously. The good news is that it does not have to be that way. Please read on!

***

In the next chapter, Chapter 2, "The Impact of Social Media on Friendship," we'll look at social media, probably one of the biggest developments in how we interact with our friends to occur since the invention of the telephone attributed to Alexander Graham Bell in 1876.

Chapter 2
The Impact of Social Media on Friendship

"Facebook is a very distant fourth place in ranking my preferred way to communicate with my friends as I don't think FB is a good tool, except I do use Facebook Messenger sometimes. But I prefer Skype for sound quality/user features when voice/video chatting."

—50-year-old single Midwestern administrative assistant

"I had an online friend who died; she and I were very close. I found out later how much she adored me through her surviving husband."

—44-year-old married homemaker with a 16-year-old son

An interviewee shared with me how she lost a friendship over a Facebook post. She was surprised and saddened that the post ended their long-standing friendship since her negative comment was actually posted anonymously. She had made a joke about how awful her friend's cake was. Even though she didn't mention her friend's name, and she meant it in a joking way, her friend still knew it was about her and her cake, and the insult went too deep for her to ignore despite many apologies.

In another interview, a different woman shared how she actually shut down her Facebook account and also started pulling away from certain friends because, from time to time, they would badmouth her husband. A few years later, however, she returned to Facebook but not to those friendships.

Communicating with friends via social media gives you the option of having free, private conversations with those you are connected to via a particular site, or with everyone should you wish to share something with all of your friends and acquaintances. You can also communicate with groups of connections.

Although reconnecting with old friends is one of the pluses of all those sites, they can also be a way to make new friends. Some online connections blossom into friendships and even move offline. Some might stay online and do not go too much beyond being a connection, even though Facebook gives all those who connect to each other the often unfounded term of "friend." Most would agree that a fraction of their Facebook "friends" are actual friends rather than just acquaintances or even "contacts." What needs to be emphasized, however, is that it's okay for many or even all of those "friends" relationships that start online, to stay online. We are in the realm of "new rules" and there is no rule that every single connection, or what I refer to as an FBF (Facebook Friend), must be a close or best friendship that involves having a cup of coffee or going to the movies together.

But as we saw in Chapter 1, which addressed social media and its impact on longevity, we know that isolation and loneliness are linked to depression, and that depression is associated with a higher risk of suicide. The research, including the seminal work by social psychologist Mai-Ly N. Steers and her colleagues, has found a link between Facebook usage and depressive symptoms. So, if too many of those online "friends" are not friends at all, and those who are spending too much time on Facebook are finding their real-world universe of friends diminishing because they are being ignored, that can be a red flag about the consequences of social media friendship. But it could also be the chicken and the egg phenomenon.

Years ago, when my children were small and it was harder for me to get out and connect with friends in person, I was participating in a working mother online site. None of us ever met in person—we were spread out all over the United States with young children to care for— nor did we even call each other on the phone. We communicated purely by email. However, as a friendship researcher, I decided to interview a couple of the participants on our working mother site about how social media—it wasn't called that back then, it was just the Internet or the World Wide Web—was impacting their friendships. One woman told me that she was happy that she didn't have to meet any of her new friends in person. She was shy, and she also wasn't happy about her appearance. She shared that she had more friends because of the Internet than she had ever had before. She liked that she didn't have to worry about meeting someone face to face, which she had always found just too much for her to handle. In a communication, however, another online participant shared her frustration that if her car broke down and she needed a friend to give her a lift home from the gas station, she would not have anyone close by she could call. All her friends were online.

So, the question is: Is someone spending too much time on Facebook and other social media sites because they are lonely and without a robust friendship network in the "real world"? Or is the time spent on social media helping those individuals who would be even lonelier if they did not have their online friends to post to and check in with?

This chapter is a lot more positive about social media and how it is impacting friendship than it might have been just a couple of years ago, before I began doing more concerted research on friendship and social media. We know that many people report that they are spending too much time on Facebook and not enough time in the "real world" with their friends. There are also some very hurtful things going on related to friendship and social media. But, fortunately, most people I surveyed or interviewed shared with me that they are finding a way to use social media, Facebook especially, to the benefit of their friendships and their lives.

Social Media and Friendship Survey Results* N = 203
Q2 Are you on Facebook? Yes – 70.94%
No - 27.09%

Q3 If you answered "yes" to the previous question, how much time EVERY DAY do you spend on Facebook?

2 minutes to 15 minutes	44.67%
30 minutes to 1 hour	35.33%
1-1/2 to 3 hours	14.67%
3-1/2 to 6 hours	5.34%

Administered on July 3, 2016

Since this was an anonymous survey, follow-up was not possible. Assuming respondents were honest—since it was anonymous, as long as they were honest with themselves there was no reason for them to inflate or deflate their answer—the majority of respondents have their time on Facebook under control spending only between 2 minutes to 1 hour. However, almost 15% are spending between 1-1/2 and 3 hours on Facebook with a small number, but a number that probably needs to consider seriously whether there are any relationship or even work-related consequences to all this time on Facebook, is the relatively small but important number, 5.34%, or eight individuals out of the 203 surveyed, who are spending between 3-1/2 and 6 hours on Facebook.

As an observer of friendship and social media, I have some tips I'll share later in this chapter about how to make social media even more helpful, not hurtful, in your friendships. There is the occasional dark side to social media and friendship, such as online bullying, and I'll address that as well.

In one of my other surveys—the international snowball sample of 178 men and women—I asked a question about bullying; unfortunately I didn't narrow it down to cyberbullying. So we do not know how many of the 60.82% who answered *yes* that they have been the victim of a bully were referring to cyberbullying. In reality, however, cyberbullying is bullying that occurs online so whether or not the bullying was happening in the workplace, at school, or in cyberspace, it is an interesting statistic that almost 61% of those polled had been the victim of a bully.

In my Survey Monkey Audience survey of 203 men and women, however, I asked respondents to check off statements that applied to them and social media. Two of those statements related to cyberbullying. Here are the results:

"I have been the victim of cyberbullying" (11.33%)

"I have witnessed at least one case of cyberbullying" (15.76%)

So a total of 27% of that sample have either been the victim of cyberbullying or witnessed it.

On a cheerier note, here are the positive statements related to social media and its impact on friendships and the percentage in that sample that agreed with these statements:

"It has led to the formation of at least one friendship." 25% "Social media helps me to reconnect with old friends from work and school." 53% "Social media helps me to stay connected with all my nearby and far away friends." 55%

What Social Media Platforms Are People On?

LinkedIn was launched in 2003 and Facebook was founded in Cambridge, Massachusetts a year later, going wide in 2006. But the Internet has been trying to put friends together since long before then. Twenty years ago, when I was researching *Friendshifts* (1997; 1999), there were sites I learned about that were dedicated to helping old friends to reconnect—although none took off the way the better-known sites introduced in the early 2000s and still thriving today did. Classmates.com, one of the earliest sites for finding old friends, started in 1995. Not as well- known as Facebook, LinkedIn, Pinterest, Snapchat, and Twitter, Classmates came in a distant sixth in popularity in my most recent May 2018 survey of 117 men and women, far behind Twitter. But the 4.72% who noted that they used Classmates was a very far cry from the 81.13% who stated they used Facebook, the most popular social media site among those respondents.

Q6 Check off any and all of the social networking sites that follow that you participate in.
Answers in order of descending popularity

Facebook	81.13%
LinkedIn and Pinterest (tied)	45.28%
Instagram	33.96%
Snapchat	28.30%
Twitter	25.47%
Classmates	4.72%

Facebook, as well as LinkedIn, which is mainly for business connections, initially focused on connections or friendships that you already had. Today, Facebook allows anyone to send you a request to "friend" each other, although you can always decline or just ignore the request.

We have all heard that Facebook is popular, with over 2 billion users. The results of these surveys substantiate how prevalent Facebook is as the number one preferred social media site. Here are the results from all seven surveys about Facebook participation. Each survey represented not just males and females but singles and married as well as a wide range of age groups.

Facebook participation
Snowball sample N = 178 Facebook participation – 92.68%

SurveyMonkey Audience (Australia)
N = 58 Facebook participation – 86%

SurveyMonkey Audience (United Kingdom)
N =51 Facebook participation – 75.51%

SurveyMonkey Audience (USA) N = 339 (January through April,
2016) Facebook participation – 81.90%

SurveyMonkey Audience (USA) N = 203 (July 2016)
Facebook participation - 78.49%

SurveyMonkey Audience (USA) N = 105 (March 2018)
Facebook participation – 77.14%

SurveyMonkey Audience (USA) N = 117 (May 2018)
Facebook participation - 74.36%

The Positive Benefits of Social Media for Friendship

Dave Koco, an entrepreneur, and novelist (*Operation Freakshow* and *Lucky the Orphan*) from the U.S. who lives in Tokyo with his family, says, "If it wasn't for Facebook, I would have lost contact with a lot of friends." Dave is not alone in seeing social media as helpful for keeping long-distance friendships going, or even for enhancing friendships.

Mike Kiger, of Lake Oswego, Oregon, and the head of a company called Missing Inc., says that Facebook "has helped me to get to know some friends better."

Thirty-five-year-old Jane, married without children and working in an office, finds Facebook has helped her friendships: "Pictures and status updates create conversation for when we see each other in person."

Fifty-seven-year-old Jennifer has found that Facebook "rekindled some old friendships and elevated a few acquaintances to friends."

For my cousin Phyllis Silver Henkel, who is single, retired, and living in Florida, Facebook has "brought me together with school friends. Facebook keeps my long-time friendships intact." It also makes it a bit easier for her to keep up with the activities of her five grown children and seven grandchildren, as well as to share pictures and news about her family members with her friends and other relatives.

Marketing consultant and author Shel Horowitz expresses a similar view when he shares about how Facebook helps new relationships to start off faster when you finally do meet face to face: "I find in those situations, you don't focus on small talk," says Shel. "You've already done that [through social media]."

We hear so much about the negatives of social media on our relationships. I want to take just a little time to highlight some of the positives shared with me in one of my SurveyMonkey Audience surveys from 2018 based on responses from 105 men and women in the U.S.:

- "I use Facebook chat to keep up with long distance friendships. It is free as opposed to texting."
- "Casual friends from Facebook"
- "I became friends due to a disagreement. Through further dialogue, we began to see each other's points and agreed to disagree, but found common ground on other issues."
- "Met casual friends playing games and met a distant cousin who has become a friend."
- "Sometimes politics have drawn me to make new friends online. Others who are passionate about animals and their welfare have become my friends. In general, having the same passions."
- "Facebook, few casual. But do have a best friend that meet off fb."
- "Through a mutual friend on Facebook. It's a very close friendship."

The Negatives of Social Media for Friendship

Dave Koco, who shared about the benefits of Facebook to his friendships, also commented on how it's hurt his friendships. Says Dave, "Usually just people who [you] thought you knew or they knew you but being way different in a bad way. A lot of extremists on Facebook who acted ruder online than in person. I try to live by a code of treating people the same online as in real life."

Mike Kiger also says Facebook has impacted a friendship: "It allowed me to see someone's true colors as to who they really are and not simply the front they put out for the public."

The two topics that can get you in the most trouble with friends on social media seem to be politics and religion. Ajeet Khurana, an entrepreneur based in Mumbai, India, who is married with two teenage sons, says, "When sharing political views, Facebook has created misunderstandings with friends."

An example of how Facebook could potentially be a negative is that it takes up time that could be used to get together with friends in person.

A 65-year-old single woman who has 5,000 connections on Facebook admits that she has zero best friends and zero close friends on Facebook. She actually considers her 5,000 Facebook connections to be "casual friends" with several hundred of those Facebook friends are also former coworkers from various jobs. She admits to spending three hours a day on Facebook. What if even two of those three hours could be spent meeting face-to-face with people, or even going out to activities in the world as another way to meet new people with whom she could interact with off line? What about just taking some of the time spent on Facebook to meet up with new acquaintances at a local coffee shop to see if a friendship might ensue?

Cyberbullying is a challenge that too many are having to deal with. If it is anonymous it can be harder to confront and deal with. Sadly there are too many instances of cyberbullying leading to pre-teen, teen, and adult depression and even suicide. Cyberbullying is the exception. Based on my survey results, and interviews, and my own observations, it is more of an exception than a rule.

Bragging about how wonderful things even if times are tough,

is more common than cyberbullying. The main reason bragging on social media when it is far from true on social media can have negative repercussions is that someone who genuinely needs to get support and help will be less likely to get any because friends and acquaintances are unaware there is a problem.

Five Rules to Help Smooth the Impact of Social Media on Friendship

Fortunately, many social-media-related conflicts that hurt or end friendships are probably preventable. Here are a couple of typical ones:

Reading on Facebook, rather than learning about it directly, about something that happened to a close or best friend the day before. It's already gotten more than 25 comments by the time the friend reads about it, further emphasizing that she didn't hear about what happened *directly* from her friend *before* everyone else.

An event that a friend was not invited to is discussed on Facebook, complete with pictures of the event showing lots of other shared friends in attendance. That just makes the friend more infuriated than she would have been about being left out.

Posting political opinions that demonstrates that the friends have diametrically opposed views.

Sharing about a bodily function that some consider to be TMI (Too Much Information) or offensive to read about.

Using language that is offensive or sharing intimate details about a work or personal situation that borders on cringe-worthy.

Below you will find five social media-related guidelines to consider that might help to avoid the common FB or social media pitfalls that challenge friendships. These rules refer to personal social media pages or profiles, not to business pages, which have a whole other set of rules and considerations.

Rule #1 - What to Post

Here is a prime example about the challenges of what to post. Your daughter is getting married and you are having a relatively small wedding, so most of your Facebook network will not be invited to the wedding ceremony. What should you do? Is it okay to post pictures about the wedding? Should you create a subgroup on Facebook of just those who are invited and attending so your other friends will not feel left out by the posts? Should you have a separate friends party to celebrate the upcoming wedding as a way of minimizing the hurt feelings, or will that create an even worse situation for those who did not make the cut for the main wedding invitation?

Before you post something, consider each and every person you are connected to on Facebook or other social media platforms when you create and launch a post. Is this something everyone that you are connected to will want to see or should see? Even alienating or offending one person with one social media post is one too many. The old maxim of "When in doubt, leave it out" applies.

Send information directly to someone through Facebook Messenger if you think you are posting something that too many will feel offended by, whether it's because they will feel left out or ignored.

If someone has a couple of hundred or even a couple of thousand connections on a social media platform, very few are going to be close or best friends, and some may even be acquaintances or strangers, and not even casual friends. Another approach to this challenge is that everyone in your network should know where they stand with you so it's less likely they will be offended. For example, Manhattan-based David Hochberg, an agent for artists, noted that Facebook has indeed hurt a friendship because he found out he had not been contacted: "If an out-of-town friend comes to NYC without telling me nor attempting to get together!"

Rule #2 – When to Post

Knowing *when* to post information on social media can be as important as what you post or with whom you share it. A key finding about friendship is that the more intimate you are with a friend, the more exclusive should be the information that is shared, as well as the speed with which it is conveyed. You do not want your best friend of 30 years to see the post announcing big news—that you're having a baby, or getting married, or that you just signed a new book deal—at the same time, or even after, your casual friend from work.

You want to be sharing that information with your closest or best friends *before* all others. (I have been told that some users of social media, especially younger ones, may create what is known as a fake account" to only friend a few of their closest friends. As it was explained to me, it is "so they can be silly or complain about people in their daily lives who follow them. If it's an Instagram, it's colloquially known as a "finsta" the term for a fake Instagram account.

So, pick up the phone, send a text, an email, or a private message on Facebook so that when you do post about that event to your vast social media network, your close or best friend or friends can all say, with a big smile, "Oh, yeah, I already knew that."

Rule #3 – Who to Post to

I found one person's Facebook posts so upsetting and off-putting that I had to ask my older son Scott how to "hide" their posts so I couldn't read them again. I didn't want to "unfriend" her. She's a powerful person in the industry that I still associate with professionally, so "unfriending" her would not have been cool.

That's an example of why it's so important to be careful about who you let into your social media network. If you have to, go through your contacts on each and every social media site and "hide" or delete contacts that are not in your best interest to be connected to. (There may also be a newer option to "mute" posts on Twitter and Instagram that will not allow someone to be aware of your activity.) There is no reason to continue to share your own posts with them or have to see their posts since it takes up your mental space as you wade through them even if you try to avoid reading those posts. Since you are simply "hiding" that person's posts, you are successfully uncluttering your mind without offending them.

Make sure you know the difference between private messaging someone on Facebook or in LinkedIn versus posting and publishing to the world. If you don't know the difference, ask someone savvy about social media to teach you what you need to know so you don't embarrass yourself, hurt someone, or even unwittingly end a friendship or two.

Rule #4 – How Often to Post

There was a second non-friend contact on Facebook that I was about to have to "hide" because he posted so often it was making me crazy. He was posting 10 to 20 items, in quick succession, and several times a day. I could scroll through everything and even avoid reading most of them, but some of them were actually interesting and I also felt guilty completely ignoring his posts. But before I had to "hide" him, the way I did the other woman, he stopped posting as often. Maybe now he posts only once a week. It's so much more manageable this way.

So that's the question you have to ask yourself: how often are you posting? Is it too often, not often enough, or just right? This number may of course vary as your situation changes. For instance, if you go off on a dream trip for 14 days to different countries throughout Europe, it might be justifiable to post several times a day as you go to different places, especially if you're including the photographs.

But if that's not the case, unless there's something really interesting and dramatic going on, maybe post just once a day, so your world of friends and contacts know you're around but you're not overwhelming everyone.

Rule #5 – Language and Tone to Use when Posting

Numerous respondents to my survey pointed out that too often some people seem to lose their boundaries when they're posting, and that they also share about politics and topics that have ended up hurting their friendships. But in addition to considering what you post, you have to be careful about the language you use in your social media posts and the tone. Avoid using swear words. It's offensive and it gives a very negative impression of you.

Also try to avoid a combative or confrontational tone. No one likes the "know it all" and that's true on social media as well. So, try to be humble and let people know that what you are sharing is IMHO—In My Humble Opinion—without being overbearing and bossy.

Be especially careful about how you criticize someone else. As the example at the beginning of this chapter, even sharing anonymously on a social media site in a negative way about someone's pie can hurt feelings and end a friendship. Of course, offering feedback in a constructive way is a lot different than hurling insults or just outright putting down someone because they have another opinion or do not agree with you. But you need to be careful about even sharing what you see as helpful feedback. Unless you know someone fairly well, some people simply cannot take it. Yes, some people like to share just to share not to get comments or reactions.

Social Media as a Way to Make Friends

Have you ever made a friend through any social media sites, including Facebook? I have made many casual friends through Facebook; for me it is also a great way to maintain my friendships, especially with those who live in another state or country. I have also reconnected with friends from high school because of Facebook. Here are the results from several of my surveys to the question about making a friend because of Facebook.

Q4 "Have you ever made a friend because of any social media sites including Facebook?" Yes – 24%   No -   77%
SMA (Survey Monkey Audience) N = 105

Here are follow-up comments from some of those who answered "yes":

- "Through a mutual friend on Facebook. It's a very close friendship."
- "VERRRRRY, VERRRY close-best friend."
- "A friend of a neighbor asked to 'invite me' on Facebook. Great person to meet."
- "Casual friends from Facebook."

Yes – 34%
No - 65%
SMA N = 117

Here are some of the comments that were also shared related to that question:

- "Reunited with old friends, but didn't make any new ones."
- "I have made friends in a Facebook group for others who have suffered from the same illness I have. One girl that was local to

me actually paid me visit, which was very beneficial. And I am currently making plans to meet with another friend. It's a great support."

- "I've made friends on Facebook. They run the gamut from casual to intimate."
- "Met 2 good friends on a page for former soldiers. In one case we met face to face within a month. In the other we didn't actually meet for over 4 years. We still are all friends."
- "Casual, he's a friend of a friend but turns out to be a funny dude."
- "I have made friends through Facebook. Not best friends but casual. Started with a comment here and there, then message, then real life."

In my snowball sample of 178, questions 34 and 35 related to the most recent friend that the respondent had made. Of the possible ways that the friendship could have started, only 5% noted that it started online. The other more popular answers were "through work" (37%), "through another friend" (19%), and "lives nearby/neighbor" (14%).

There would probably be a much higher percentage of those who have met a friend through an online social media site if a respondent was on a site or using an app dedicated to friendship formation. As noted before, the main goal of most Facebook users is to stay connected with family, friends, colleagues, or co-workers. Making friends through Facebook and other social media is a side benefit that may or may not occur. There are, however, quite a few websites and apps that are dedicated to helping people connect and start friendships, especially women. These sites are listed and briefly described in the Resources section in the back of this book. Some of those social media sites for starting friendships include GirlfriendCircles, which relaunched in July 2016, and was started by Shasta Nelson, who's published three books on friendship, *Friendships Don't Just Happen!*, *Frientimacy*, and *The Business of Friendship*. Other friendship-formation websites catering to women include Girlfriendology, founded in 2006 by Debba Haupert, which claims to have more than 90,000 followers. An app called Bumble, founded in 2014 by Whitney Wolfe Herd, co- founder of Tinder, the dating app, added a friendship version in March 2016. It is known as Bumble BFF for finding new friendship (platonic, non-romantic) relationships.

The Friendship Page was started by Australian Bronwyn Polson in 1996. It includes a Find a Friend function.

Patook is a free website and app for making platonic friends that started in 2014.

SKOUT, founded in 2007, is a free app for finding people around the world for friendship or for dating. Its tag line is "Meet, Chat, Friend."

Tips for Improving Your Safety if You Make Online Friends*

Here are some tips for helping you to be more self-protective if your friendship starts online:

Whether it's friendship or romance, the number one rule is: never meet alone in an isolated place or at someone's home. Stay in public places surrounded by others until you are absolutely secure about this new potential friend.

Don't reveal your complete name, your phone number, or your home address to a stranger whether you meet over the Internet, through a MeetUp activity, or at a conference. For safety reasons, use a post office box, or a mailing address besides your home (such as a UPS store), or only use email.

Be very careful about what personal information you reveal, and certainly do not brag about any financial assets or personal wealth.

Never reveal personal information to anyone who is trying to befriend you, such as your banking information, Social Security number, or anything that might put your identity at risk.

Review the subject lines of any emails you receive, and only open emails from those you know or that you feel confident are from a reliable source.

Be especially careful if you are using a public computer.

Do not share your passwords to your key accounts with anyone else.

You might want to create a new online name that you will use for your online friendship activities so it is easier to track responses to your listings. It will also enable you to keep those responses separate from your other personal or work-related email communications.

Generally, online friendship sites and apps do not do criminal background checks on those using their services, so you might want to do your own checking. Consumeradvocate.org, in its article, "Top 10 Best Background Check Services" lists the following sites, with a link to each one: Intelius, Inc.; Truthfinder, LLC; BeenVerified; Peoplefinders; USSearchforPeopleData, Instant Checkmate®, DeepsearchPr, PeopleLooker®, GoodHire, and PeopleLookup.™

Do not open links to attached files, because doing so could open you up to having your identity stolen.

Once you meet or connect with someone, keep your eagerness to start a new friendship under control while you weigh carefully what someone says in terms of how reliable or believable it sounds.

If you have an instinctive feeling of fear about someone, trust your gut and keep yourself safe.

If you need a second opinion, consider bringing another friend along to meet this new potential friend.

If necessary, check out the implausible parts of someone's autobiography so you feel more comfortable that what this person is sharing with you about herself or himself is true.

Take the developing friendship at whatever pace is comfortable for you. Do not let anyone pressure you into a friendship if you just want to be acquaintances until you're really secure and comfortable with this person.

Make sure at least one person knows your whereabouts at all times. If you are meeting someone new, even if it is in a public place, give his or her name and contact information to someone you trust so there is documentation about your whereabouts. Keep in mind that many phones today have apps or systems that enable the user to "share your location" through a GPS tracking system. This information could be shared with a friend or dependable parent.

Carry a fully charged cell phone with you at all times so you are able to call for help or a taxi or car service if you have car trouble, or if you want to get out of a situation.

Whether you're 60 or 30, the advice your parents told you when you were a child or teen still holds: Never ever get into a car with a stranger even if it's a same-sex potential friendship situation. You are still putting yourself at risk.

Be careful about attending any private or commercial establishments where there is drinking; you must be of legal drinking age, and there has to be a designated driver who does not drink.

If you do meet a potential new friend in a public place, since you do not know this person well yet, never leave a drink unattended so go to the rest room or to go outside to take a call. Although this is an extreme rare case, you do open yourself up to having something slipped into your drink, such as a tranquilizer (that could put cause you to lose consciousness).

Keep in mind the tragedy in Rhode Island in 2003 where 100 people died because of a fire that broke out at a club. Be careful that you and your potential new friend choose to attend concerts, clubs, or restaurants in safe buildings, and that there are ample available exit signs in case of an emergency.

* *These tips are edited and reprinted, with permission, from my book* 125 Ways to Meet the Love of Your Life (Second edition) (2016), *with a platonic, not a romantic, emphasis.*

The Potentially Darker Side of Social Media
Time Spent on Social Media

Unfortunately, most people are unaware of how much time they spend on social media till they are asked to consider it for something like my survey. Or they see their productivity going down at work. Or, in their personal lives, they see themselves interacting with friends and relatives, but they don't seem to be getting together as often. And they are also feeling lonelier than they used to, which they find peculiar, since they have so many posts to read and comments to share about their friends' activities.

Would you be surprised if I told you that out of the 203 men and women surveyed about how much time they spent on Facebook every day—just Facebook, mind you, not all social media platforms—that out of the 149 people who answered this question, 51 (34.22%) are on it for 1–6 hours a day. Granted, only two people were on Facebook 6 hours a day, one for 5 hours, 1 for $5^{1/2}$ hours, two for 4 hours, and one for $4^{1/2}$ hours—but think of the amount of time we're talking about.

I am the author of eight books on time management, so, in addition to friendship and work relationships, time management is an issue I've been studying since the early 1980s. In one of my books, *Creative Time Management for the New Millennium*, I advise my readers how to find "hidden time" in their day. I help them to look over their day—something I do again in my books *Work Less, Do More* and *Put More Time on Your Side*—with an emphasis on finding "another hour" that they can use productively.

If you are spending too much time on Facebook, taking some of that time to do other things could be your "hidden time."

Do you even know how much time you are spending on Facebook if you're on Facebook?

Take a few minutes to consider it. Also consider what you accomplish when you're on Facebook.

Consider what one of my respondents wrote about Facebook: "It has often made me (and my friends) too reliant on it to keep us connected instead of making time to call or see each other."

Does that sentence describe you? If it does, take this opportunity to make a commitment to yourself that you will monitor how long you're spending on Facebook, what you're getting out of it and whether or not you should be picking up the phone, using FaceTime, or even texting, or setting up a time to get together in person with your friends, especially those who live and work nearby.

Please note: I invite you to refer again to the section in the Introduction on The Impact of the Pandemic on Friendship. All of the information in this chapter on social media, written before the pandemic, has to be reconsidered in light of the pandemic and how being forced to stay home more and not interact in person is making social media sites like Facebook and videoconferencing sites like Zoom lifesavers. When it is possible to get back to more in-person activities safely and without fear of getting a virus, hopefully everyone will also modify their habits again, putting in-person gatherings before electronic or virtual ones.

When Social Media Becomes an Addiction

One of the most outspoken critics of Facebook is CNN producer Rachel Ruff, who wrote about her four-year addiction to Facebook in her 2014 memoir, *Defriending Facebook: How I Deactivated My Account & Re-Activated My Life.*

Before you discount Ruff's account of her addiction to Facebook as a rare occurrence, let's review the results of my survey with responses from 149 men and women about how much time they spent daily on Facebook. Remember the finding that 51 reported being on Facebook one to six hours *a day*! But it's not just the number of minutes or hours on Facebook that need to be considered, it's whether or not going on Facebook has become an addiction.

Here's a quick quiz I devised that you can take to help you decide if Facebook has become an addiction or not.

Self-Quiz: Have You Become Addicted to Facebook?
Do you feel compelled to go on Facebook at least once a day?
Yes _____ No _____

Do you feel compelled to go on Facebook frequently, even if you're busy with your personal and work commitments and the time would be better spent in other ways?
Yes _____ No _____

Are you spending a lot less time, or no time, with your friends than you are with the people you are connected to on Facebook?
Yes _____ No_____

Are you on Facebook an hour or more a day, and it's not for business reasons?
Yes _____ No _____

Do you find yourself needing to post on Facebook, or read the posts of others, as a way of figuring out how you are feeling, how your day is going, or as a way of validating yourself?
Yes _____ No _____

Has your romantic partner, family member, or roommate called you for dinner and you said you'd be there soon, but time goes by and you're still checking or writing posts on Facebook 30 minutes to an hour later?
Yes _____ No _____

Do you find yourself getting turned on by the posts you read on Facebook more than you do by sexual intimacy?
Yes _____ No _____

Are you obsessed with Facebook and keeping up with all your connections at the expense of your family, non-Facebook friends, job, or school commitments?
Yes _____ No _____

Do you find yourself fearing what you'll do if you go on a trip and Facebook won't be available to you in your hotel room or in the new location?
Yes _____ No _____

Do you find yourself more focused on taking pictures and sharing about what you're doing in your life than actually experiencing it?
Yes _____ No _____

If you answered *yes* to three or more of the above questions, you should consider whether you have become so addicted to Facebook that it's getting in the way of your everyday life. An addiction is when something, whether it's Facebook, eating, drinking, or working, has become such a psychological necessity that your investment of time and energy in that particular activity or substance takes up a disproportionate amount of your focus. The substance or activity seems to take control of you rather than you being in control of it.

For some, just limiting the amount of time spent on Facebook daily may be the answer. Starting to sign on to Facebook every couple of days, instead of daily, may be a way to wean yourself from the addiction to Facebook.

For others, going "cold turkey" and quitting Facebook altogether may be what is needed. That is what Rachel Ruff had to do. She shares this in the following excerpt from her memoir, *Defriending Facebook*:

"I joined Facebook in 2006 and my friend list grew from 1 to 1,500 friends in just over two years. Facebook was a way for me to medicate my real-life boredom pains. I began spending my days looking at what my thousand-plus friends were busy doing in life, or at least I thought they were doing, and I couldn't help compare myself to them."

Unfortunately, her real life was losing its appeal. For Rachel, going cold turkey and deactivating her account was the only way she could deal with her addiction. Like the cigarette smoker who knows she can never have another cigarette again or she will go right back to being a chain smoker, Rachel had to quit Facebook all together.

Here are some of the benefits of deactivating Facebook that she shares in *Defriending Facebook*:

> *Happily as time went on I increasingly found myself cultivating friendships with people I knew from the gym or the neighborhood who I realized had given up asking me to hang out thanks to my lackadaisical friendship format at the time: No Facebook account = Digital Dark Age member. "Going to lunch with Kelly" posted to my wall was more important back then than actually going to lunch and enjoying the company of a friend with true sincerity like I do now. No announcement to others needed.*

When Social Media Leads to Cyberbullying

We need to consider the issue of bullying, not just cyberbullying, although once bullying moves to the Internet it can be a 24/7 event, not just a case of someone teasing someone else at school or saying something nasty at work.

The darkest side of social media is when it leads to cyberbullying that in turn drives someone to turn to suicide. Tyler Clementi jumped to his death off the George Washington Bridge on September 22, 2010, allegedly because of some compromising video filmed by his college roommate that was being shared on social media. Amanda Todd hanged herself on October 10, 2012, a month after posting a video in which she shared her story of being cyberstalked and cyberbullied since she was in the seventh grade.

Francie Diep wrote in *The Atlantic* online edition on September 30, 2014, about how she confronted her cyberbully 13 years after she was bullied from the age of 13 to 16. At that time, her cyberbully got into her email account and sent her emails telling her to kill herself. But Francie Diep did not kill herself. She survived, eventually went away to college, and became a freelance science journalist based in New York.

In her article, Diep shares what her former friend, whom she calls Amanda, did to her, and how she never told any other friends or adults about what happened until she was 29. Amanda does write back to Diep, who contacted her victimizer after all these years: "OMG no! That's horrible. I'm really sorry." But when Francie confronts Amanda about what she did, as Diep writes, "She has still never admitted to leaving the calendar reminders" telling Francie to kill herself.

Francie Diep's story, in a way, has a happy ending because she survived and has become a successful journalist despite what happened to her all those years ago. However, she did have to experience the emotional distress of those three years of cyberbullying, as well as having to carry the secret of it for more than a decade.

Not all victims of cyberbullying are tweens or teens. There are also adult victims of cyberbullying and cyberstalking. Sameer Hinduja, Ph.D. and Justin W. Patchin are co-founders of the CyberBullying Research Center. Here are the highlights from their handout, "Responding to Cyberbullying Top 10 Tips for Adults Who are Being Harassed Online," available at their website, Cyberbullying Research Center (www. cyberbullying.org).

- Do not retaliate.
- Record everything.
- Talk to your employer (if it is a coworker).
- Contact law enforcement.
- Report abuse.
- Consult with an attorney.

- Talk about it.
- Cut ties.
- Block the bully.
- Change your contact information.

***

In the next chapter, Chapter 3, "Assessing Your Friendship Skills and Current Network," we will explore your friendship capabilities as you review your friends with the goal of helping you to decide if you need to make any changes.

Chapter 3
Assessing Your Friendship Skills and Current Network

"When I was younger (17–20), several friends (or perhaps I should say their parents, LOL), let me stay with them for a few weeks/months during a particularly difficult home situation (abuse, etc.)."

—42-year-old woman involved in a living together relationship

Taking a Friendship Inventory

I am often asked if you can have too many friends. Most expect me to answer no. But there's research indicating that the number of friends you need depends on several variables. Although research shows we need at least one close or best friend besides our spouse or family to confide in, just how many close or best friends you need depends on your personality, the other competing demands on your life, as well as whether those friends are "easy" or "high maintenance."

Furthermore, it depends on whether or not you're still in the same physical place you've been in for the last umpteen years, or whether you've relocated to a new community, and whether you started a different job or career, or there have been changes in your life that are forcing you to need friends. You may be forced to reevaluate the friends you do have. Changes such as getting married, getting divorced, becoming widowed, having a child, going back to work after maternity leave, becoming an empty nester, retiring, experiencing a friend's serious illness or death, or you or your friend moving to a senior living community, or any number of other life-changing occurrences, may mean some friends are no longer available to you.

The bottom line is whether or not you have enough friends *right now*, not ten years ago, or even two weeks ago. It depends on circumstances, and it is also based on your personality, how much time you have available for friendship, and even how many friendships you can handle.

Evolutionary psychologist Robin Dunbar of Oxford University concluded that anything more than 150 friends would be too complicated to handle. Dunbar's research led to "Dunbar's Number" of 150 from his book, *How Many Friends Does One Person Need?*

There is no ideal number because we are all unique. What matters is what works for *you*. You may be able to juggle the time and energy it takes to maintain four best friendships, or you might find that just one close friend is all you can handle right now. You may have 20 casual friends and you thought that was simply fine until you had a party for the latest release from your company and only 5 showed up—but you needed at least 20 so the media wouldn't walk into a near empty room. So now you're on a mission to get at least 40 people who care about you—casual friends—since that will increase exponentially the likelihood someone will show up at a business function.

Take the following self-quiz to help determine if you have enough friends right now. Then consider the analysis of the self-quiz that follows to help you distill what your answers might mean.

Self-Quiz:
Do You Have Enough Friends?

1. If your car broke down, you have at least one friend nearby who could pick you up and drive you home after the service station or automobile service towed your car.
    Yes _____ No _____

2. If something really good or very bad happened to you or a family member, there is at least one close or best frsiend in whom you can confide.
    Yes _____ No _____

3. If someone asked you, "Do you feel like you have enough friends right now?" your honest answer would be yes.
    Yes _____ No _____

4. Especially if you've gone through any major changes, you have made at least one new friend within the last few years

who knows you from that point on in your life, and not from your previous careers or stages.

Yes _____ No _____

5. You have interests and activities that you enjoy doing with casual friends, and you always have at least several casual friends available to you *nearby* to do things with.

Yes _____ No _____

6. Your close or best friend died or moved far away and you have another close or best friend nearby available to you.

Yes _____ No _____

7. You like the friends you have, but you still feel that there is something missing in your life, a void that a special friend could help fill.

Yes _____ No _____

8. You've never had a close or best friend, and you would like to have one.

Yes _____ No _____

9. You could not handle another friend right now.

Yes _____ No _____

10. You would like to become a better friend to the ones you already have.

Yes _____ No _____

Look over your answers. What do your *yes* answers say about you? If you answered *yes* to questions 1 and 2, you have at least one friend nearby to help out in a crisis and one close or best friend to confide in. If you answered *yes* to question 10, and especially if you answered yes to question 9 as well, you want to become a better friend to the ones you have now, but forming new friendships is not a priority for you right now.

If you answered *yes* to question 3, and yes to question 7, even though you are satisfied with your current friendship network, you are still open to starting a new friendship. This can be a very controversial admission; your current friends might even be offended if you confide this need as they ask themselves, or even ask you, "Why am I not enough?"

In our monogamous society, you are expected to have only one spouse. Fortunately, having a multiplicity of friendship relationships is not only acceptable but sanctioned, and is preferable to over-relying on just one friend. Still, it can be hard to get support for your wish to find another friend or two from your current friends; even relatives might be jealous that you want to put your precious time into new friends rather than the relationships that you already have.

If you answered *yes* to question 8, that you have never had a close or best friend but you would like to have one, I commend you for having the courage to admit that. I have been very surprised at how much more common that situation is than I was aware of when I first began my friendship research. When I did a radio interview with teens in Asia, a boy admitted on the radio, "I have never had a friend." Over the years, men and women of all ages have confided that they have never had even one close or best friend or, if a friend betrayed them, they had not yet recovered and had another intimate friendship. Obviously if you answered yes to question 8, your friendship inventory is going to be small, but the good news is that you will find hope in these pages. You're willing to put some effort into doing something about it since you're reading this book and taking this self-quiz.

Before any of you with a thriving friendship network starts to feel grateful that you're not the one without even one friend, think back to the times in your life when you suddenly found yourself friendless, for any number of reasons. I know it has happened to me over the years. It wasn't that my long-standing friends from childhood or school or previous jobs or neighborhoods were not there for me any longer, but I had physically relocated to another place or I had changed career paths and did not have a confidant who could share with me about my new interests. Until I found and cultivated a close or best friend in those new physical spaces, or mental or professional places, it was lonely and tough, whether I was single, married, or a parent.

As most people know, layperson and social scientist alike, friendship is a unique social relationship connecting us with peers with whom we are not connected through blood ties, marriage, or another formal role like co-worker or neighbor. It is something that we all need, and we need it from those who are nearby, not a telephone call or email away. You may be in such a place now because of a recent relocation or change in your life. You're not alone in wondering how, right now, you're going to find and cultivate a new positive friendship.

Whether you've done it once, twice, or a gazillion times before, starting out on a relationship that might become a new friendship takes courage and the ability to take emotional risks. You're putting yourself out there, opening yourself up to potential rejection, criticism, and even betrayal. But, alas, the old adage is as true about friendship as it is about romance or any important next steps in your career: nothing ventured, nothing gained.

Activity Sheet:
How Many Friends Do You Currently Have?

Take this short inventory focusing on the number of casual, close, and best friends you have.

Personal Relationships
How many friends do you currently have in the following categories? Casual ____ Close ____

Best
How many of your close or best friends live nearby or within 20 minutes of your home or apartment?

Close (nearby) ____ Best (nearby) ____

At Work/In Business
How many friends at work or in business do you currently have in the following categories?
Casual ____
Close ____
Best ____

How many of your work close or best friends work nearby, in the same building, or within 20 minutes of your office?

Close (nearby) ____
Best (nearby) ____

The self-quiz that follows will help you explore the quality of those friendships now, not when your friendship started or when you lived nearby or worked together. This is a contemporary assessment of each of your close or best friendships. If you do not currently have a close or best friendship, you can read over these questions and keep them in mind as you form close or best friendships, or you can just move along to the next section, "Fifteen Friends That Everyone Needs."

Self-Quiz
What's Your Friendship Quality Quotient (FQQ)?*

*Excerpted, with additional editing, with permission, from Friendshifts : The Power of Friendship and How It Shapes Our Lives *by Dr. Jan Yager, 2nd edition (Stamford, Connecticut: Hannacroix Creek Books, 1999).*

Consider asking yourself these eight questions about your close or best friendships to assess the quality of the friendships.

Do you and your friend communicate—by phone, fax, letters, email, or through social media—or get together as often as you and your friend want to?
Yes ____ No ____

Do you and your friend have fun together?
Yes ____ No ____

When you and your friend speak on the phone or get together, do you feel connected and appreciated by your friend?
Yes ____ No ____

Is this friendship basically reciprocal (rather than one-way)?
Yes ____ No ____

Do you and your friend share the same values on issues that matter to you both or, if you do not, are these value disparities easily overlooked? Yes ____ No ____

Do you like this friend? Yes ____ No ____

Has this friendship stood the test of time and structural changes such as graduating, moving, getting married, having children, or switching jobs or careers? Yes ____ No ____

Is conflict with this friend minimal or, if it does occur, are you able to resolve it without long-term resentment?
Yes ____ No ____

If you answered no to one or more of the above questions about a particular friendship, it may indicate that you or your friend need to do some work on your relationship.

How Well Do You *Really* Know Your Friends?

How well do you really know each of your friends? Have you ever thought about that? Especially if you met later in life, unless you did a formal interview with your friend, you might not know as much about him or her as you would like to know. To help you out, I've created a list of 15 questions. You can answer these questions on your own and see how much you know about your friend, or you can use them to interview your friend and find out the answers.

Hopefully, you'll both be able to answer question 3, but if you can't, if you're friends on Facebook you can probably find out your friend's birthday there.

Fill out this self-quiz with one particular friend in mind. You can also photocopy this list and have your friend fill it out about you. If you're very clueless about a lot of the answers, do the quiz over the phone, in person, or electronically with your friend. A blank self-quiz is included in the Appendix so you can interview/fill in the answers for each other.

Important caveat: If you go over these questions with your friend, please be respectful if he or she prefers not to answer any particular question out of shyness, concerns about privacy, or for any other reason. The goal of this activity is to strengthen your friendship and bring you closer, not create conflict or anxiety. So, let your friend lead!

Self-Quiz:
How Well Do I Know My Friend?

Friend I'm writing about:

My friend's favorite color is _____.

My friend's favorite movie is _____.

My friend's birthday is _____.

If I asked my friend to tell me the truth about how an outfit/suit looked, she/he would say:

"It looks terrific" even if it did not.
"You look great" because I always look great to her/him.
"Do *you* like the way it looks, that's what counts."
None of the above.
Other _____.

My friend grew up in _____.
Her/his father's occupation was/is _____.
Her/his mother's occupation was/is _____.
If my friend had three wishes, this is what she/he would wish for:
1. _____
2. _____
3. _____

If my friend could change one event in his/her life it would be:
The last book my friend read was _____.

I would describe the job that my friend does in this way:
_____
My friend met her/his spouse (romantic partner)

- Through school
- Through friends
- At work
- Through a dating website or app
- None of the above
- Other

The most important trait in a friend to my friend is:
_____

My friend's biggest regret is _____.
If my friend could travel to any country in the world, she/he would want to travel to _____ because _____.

My friend's favorite childhood memory is: _____

_____

_____.

If You Want to Improve Your Friendship Skills

If you feel your friendships are not as strong as you would like those friendships to be, how do you start to make changes? One way is to look back and consider how your earliest relationships may have had an impact on the friendship skills that you developed. Here is a self-quiz to help you think about those key issues:

Self-Quiz:
Consider How Your Childhood Might Be Impacting Your Friendships

Answer the following questions to discover some factors in your childhood and formative years that may be impacting your current work relationships.

How did you get along with your father?
- Excellent
- Good
- Fair
- Poor
- Varied between okay and poor

How did you get along with your mother?
- Excellent
- Good
- Fair
- Poor
- Varied between okay and poor

How did you get along with your siblings?
- Excellent
- Good
- Fair
- Poor

- Varied between okay and poor
- I am an only child.

Sibling #1
- Excellent
- Good
- Fair
- Poor
- Varied between okay and poor

Sibling #2
- Excellent
- Good
- Fair
- Poor
- Varied between okay and poor

Sibling #3
- Excellent
- Good
- Fair
- Poor
- Varied between okay and poor

Sibling #4
- Excellent
- Good
- Fair
- Poor
- Varied between okay and poor

Sibling #5
- Excellent
- Good
- Fair
- Poor
- Varied between okay and poor

(If you have more than 5 siblings, photocopy a blank version of this page and use that to complete the self-quiz in as detailed a way to fit your particular family situation.)

What was your first experience with friendship? Was it positive? negative? _____

How did you deal with anger during your childhood and teen years?

Does competition inspire you, enrage you, or shut you down?
- Inspires me
- Enrages me
- Shuts me down
- Depends on the person

Did your family members make you feel as if you counted and were important?
Yes ___ No ___ Sometimes ___

Was honesty valued in your family?
Yes ___ No ___ Sometimes ___

Did your parents have friends when you were growing up?
Yes ___ No ___ Sometimes ___

What were those relationships like? Did you feel valued by your parents' friends? Did any of their friends send you birthday cards or presents or see you regularly during your formative years?

***

In the next chapter, "Making Friends," we will explore in greater detail about the various types of friends we all have, the process that turns a stranger or an acquaintance into a new friendship as well as a list of tips for making friends during your adult years including the older ones.

Chapter 4
Making Friends

"One incisive comment from a friend can be enough to inspire us, allow us to see our situation in a different light, or even drag us out of a particularly dark place."

—Carlin Flora, *Friendfluence: The Surprising Ways Friends Make Us Who We Are*

Who do you consider a friend? At one end of the spectrum are people who donate kidneys to friends in need. At the other end are those who find it hard to make the time to have a cup of coffee, even if they live only ten minutes away. Before you cross that friend off, continue reading this chapter and the rest of *Friendgevity*. Hopefully, you will learn that friendship, although it's supposed to be an "easy" relationship, is not as simple or as obvious as it seems.

As a friendship coach, I've learned that rushing to judgment can strain and sometimes prematurely end a friendship. Fortunately, I've been able to help clients reconnect with former friends and patch up their differences by reinterpreting words or actions. Hopefully, you'll find that what you learn about friendship here will help you handle strained friendships and situations differently, making them better and stronger.

From Stranger to Acquaintance to Friend

Every friendship starts with that first connection. Until the Internet, and except for occasional pen pals, where you were matched with someone across the country or around the world through letter writing, friendships began when two strangers met face to face. Whether that was because you were neighbors, like my childhood best friend, Ginny, who lived next door, or you went to school together, like Dara Tyson, who is in her fifties and is still best friends with Phyllis, whom she met in seventh grade, two strangers met, got acquainted and, in time, became friends.

There are such things as "fast friends," like 76-year-old Lynn Rosenberg and her best friend Pam Lane. They met three years ago at a conference and both told me they considered each other friends almost instantly. But for most of us, going from a point of connection to becoming a friend takes time and a "testing out" of that relationship. In conducting research for my dissertation, I discovered that it takes, on average, three years from meeting to becoming friends to feel that someone is a "tried-and-true" friend. That does not mean that you do not feel like friends long before that but the relationship goes through enough situations and potential or resolved conflicts that you, and your new friend, are mutual committed to this relationship that has become elevated to the status of a friend.

The Internet has changed how friendships are initiated with some friendships starting out online and, in some instances, those friendships becoming closer although the friends, who live far away from each other, never meet. When you consider the concept behind friendships that start without physically meeting initially, it really hails back to the days of the pen pal. Encouraged through associations or clubs in school, it was not unusual for students to have pen pals and back in those days, when it was very expensive to travel internationally or cross country, the pen pals might never meet. The pandemic of 2020 meant that more and more in-person and online friends had to meet virtually or call each other on the phone.

Friendship Choices

There are no right or wrong reasons to choose a friend. The reasons also may change as you go through your life cycle, as I review in greater depth in Appendix I, "Friendship Over the Life Cycle."

What matters is that you and your friend have similar goals for your friendship. If you want a friend who is someone to have fun with and your friend wants someone for emotional support, you can see that it might lead to some unmet expectations for both.

Here are the most common reasons that friends are chosen:

- Companionship
- Someone to do things with
- Emotional support
- Shared activities
- Someone to have fun with
- Someone to talk to

In conducting my friendship research, I found the best predictor of longevity in a friendship was shared values. However, you don't usually choose someone because they share your values. It's just something you learn about each other over time. But since it's the number one predictor of longevity in a friendship, it's something you might want to consider as you go from stranger to acquaintance to friend.

What Should You Expect from a Friend?

What can you reasonably expect from a friend, whatever the level of intimacy, and what should they anticipate from you? To answer this question, I came up with something I call the Friendship Oath (in the Appendix). The basic conditions of a friendship are to be open and honest with each other and to respect each other's boundaries. Since it also depends on the level of intimacy, there are more details below about what to expect from our various types of friends.

Types of Friends: Casual, Close, or Best

"Friendships are the crown jewels that one owns. The stock market might go up and down, but friendships only grow in their value."

—Gladys Barkas (1925-2013), a quote from my mother, at age 74, originally included in *Friendshifts*, Chapter 2, "What is a Friend?"

In my 3+ decades of friendship study, one thing has remained consistent, which is that there are basically three types of friends: casual, close, and best.

Casual friends are those you consider more than acquaintances but are rarely those you'll entrust your deepest secrets to. Casual friends are still important, though, because they could become a close or best friend. Also, even if the friendship stays at the casual level, the information a casual friend provides, as well as the companionship—having someone to play tennis with or go to the movies with—is still valuable. Most careers, especially if you're in business for yourself, depend upon casual friends to help recommend you for jobs or refer you to others for work or business opportunities.

A **close friend** is just that: someone who is cherished, dear, someone you confide in. For some, a close friend is synonymous with a **best friend**. For others, such as the French essayist Montaigne who wrote so eloquently about friendship, there is only one best friend, for if two friends were to need you, which one would you respond to?

Ken Immer, president of Culinary Health Solutions, his company in Charleston, South Carolina, shares about the nicest thing one of his best friends has ever done: "One of my best friends has been there for me to help me in financial dire straits when I needed it most. The best part (and the most important part) was that she worked hard to make sure that I never felt like I 'owed' her. She always made sure that I didn't pay for the loan with my dignity."

Linda Swindling, a Texas-based speaker, former lawyer, and author, shares about one of her two best friends as well as her ten close ones: "I love my friend Ginger. We are similarly situated with kids and husbands. We think the same and help each other out of situations. We met at a speaking meeting. She lives 20 minutes away and we talk almost every day. We get together for nails and wine. I have several friends, one I've known since I was five. Another that I suffered through a terrible job experience [with]. I like different aspects of each friendship. All make me a better person. I would do just about anything for them and they have for me."

Some will say their spouse is their best friend, but social scientists tend to accept the definition of friend as someone unrelated by blood ties (not a relative) or marriage (not a spouse).

In the workplace, as you'll see in greater detail in Chapter 8, "Making Meaningful Connections at Work and in Business," I discuss a relationship that is more than an acquaintance but less than a friendship. I call it a *workship*.

A recent addition to the relationship category is something I call a "Facebook friend," or an FBF. In some cases, the friendships are real, reflecting a more traditional friendship with face-to- face get together as well as occasional phone calls, text messages, or e-mails. But in a majority of the FBFs, especially if someone has several hundred, or even several thousand FBFS, it is a connection that was made, and is maintained, only through cyberspace and social media.

Facebook designates those you're connected to as a "friend." Only you know whether he or she is really a friend, or merely someone you connected to on Facebook but who you don't really know all that well or even at all.

Social Media Friend/Connections

As noted before, in researching *Friendgevity* I studied the connections made by 1,051 men and women from throughout the U.S. and 17 countries around the world – 873 in several SurveyMonkey short Audience surveys and 178 in a 50-to-100-question confidential survey that was distributed to friends and acquaintances who often shared the survey with their networks. (The URL for the survey was also posted in a magazine in the Netherlands in 2015 which led to receiving completed surveys from 31 mostly women from Holland and Belgium.) What I learned from all those responses is that the concept of a Facebook friend (FBF) needs to be expanded to the category of social media friend (SMF). That category covers those connections you've been making on whatever social media platform you choose to be on, including Facebook, LinkedIn, Twitter, Instagram, and even Pinterest and Myspace.

What is so amazing about these SMFs is that you could know more about some of them if they post regularly on their favorite social media platform than you do about even your closest friends. For example, there's one SMF that I have on Facebook who shares in detail about her family as well as the causes that she's involved in, the fundraisers that she's organizing, as well as about her upcoming speaking engagements and family reunions. Yet she and I have never met or spoken on the phone, never even had a direct message or email exchange with each other. Maybe we will someday, but for now we are both content to be SMFs.

Friendship Dynamics: Twosome, Threesome, Group of Four or More

Just as each kind of friendship—casual, close, or best—offers something to our lives, each type of friendship dynamic provides something distinct and valuable. Size does matter. There are pluses and minuses to each type of friendship pattern, something to keep in mind if you have a two-way friendship and you're thinking of adding a third or fourth to your group.

Two-Way Friendships

The most common type of friendship is the friendship between two individuals, also known as a twosome or a *dyad*. Usually the friends are of the same sex but, especially in generations beginning with the introduction of coed college dormitories that offered an increased chance to befriend the opposite sex in a non-sexual way, they could be of the opposite sex. It also used to be a truism in social scientific circles that a friendship also meant there was no current sexual relationship. With the growth of the phenomenon "friends with benefits," that can no longer be stated unequivocally. A twosome friendship is the most private of all friendships, especially if the two friends do not have other friends in common.

The twosome friendship has the greatest promise of secrecy and intimacy as self-disclosures are less likely to be the source of gossip, as may happen in the threesome friendship.

Three-Way or Triad Friendships

The threesome friendship is, by definition, between three friends but, as social scientists studying group dynamics have pointed out, there cannot be a truly equal three-way friendship. It is actually two friends, plus one; who the primary tie is to and who is the plus one may shift from time to time, day to day, or depending upon which friends are in proximity and which friends have relocated elsewhere or whose interests or other pulls have changed.

What the three-way friendship gives up in terms of intimacy and secrecy it gains in longevity since the three friends always have each other to talk about and tie them together. By contrast, if one of a twosome wants to end the friendship, it is over. Not so with the three-way friendship, which will still have two to keep it going.

Four or More, the Group Friendship

The four or more group friendship expands the possible connections among the friends in proportion to the number, with each additional friend exponentially changing the possible links. It is a hybrid of this principle that is, in essence, at the basis of some of the online friendship sites, such as LinkedIn or Myspace, whereby each friend asks another friend to be part of one's circle. As those friends tie to others and the friendship network expands, the universe of "friends" rapidly multiples till one, two, three, four, five, or six friends can easily become hundreds in no time.

Sometimes intimacy may suffer in a larger group of friends, but not always. Getting lots of information about the various friends in the group is a way of keeping the group going. Also, if you like to, or need to, have celebrations with more than just one or two friends in attendance, especially if you like to have big parties for social or professional reasons, having strong and active friendship networks will make the difference between easily filling up a room or having just a few lone intimate friends present.

For example, one of my friends, Dara Tyson, has two best friends as well as being in a group friendship of nine women. Dara, who is in her 50s, with two grown children, says the common thread of her network of nine friends is that they were all cheerleaders in high school and sang in the glee club.

Whereas most people will say that they have four to six close friends, on average, Dara tells me that she has twenty close friends, including her friends from high school. The fun factor is strong for Dara and her eight friends from high school. As Dara explains:

> We did our 50th birthdays in Vegas, all nine of us. We went to the Cirque du Soleil Beatles Love Show. This was a great group bonding activity and such a powerful show to see with well- loved friends because of the theme and the fantastic staging. We had great dinners out and even rented a limo to shuttle us around—it was our little enclave. One of our friends used to have a beach house so we'd go there regularly. The beach house getaway is great for chilling together and having those heart to hearts that are inspired when we're at our most relaxed by the ocean with salt spray in our hair and lungs.

Gender Similarities and Differences

If you're wondering whether there are gender differences when it comes to friendship, the answer is yes. The groundbreaking research of UCLA psychology professor Shelley E. Taylor, originally shared in scholarly articles but expanded on in her popular bestseller, *The Tending Instinct*, emphasized those sex differences in how men and women deal with stress.

Although men tend to react through "fight or flight", meaning they either get physical and fight or they run way, women, by contrast, have what Dr. Taylor calls the "tend and befriend" instinct.

In her 2006 journal article, "Tend and Befriend: Biobehavioral Bases of Affiliation under Stress," Dr. Taylor addresses the female "befriending" instinct: "A large social-support literature documents that 'befriending' leads to substantial mental and physical health benefits in times of stress. Social isolation is tied to a significantly enhanced risk of mortality, whereas social support is tied to a broad array of beneficial health outcomes, including reduced risk of mortality [. . .]"

It has been a truism for generations that women live longer than men. In 1990, according to the Population Reference Bureau (PRB), women in the U.S. lived seven years longer than men. But by 2014, according to the World Life Expectancy website, the gender gap had shrunk to just five years, with women in the U.S. living on average until 81.3 years and men to 76.3. The men are catching up! The PRB attributes the narrowing of the gap between life expectancy for women and men in the United States to the increase in smoking among women.

But what if increased smoking trends is just part of the reason? What if the decline in face-to- face "tending and befriending" by women, and the increase in "befriending" among men, are other contributing factors to this trend?

One of the predictions in *Friendshifts* (1997, 1999, 2014) was that female friendships were becoming more "male like," meaning based more on doing activities together rather than confiding in each other, and that male friendships were becoming more classically female, meaning that men were sharing more and being more trusting with each other, with more self- disclosures. In my friendship research over the last decade, especially in the last few years, I'm seeing the evidence of these tendencies that I once predicted. Interviews with men of all ages, as well as my observations, confirm the increased willingness of men to share with friends whether or not they have a romantic partner in their lives.

Similarly, as more and more women are working, especially those with school-age children at home, friendship simply has to be something that they get to after all the work and family obligations are met. The time that might have been spent with friends before—having coffee while the children were at school or working out together at the local health club—is being spent at work and, in non-work time, they have to spend the limited time they have reconnecting with children, teens, or romantic partners.

Hopefully the narrowing of the gender gap in life expectancy will be a wake-up call to women that we all have to do more of the "tend and befriend" that the neurological, scientific, and psychological research done by Dr. Taylor and others has shown will help us to live longer.

More and more men have been realizing the value of friendship but there are still some men in marriages or serious romantic relationships who cling to the idea of "my wife is my best friend," as a 67-year-old man recently shared with me. He has a male close friend who he talks to and, until his wife died last year, the two couples would travel together and go out to dinner regularly. However, his wife was his confidant and he liked it that way. "Friendships aren't really that important to me," he added.

The Most Common Blocks to Forming a New Friendship and How to Overcome Each One

One-Sided

This is probably the biggest obstacle to overcome in turning an acquaintance into a friendship. What is shared need not be equal in a friendship, but the wish to become, and to remain, friends must be shared. It is much like romantic love whereby if, at a certain point it seems clear that it is unrequited, the person who cares more has to back off and take a "wait and see" attitude to avoid being accused of being too pushy with someone or even getting into stalking territory.

No Time

I have observed that the most common block to forming new friendships today is the time factor—or at least the belief that there's not enough time. For some, it truly is a question of not having enough time. This is especially true during the parenting years, when there are young children to be attended to and possibly also spouse or a romantic partner, a part-time or full-time job, and a home to be taken care of. Finding time for the friends you have, let alone starting a new friendship, can be difficult

How do you deal with someone who says, "I'd really like to start a friendship with you, but I just don't have the time?" Or what if you're the one saying that to someone else? Let's start with what you can do if someone says that to you.

First of all, make sure that their lack of time is a reality and not what I like to call the "time excuse." The time excuse is what people will say to you when they really don't like you or don't want to make the time, but it would be cruel and impolite to state that directly. So instead, someone says, "Sorry, but I don't have the time." So, it's up to you to see if it's really true that your potential new friend doesn't have time, or if it's just an excuse to push you away.

The concept of having enough time is very subjective. One person could have one toddler and a part-time job but feel like there's no time, and someone else could have two children, including an infant, and a full-time job and feel she has lots of time. So, you need to look at what the person you're trying to befriend is telling you about their situation and what they can handle—not what you would be able to handle if you were in their place.

If it is true that your potential friend just doesn't have enough time, respect that, acknowledge it, but also point out that you're happy to revisit the possibility of getting together at another time. If, however, it is the time excuse, and this potential friend does not really want to become your friend, take the hint and go on to another possibility with as much of your ego intact as possible.

If you're the one telling a potential friend that you don't have the time for starting a new friendship, but you would really like to, look at whether or not there are ways you could free up even a little time. Perhaps you could go for a cup of coffee or do something together that you have to do anyway, like shopping or working out.

Look deep inside yourself to see if there's something about this potential friend that's pushing you away and so you're using the time excuse yourself. Perhaps it's hard for you to admit that you really don't want to become friends with everyone just because they want to become friends with you, so you use the time excuse. It's okay to not reach back just because someone reaches out to you. You don't have to be cruel about it, and you can still use the time excuse if that makes you more comfortable. But be up front with yourself so you won't keep worrying about finding the time for this potential friend or feeling guilty that a friendship did not ensue.

By being clear about what the "no time" reason for a friendship's failure to move forward really means, you can see it for what it is and free up that time and energy to possibly befriend someone who does have the time. Or, you can remind yourself to contact this person again when you have enough time as well.

Past Hurts

Romantic disappointment stopping someone from having the courage to love again is often the subject of films, plays, and literature. Less well known is that the same kind of fear of being hurt can stop someone from pursuing a new friendship.

One way to work through letting a past hurt stop you from starting a new friendship is to build up your self-esteem. Whether your friend dumped you, you dumped your friend, or the ending was mutual, the more you think of yourself as having value as a friend, the more confidence you'll have to try another friendship.

If, when you try to befriend someone new, you see the image of your former friend who hurt you, or you hear some of the painful things that you or your former friend said to each other, try to replace those negative images and words with positive ones from other wonderful friendships.

Use positive self-talk to work through this block. "I am wonderful."

"I won't let the friendship with stop me from starting a new friendship." "This is a new friendship and I will give it a chance." If the person you want to befriend tells you that a past hurt is stopping her or him from wanting to become your friend, offer to listen to what happened, if he or she wants to share.

Listen, really listen, and don't just dismiss what's said with the response, "Oh, but that was then, and this is now." Instead, be empathetic and acknowledge that some past hurts, no matter how old, can seem as new and painful as if they happened yesterday.

Offer to take the friendship slowly, and at the pace that your new potential friend can handle. Express your understanding that as you get closer, going from strangers to friends, your new friend may have fears and memories of the past hurts.

If you are the one whose past hurts are getting in the way this new friendship, ask for the same understanding that you'd be willing to extend to someone who has this block. Ask for patience and understanding as you work through your fears.

If you or your potential friend find your past hurts so insurmountable that you can't get past them to pursue your new friendship, working with a professional therapist might be an option. Help is available in a variety of ways, such as psychologists, social workers, psychiatrists, psychoanalysts, or specialized therapists, in individual sessions or in group therapy.

Most important of all is to be aware of how your past hurts are blocking you (or your potential friend) from going forward with your new friendship. Becoming aware of this block, as with all of these blocks, is the first important step on the road to recovering from its hold, so you can try to go forward with new friendships.

Other Competing Relationships

Whether it's the new great-nephew of a single, older, unattached retired woman, a married couple's excitement about the birth of their first child, or a promotion that will have someone working 24/7 for a very demanding boss for the foreseeable future, there may be other demands on a potential new friend. Keep in mind that those concerns are legitimate reasons that a friendship with you is just not a priority right now. That might change in a week, a month, a year, or never. Be sensitive to whether someone's priorities are genuinely divided to the point that you have to be patient, or whether you're being given a polite brush off.

Physical Distance

These days, this should not be a real reason not to let a friendship develop. A respondent to my confidential survey from the United Kingdom, a middle-aged married woman who works as a publisher, shared that the last ten friends she made were all through Facebook and all live far away from her. But she considers each and every one of them a close friend.

Value Disparity

As I mentioned before, my research has found that the number one predictor of longevity in a friendship is shared values. You have to be very aware of the potential new friend's values and whether or not you can live with any major disagreements. That same respondent who shared about how distance does not stop her from developing new friends shared how painful it was that she lost a friend whom she had been there for even at his darkest time after his wife died. He found out that she was voting yes in the Brexit referendum, in accordance with her belief that the U.K. should leave the European Community, which was a viewpoint diametrically opposed to his. Their friendship could not survive that disparity.

In the beginning of a new potential friendship, you can take a couple of different approaches. You can state your beliefs right up front with the knowledge that your friendship just might stop cold in its tracks because of it. Alternatively, you can keep some of your opinions to yourself that you instinctively know might sabotage your attempts to form a friendship, consciously downplaying those differences.

Gender Issues (Cross-sex or Platonic Friendships)

Research has confirmed what many always suspected: in a platonic relationship there is sometimes a little underlying hint that at least one of the people has an attraction to the other that goes beyond friendship. Sometimes, it seems, it can go even beyond an "underlying hint." As reported in "On being 'just friends': the frequency and impact of sexual activity in cross-sex friendships," a scholarly article by Walid A. Afifi and Sandra L. Faulkner, among the college students they surveyed "approximately half the heterosexual college student population has engaged in sexual activity in an otherwise platonic cross-sex friendship." Their article, published in 2000 in the *Journal of Social and Personal Relationships*, was based on 315 male and female students—159 males and 150 females—between the ages of 18 and 40 at a major northeastern university. At least for their sample, the concept of "friends with benefits" seems to have some basis in fact.

Money

Financial disparity can make it challenging to form a friendship. If a new acquaintance is struggling to get by and the other one is doing so well that going out to an expensive restaurant is not a big deal, it may be more challenging for such a friendship to get off the ground. That said, it is possible if there are enough shared positive feelings about each other. Just stay clear of the money topic. The one who is hard up should avoid asking the potential friend for money, and you should do things together that are free or have a nominal cost. Meet in a neutral place like a restaurant or a coffee shop, go to the playground with your children if you have children of a similar age, or even go to the outdoor pocket park if you work near or with each other,

Jealousy

There are some potential friends who are just so jealous of you that they cannot get past it. It may even be your own jealousy that makes a friendship, which ideally is between equals, too hard to happen. If one or both of you want to give it a try, you can see if talking about the jealousy helps. You could even subtly or directly agree to revisit the relationship if things change for one or both of you in such a way that the jealousy is either under control or no longer an issue

Socioeconomic or Cultural Factors

Some cultures and religions frown upon friendships between people of certain religions, of the opposite gender, of other races or ethnicities, or even from a particular country or region of the world. If you both become aware of these restrictions that are making it hard to form a friendship, and you think you can work around it, that's great. But if you cannot, try not to take it personally. There are other issues at stake that may have nothing to do with you. I am reminded of several so-called honor killings that I have read about whereby young girls in the Middle East as well as in India have been killed by their parents because they went against the father's wishes and befriended a boy, which was not allowed. As recently as March 2018, as reported in an article by Madhavi Pothukuchi, a 13-year-old girl in India was killed by her father. He confessed to the crime, which he allegedly committed because she befriended a boy from a local mobile shop in their neighborhood.

Shyness

In some ways, the Internet and social media, especially Facebook, have made it easier for those who are shy and find it hard to connect in person to make friends. On the other hand, spending so much time online or on a smartphone instead of connecting in person and developing better social skills (so it might be possible to overcome shyness) can exacerbate this tendency. Books have been written about the causes of shyness and how to overcome it, and there are places to get help just for shyness. So, whether you are the one who is shy, or the person you are trying to befriend has this tendency, there is help if you want to become friends. (Related to shyness are those who consider themselves introverted.)

Too Critical

Most people get enough criticism from other people in their lives, whether from work, their extended family, or even a spouse. The last thing most people want in a new friend is someone who is going to scrutinize them. If you have this tendency, work on it or you may push more people away than you can imagine. If the person you are trying to befriend is being too critical of you, and you really want to give this friendship a try, at least tell this new potential friend that criticism does not sit well with you. You might be open to some occasional feedback, especially if you have asked for it, but chronic, unrelenting criticism simply will not be tolerated. See if your potential friend can control this tendency enough to give your new friendship a try.

Too Controlling

Related to being overly critical is the tendency to have to control everything—when you get together, where you go, how long you spend together, who is present at your get-togethers, etc. Like with the overly critical person, let your potential new friend know that this is a trait and tendency that you find quite off-putting. How about taking turns making the decisions?

Alternatively, why not make the decisions together in a joint discussion through text messages, the comment section on Facebook, email exchanges, or over the phone?

Red Flags You Should Notice

At the beginning, when you and your new acquaintance are deciding if you want to take the relationship further, to the friendship level, be aware of any red flags that might put you or your loved ones in harm's way or become issues down the road. Being able to keep a secret is an important trait in someone who you are considering for a friend. Being trustworthy, kind, empathetic, reliable, and genuine are other traits that you might care about. No one is perfect, and that includes you as well as your potential new friend. But some behaviors are red flags or even deal breakers, such as drinking and driving (especially if you plan to get into this person's car), involvement in any kind of illegal activity, addictions that might put you in jeopardy, and a whole host of other issues that are more than just your garden variety collection of idiosyncrasies that you need to decide if you can tolerate. Now, in the beginning of this relationship, is the time to have your eyes as wide open as possible before your emotions and lives get too entwined.

Fifteen Types of Friends We All Need

You want to go to a movie with a friend, but your best friend Gloria is busy, or she just moved away. You really like your close friend Glen, but he's not very keen on committing to a weekly run with you. That's what makes friendship such a marvelous relationship when you get the hang of it. You can have as many friends as you like and still be loyal and true to each one.

I put together a list of 15 types of friends that I've observed over the years that would really help us all to have a wide range or repertoire of friendships. (This section of *Friendgevity* is an edited and updated version of the article I wrote on 15 types of friends every woman needs when I was a friendship consultant for Kimberly Clark Corporation. That article was widely published as an advertorial in a number of major magazines. This new version, however, includes men as well as women. It also has new examples from the interviews I have conducted and the surveys I have received and analyzed.)

You do not actually need 15 completely different people to cover all 15 types of friends.

Categories might overlap. For example, you could have a friend who is the Fun Friend and also your Best Friend as well as a Nonjudgmental Listener. The Athlete Friend might be your Close Friend as well as a Same-Sex Friend. Or your Best Friend might be an Opposite-Sex Friend who is also a Role Model Friend.

This is just a guide and not a hard and fast set of rules. But if you try to find and cultivate these 15 types of friends you will have a very fulfilling and diverse friendship network. You can also work at being some or all of these 15 types of friends to your network.

The Athlete

He or she will play squash or tennis or get together a Friday night basketball game. He may just talk between taking shots, but this friend pulls you out of your sedentary lifestyle, helping to lower your stress level because you work out together. She may ask you to get on the treadmill at the same time every day for a quick workout, or she may convince you that a weekly exercise class together is the way to combine your friendship and your shared need for regular workouts. You may be neighbors who regularly walk together around your cul-de-sac and it's okay that you're not close or best friends. But you're still friends even if you don't share your innermost secrets, and you both know that you're more likely to keep up your walking because you do it together.

Tom Ingrassia, a Boston-based motivational speaker and author, shared with me how his Athlete Friend, Jared Chrudimsky, a massage therapist, made a big difference in his life. Tom had never been considered athletic before. He also had been having a very tough time emotionally due to several deaths in his family. It was back in 2009 to 2010. Within just 18 weeks, Tom lost his mother, father, and mother-in-law. To say it was a tough time for Tom would be a gross understatement.

As Tom puts it, "It was Jared who pulled me out of the black hole I found myself in." Jared, who was a lifelong runner, decided to get his friend into running. "I was bullied as a kid because of my lack of athletic ability," says Tom. But Jared would not take no for an answer. He knew, in his heart of hearts, that his friend had it in him to become a runner. Together, they went on runs, Jared encouraging his friend every step of the way. Within six months, Tom managed to run his first 5K race. As Tom explains, "This former wimpy kid had competed in his first-ever athletic competition at age 57 and did pretty well. Thanks to Jared's training and mentoring, I no longer felt like a loser."

You will find the rest of this story about a best friendship between two married men who are now ages 65 (Tom) and 43 (Jared), which includes their participation in the legendary 2013 Boston Marathon, in Chapter 5, "Healing Friends."

The Work Friend

This is someone to share frustrations and triumphs with at work. The

Work Friend is someone you can bounce ideas off of and, because he or she is a friend, you don't have to worry that your friend will steal yours and claim everything as his or her own. Going on vacation and you need someone to cover for you? This Work Friend volunteers to deal with any priority emails that are sent to you while you are gone, including forwarding them on to you if necessary. Just another example of how he or she has your back.

Having the Work Friend means you don't have to eat lunch alone. It also means you are more likely to look forward to Monday morning because you know someone is going to ask you how your weekend went. Your friend is going to care about what you share with him or her.

Bestselling romance novelist Loree Lough has a friend who is somewhere between a Casual and a Close Friend and who is also the Work Friend. His name is Rev. Robert A. Crutchfield and they met through work. About six years ago, when Loree was researching the first novel in her First Responder Series, *From Ashes to Honor*, she did a Google search for a first responder prayer. That led her to Rev. Robert A. Crutchfield's blog. "He struck some nerves with that prayer," says Loree.

From that simple early exchange, their friendship has grown over the years. They communicate via email or Facebook. "Every now and then, Robert will send me a private message on Facebook," Loree explains from her Baltimore home office. Rev. Crutchfield lives outside of Houston, which is one reason at the time I interviewed both that they still had not met. But the friendship is solid and a source of strength to both. As Rev. Crutchfield explains, "A lot of people look at social media as a toy. For me, social media has always been a tool and because I have social media, I have Facebook, Twitter, and a blog. It's set up to be a tool. It has led to productive relationships like the one that Loree and I have."

The Good Friend

This is the friend you do well with. This friend helps you to reach outside of yourself and your world as you contribute time, money, or whatever together, reminding you that giving is better than receiving, especially if you do it with a friend. Maybe this is the friend who suggests you volunteer at the homeless shelter once a month or train to become volunteer clowns at the local hospital or nursing home.

It was two friends who started the nonprofit organization called Together We Can Change the World (TWCCTW). Those friends are international speakers Scott Friedman and Jana Stanfield. Scott is also an author and Jana is also a songwriter and performer. Scott Friedman explains how their foundation got started:

> *I've known Jana for 25 years through NSA [National Speakers Association] and we both had compared notes about Southeast Asia over the years and we just decided that we wanted to do something. Jana had been to Bali to do a speakers' volunteer trip which in 2008 became our very first trip. We work with a lot of organizations helping to rescue girls and women from bad situations or giving them a better next step in life. A lot of friendships have started from the trips. At some level, everybody would like to make the world a better place. And there's no better way than sharing that experience with friends. It gives you a chance to grow the friendship you already have and to meet new friends as well along the way. We started with one trip four or five years ago and we've taken a second trip as well as a family trip.*

A few examples of the projects they have done? Continues Scott Friedman, past president of NSA:

Right now, there's a young lady that we found out about that was working in a factory and her mother was dying of cancer. We are now sponsoring her to go to nursing school. This is her first week. We've also built a technology center in Cambodia and helped rescue kids out of trafficking in Thailand. We've provided them with new lives as well as scholarships that allow them to go on to college.

Business executive Deidra Williams, who is 47 and married with two grown daughters, shares about her Good Friend that she met back in 2013:

> *We met at a breast cancer survivor's luncheon where she was the keynote speaker. We connected instantly and I have a lot in common [with her], from being driven professional black women on Long Island, New York to loving music and laughing, being the daughters of artists, and wanting to do work that positively impacts our community.*

The Nonjudgmental Listener

Whatever the level of intimacy in this friendship—Best, Close, or Casual—she or he is always there to listen and not to judge. This friend usually just makes little noises or nods her or his head when you get together in person. If you're looking for confirmation for what you're feeling, thinking, or doing, she or he is the one you'll turn to. This is the friend that you will probably associate with the phrase "I can tell this friend anything at all." A 54-year-old married woman I'll call Beverly shared about her Nonjudgmental Listener friend: "When my oldest son became involved in drugs and eventually served time in prison, she showed complete empathy and helped me through it just by being there to talk and make me laugh as much as possible."

The Casual Friend

A Casual Friend is someone you like and who likes you, but the friendship is far from intimate. In contrast to acquaintances or those with whom you merely network, casual friends do know enough about you that there is a connection and a friendship. This is the easiest friendship to maintain because it lacks the emotional connection or exclusivity associated with close or best friendships. But casual friends still are important; we learn a lot from our casual friends since information is often the basis for exchange in this type of friendship.

Judy has a casual friendship that started three years ago through work. Judy, who is 61 and divorced with three adult children, explains: "We are friends because we meet up for lunch and talk about things going on with us. We have similar situations: ex; divorced. We both want to find a man for a relationship, so the plus [of our friendship] is a common goal, but we have very different . . . things we like to do."

Twenty-five-year-old Ray started a new casual friendship five months ago and "the challenges of this friendship are nonexistent," he declares. They met through another friend and get together at least once a month. They are friends because they "share common interests," which is one of the primary benefits of the Casual Friend. Jim has 30 casual friends and, because of social media, especially Facebook, he is not alone in having that many.

Fifty-five-year-old Rose, who is married and the parent of four children, ages thirteen to twenty-one, has 30 casual friends as well. A woman I will call Carla is 40; she has 50+ casual friends (as well as two best and three close). Thirty-seven-year-old Joe notes he has hundreds of casual friends, but that might be because his full-time job is as a fundraiser for a college. (He notes he also has six best friends and twenty close ones.)

The Close Friend

A Close Friend is one to whom someone confides private thoughts or feelings without fear of repercussions, because there is a mutual trust that confidences will not be shared. The key difference between a Close Friend and a Best Friend is that you can have several or many close friends; it is difficult, especially in the same geographical area, to have multiple "best" friends. Twenty-five-year-old Sonia offers this definition of a Close Friend: "If I am able to be myself and they feel comfortable to be themselves around me, no matter what the situation is, I would consider them my close friends."

Rose, who was mentioned in the discussion above about the Casual Friend, notes this about her Close Friend: "[My] closest friend is someone who gets me deeply. He is busy with his nonprofit and I with my business, but we find time to walk and connect frequently."

The Best Friend

This friend is like a Close Friend, only elevated to such an intimate level that this is "the" best friend that you have. This friendship may be harder to maintain either in the workplace or once one friend marries and connects to her or his spouse as their best friend. But if you and your Best Friend respect each other's emotional and time boundaries, whatever your marital status, a Best Friend can be one of the most gratifying of friendships at any age, but especially for older singles.

Thirty-eight-year-old Brian has a Best Friend who lives in another country. Brian lives in London and his best friend lives in Australia. They met when they both went to the same school together in the United Kingdom. But distance doesn't diminish their Best Friend relationship. As Brian notes, "We see each other a couple of times a year and have started a company together. We often have disagreements, but nothing serious. I like him for his sense of humor, generosity, and positivity. We speak a couple of times a week if not over the phone, then over online channels."

Same-Sex Friend

The Same-Sex Friend helps you to validate or challenge your own perspectives and to be able to share about experiences along gender lines, as long as it is done in an appropriate way in the workplace or business settings. Some of that sharing may even be in an unspoken way; being of the same sex, there is usually a commonality of experience in terms of things like childbearing, children, aging, fashion, physical changes, and relationships.

Erin, who is 46, met her closest Same-Sex Friend in the bathroom at high school during her freshman year. "I was the new kid in the neighborhood," Erin shares. "She said she loved my shirt." Traits about her Same-Sex Friend that bond them? She continues, "She's a great listener, encouraging and supportive, knows when I am upset, can make me laugh." Erin lives on the East Coast and her friend is in the Midwest, but they talk by phone almost every day and get together in person about twice a year.

Private investigator Annalisa Berns says this about having a Same-Sex Friend, "There is something special about a close female friend; it is like having a sister of your choosing. Or, it is as if you found a long-lost sister. The most special part about it is that you don't have to say anything—the other person already knows. And, you know what they are thinking without asking them. It is a soul connection."

Deidra Williams shares about her Good Friend, described previously, who is also her Best Same-Sex Friend:

With her, there is no pretense. We are open, honest, and supportive of one another. The only challenge is the physical distance between us. We live in different states and can't see each other as much as we'd like. We communicate several times a *week*.

Opposite-Sex Friend

There are distinct benefits to male-female friendships, whatever the level of intimacy. Fortunately, it is no longer immediately assumed that the friendship must be "something else," which was the plot of the hit romantic comedy *When Harry Met Sally*. Since research has found that female friendships, in general, tend to be more intimate than male friendships, having an opposite-sex friend provides each gender with the chance to take a break from any gender-specific ways of connecting. In that way, a man can share more of his emotions with his female friend, unless he has a male friend who is comfortable sharing on a deep, personal level. And a woman can have friendships with men without the expected emotional intensity that may be more typical of her same-sex friendships.

Having an Opposite-Sex Friend, however, is not the same thing as considering your spouse your best friend. A spouse or romantic partner is a different kind of relationship than a platonic friendship. It's wonderful if your spouse is also like a best friend; I am in that category myself and I know how blessed I am to be able to say that. But we sociologists define friendship as a relationship that is not a legal one, which eliminates marriage, and which is not a romantic one. "Friends with benefits," which refers to a friendship that also includes sexual intimacy but without the emotional or legal commitment of a marriage, is also a different kind of relationship than the Opposite-Sex Friendship that I'm referring to here.

Ken Immer has an Opposite-Sex Friend who is also his Best Friend. They met around 15 years ago and, as Ken puts it, "We really get each other, we've been through a lot together." Introduced through mutual friends, they "became best friends immediately," Ken says. Ken is gay and his Opposite-Sex Best Friend is straight. "Having an opposite-sex friend is really important," Ken explains. "I don't know how to describe it. It's important having a close person with a different viewpoint that you can be honest with and have an open conversation with. The differences between men and women are so big as far as the way that their bodies interact with the world. That if you're willing to see the differences as a way to learn something, you can really learn a lot. Otherwise, it's a great opportunity to learn how to open your mind to other people's experiences."

He advocates having an Opposite-Sex Friend and as much diversity in friendship in as many ways as possible. As Ken explains, "I think the more diverse your friends are in terms of sex, economics, sexuality, age—just about any demographic that you can come up with—it's important especially when it comes to opposite-sex. I think it's really important, for sure."

The Fun Friend

Whether you're single and your friend is also single, or you're married and you do things as a couple or alone with your friend, the Fun Friend is that person you like to hang out with because he or she is fun to be around. Whether you go to the movies, take in your favorite performers at a concert, or head to the nearest bar or amusement park, the Fun Friend helps you forget about all the personal, school, or work concerns in your life. You share with each other very contrasting points of views about the fun activities that you share as you continue building up a friendship history. The fun you have together may change as you and your friend change—maybe going to a casino together or a weekend getaway has been replaced with going out to lunch or taking in a movie at the local cinema—but this friend is just fun to be around. Having a sense of humor and making each other laugh are other traits of the Fun Friend.

Christine Baumgartner has a Fun Friend named JoAnn. They met through work although neither of them works there anymore. Says Christine: "She was a good morale booster. She always makes everything into a good time because of her positive outlook." From the various anecdotes Christine shared about her friendship with JoAnn, it seemed clear that her friend is a glass is more than half full rather than a half empty kind of person.

The Nostalgia Friend

You grew up together, or you went to school together, whether grade school, high school, or college. You could have even worked together but you are no longer at the same company or even in the same field. But you need at least one Nostalgia Friend to help you have continuity in your life. That friend reminds you of where you've been as a way of reaffirming how far you've traveled. It could be ten years, two decades, or even the friend that's known you since you were children. But usually it's not the friendship you made just a few months ago or last year.

Fifty-four-year-old Beverly, married with three grown sons, who is currently unemployed, shares about her Nostalgia Friend who is also a Close Friend: "We've known each other for 20 years. She lives nearby. Our friendship has grown over the years. We are very close but not best friends. We communicate every couple of weeks. We get along great but don't have a lot of common friends or interests."

The Role Model

This is the friend who helps you go to the next level, whether she's better at hair styling than you are or works harder or has somehow managed to find the right balance in her life among her career, romantic, childcare, and friendship pulls and choices. She's great about shopping for clothes and knowing who has a sale and when. You tag along and that's fine because you learn by her example.

Thirty-nine-year-old Maggie lives in Canberra in Australia and she has a Close Friend who is a Role Model Friend because of how she stands up to people. As Maggie explains:

"She has high levels of emotional intelligence and high levels of compassion. Although she is quite gentle and giving, she will also 'bristle' when someone does not treat her well. I respect this in her, and often marvel at how such a gentle woman can transform into a fierce advocate when necessary. I also appreciate that she will 'call me out' if my behavior is questionable. As hard as it is to hear the truth, all my close friends are those who will (and have) told me truths when I needed to hear them. My friend and I often disagree on some things however we keep our disagreement respectful of each *other*."

The Motivator

When you're feeling defeated or overwhelmed, the Motivator brings you way up as she inspires you and motivates you to keep trying. Ken Immer of Charleston is a Motivator. He has been doing that for the last 15 years or so. He started with himself. "I saved my own life by starting yoga and gave up all the drugs and alcohol I was doing," Ken explains. His example just naturally made him the Motivator for his friends. "I like to see people meet their potential," says Ken. "It makes me feel good when I see somebody else wake up the way I did. The most pleasing thing I can have happen to me is to see someone make a change in their personal best interest."

But like many friends who are the Motivator, Ken had to learn to let people do things at their own pace and not have too high expectations of them. As he explains, "I had a character flaw in the past. I would fall in love with people's potential and would have high expectations for them which unfortunately they would often miss."

The Realist

This friend doesn't put you down, but she does temper your enthusiasm and wild plans with some well-meaning realism and levelheadedness. She's the one that reminds you that going blonde could be a great idea, but that you should be prepared for lots of beauty parlor visits unless you can do the coloring yourself at home. You want to go back to school and the Realist says, "Great idea," but she also reminds you that you'll need to pay for it somehow. The Realist, however, does not throw cold water on your plans or dreams. He or she just points out practical concerns that you should consider, and she or he even makes helpful suggestions about how to deal with those issues.

The Nurturer

This friend is there with a hanky when you're sad, and she even offers to babysit if you have childcare issues; she doesn't just point you in the right direction for help. She nurtures you emotionally as well. Writer and website designer Dorri Olds has a Best Friend who is also a Nurturer. "We've been friends since 1988," says Manhattan-based Dorri. "She showed me what it was like to have a friend that really loved me and offered endless patience and kindness and loyalty."

Thirty-year-old Alison shares about her current Close Friend who is also a Nurturer; they accept each other as they are. As Alison explains:

"We met ten years ago when I was a freshman in college, and she was a junior. I love her because she is incredibly generous and loving and bitchy (like me) and we love the same things. We're both introverts and we say that our favorite thing to do is hang out in the same room and ignore each other. I love how absolutely comfortable I am around her."

Tips for Making Friends During Your Adult Years Whatever Your Age

Here is a list of tips that may help you or a loved one to make more friends, whether you are 20, 35, 50, 70, or 94, or older.

- Stay active and involved in activities that you enjoy. You are more likely to make new friends if you're doing what you love. That could be running, volunteering at the local homeless shelter, taking a non-credit course in poetry, or watching movies.
- Be open to making new friends. Get it out of your head that "It's harder to make friends when you're older." Not true! It can actually be easier because you know who you are and what kind of friend you would like, and you have more free time because your children or teens may be older, more self-sufficient, or even already out of the house.
- Be a good listener. Too many focus on sharing with others, forgetting that they need to be there for their new relationships that might become friends.
- Be fun to be around. Friendship is an optional role so it's great to offer, or receive, emotional support from your friends. But especially in the beginning of a new friendship, you need to be fun to be around. Do fun things together. Go to the movies. Eat lunch out. But don't hit this new potential friend with every problem you're going through right now.
- As long as you feel safe being with this new person, move the relationship from the Internet and cyberspace to the real world. Until you know each other well enough to be completely secure about this new person, especially if you didn't meet through an introduction from another friend, you can meet in a public place. But you still want to meet rather than only communicating via Facebook, Twitter, LinkedIn, or another social media platform, or through email or text messaging. Phone calls are better than online communications but getting together in person is

still the premiere way to move an acquaintanceship along to a friendship.

My research has shown that it takes, on average, three years from when you meet till you become tried-and-true friends. You can become "fast friends," but the test of that relationship is time. So be patient with a new relationship as you both learn to share more and trust each other more. Go at the pace that your new relationship is signaling to you. If meeting for coffee once a week works for her, great. If that's too frequent, make it monthly. If bringing your spouses into the relationship is comfortable for both of you, fine. If the two couples do not particularly get along, don't force it. You can still meet your new relationship-turned-friend for lunch or an occasional girls' day or night out without your spouses in tow.

***

In the next chapter, Chapter 5, "Healing Friends," we will examine what goes into a healing friendship and, if you don't have one or many friendships that fall into that category, how you can find a friend like that or reshape the ones you have so each one is a healing friend.

Chapter 5
Healing Friends

"What I like about my best friend is that she is crazy loyal, caring, giving, and nurturing. She goes out of her way to put others before herself and is always there to help no matter what the situation is."

—Ashley, a 28-year-old single woman from Virginia

Healing Friends. What does that mean? A synonym for healing might be *positive* or *nurturing*. But there are distinct traits that we associate with a healing friend. Here is what you should expect in a healing friend. You might not have one friend who has all of these traits, and you might, upon self-analysis, realize you fall short on one or more of these characteristics yourself.

A key aspect of a healing friendship is that it can be any level of intimacy: best, close, or best. It is the healing aspect that raises any friendship, in whatever category, up a notch! It's not just a best friend, or a close one, or even a casual one, but a healing friend.

This is a guide for recognizing, or being, a healing friend and assessing whether you are in a healing friendship:

- You are equals in the relationship.
- You are loyal to each other.
- You trust each other.
- You are honest with each other, although you do show tact as well.
- You both keep your promises, and if a promise is occasionally broken, there is a good reason for it.
- You make time for your friendship no matter how busy you or your friend are.
- You have fun together.
- You like, even love, each other.
- Your competitiveness with each other is minimal and healthy.
- You have a little bit of envy, but that's okay. It's natural.

- You both return borrowed items.
- You are there for each other, through thick and thin.
- You have enough in common, and enough shared interests and activities, to keep your friendship interesting and current.
- You respect each other's differences.
- You share the same values, and if you don't share a value, you still respect the other's value.
- You keep each other's confidences.
- You rarely or never gossip with each other or about each other.
- You avoid putting each other in any kind of compromising position.
- You offer each other emotional support.
- Your friendship is flexible, changing as your lives change.

Age Is Not a Factor in a Healing Friendship

Although most friendships tend to be with someone within five years of your age, that's usually just because when you met at one point in time, such as at school or at camp, your association started in an age-related way. But when you meet a potential friend later on in life, or in a situation where there is more age diversity, such as work, a wider age difference is more common. A 22-year age difference has not been an issue in the healing friendship of Tom Ingrassia, who was 57 and married without children when he first became friends with Jared Chrudimsky, who at that point was 35 and had three children. Jared recently remarried and has a fourth child who is now $3^{1/2}$, along with his other children who are now aged 18, 16, and 13. You met Tom and Jared in the previous chapter in the discussion about The Athlete.

Here's another friendship pair where age is not a barrier to their best friendship. Annalisa Berns is in her 40s, married, and lives in a mountainous area of California. Her best friend, Landa Coldiron, is 15 years old older and lives in Los Angeles. Landa is a bloodhound handler and Annalisa is a private investigator. This is what Landa shared about her best friend Annalisa:

"I met my best friend 14 years ago while we attended a seminar to train our first search dogs. I like a lot of things about my friend. She is reliable and trustworthy. That is very important to me. I really don't dislike much about her. She is the yin to my yang. We are total opposites. Yes, we definitely have disagreements. We're like an old, married couple! We live about three hours away from each other. We communicate by phone almost every day. We get together several times a month."

Compassion

Ashley, whose description of her healing best friendship began this chapter, shared about a friend who showed genuine compassion when she had a need. As Ashley explains, "The nicest thing a friend has ever done for me was sit with my mother as she recovered from her mastectomy surgery while I headed back to work."

Forty-two-year-old Liz shares about her best friend that came through for her when her world was caving in:

> *The spring when I lost my marriage, job, house, my best friend came through for me in the usual ways of listening to my crying and letting me come visit and hugging me and calling me on it when I would go a little off the rails. But man, she did one truly epic thing. She flew in [to Seattle] from Oregon and organized a work party at my house. That sucker needed to be sold before the next mortgage payment was due, and it was coming down around my ears. She rallied my friends and neighbors and I'm 100 percent sure, based on how much money I had left over, that she got her husband to pay for a few gallons of paint and light fixtures. She literally saved me. I don't think I'll ever be able to do something like that for anyone else, but that example is seared into my soul.*

What I have learned about healing friends and compassion is that they *do something* to show they care. They don't just say, "Tell me what you need," although if they let you share about what's bothering you and share not just once but twice or three times—as long as it takes to get over the trauma—that is compassionate as well. But compassion means everything from sitting with a friend in her apartment until a service person arrives because she's uncomfortable being there alone, to knowing when to say, "I understand," or "That's awful," when you're sharing about something that's happened. And their words have feeling. They're not just words.

Empathy

You know when it's there. You feel it. Whether you are feeling it for someone else or they are feeling it for you, it is characterized by the phrase, "I feel your pain." And it's not just lip service. It's real. It's powerful.

Neuroscientists are going even further. In one study of 25 participants, "Familiarity Promotes the Blurring of Self and Other in the Neural Representation of Threat," researchers Lane Beckes, James A. Coan, and Karen Hasselmo compared the scans of strangers who held hands to those of friends who held hands. The researchers discovered that "in regions such as the anterior insula, putamen and supramarginal gyrus indicate that self- focused threat activations are robustly correlated with friend-focused threat activations but not stranger-focused threat activations." They concluded that "our results corroborate earlier social psychological suggestions that familiarity involves the inclusion of the other into the self—that from the perspective of the brain, our friends and loved ones are indeed part of who we are."

That's very powerful. According to the research by these neuroscientists, it is all about empathy. Or, as they put it, "from the perspective of the brain, our friends and loved ones are indeed part of who we are."

It is intriguing that the wise ancient philosopher Aristotle shared a similar notion, now confirmed by neuroscience, back in the fourth century B.C. when he wrote, "What is a friend? A single soul dwelling in two bodies."

Emotional Support

Offering emotional support is one of the cornerstones of a healing friendship. But there are gender differences in whether or not emotional support is the number one benefit of friendship. As mentioned in Chapter 3 in the section on Gender Differences in Friendship, according to my snowball sample of 178 men and women, of the 114 women and 37 men who answered the question, the women indicated that "emotional support" was the number one benefit of friendship (28.95%), although right behind it was "companionship" (28.07%). By contrast, only 16.22% of the men saw emotional support, which actually tied with companionship, as the number one benefit of friendship. For the men, the primary benefit was a tie between "someone to have fun with" and "someone to confide in," with both measuring 18.92%.

Someone to Confide In

It is having someone to confide in that probably most distinguishes casual friends from close or best buddies. You actually have to be careful about unloading on a close or best friend because they may feel duty bound not to share with someone else. Keeping a secret can take its toll. Because hand in hand with "someone to confide in" is loyalty. Loyalty means that you keep the secrets of the person who has confided in you. In sociological research we use the term *self- disclosure*. Feeling comfortable enough to self-disclose and knowing that your secrets and declarations are confidential are vital for most to have a healing friendship.

Listening, Really Listening, to Your Friends

Do you ever find yourself half listening to your friends, whether it's over the phone or when you get together? That you're more concerned with what you're going to say next than with listening, really listening, to what they're sharing? Or, even worse, do you have lunch with a friend but find yourself checking your smartphone every five or ten minutes, wondering who else is contacting you? Not only is that rude, but it impedes your ability to listen to your friend. I'm guilty of that on occasion, but I'm trying to cure myself of that habit. If you have your phone on, you know that you can see who it is with caller ID. Unless you're in the midst of contract negotiations with a deadline, most emails can wait an hour or two to be reviewed and responded to.

The Fun Factor

When was the last time you had fun, real fun, with your best friend? You don't have to do the kind of wild things they do in the *Hangover* or *Bridesmaids* movies to have fun. But it should be more than reading each other's posts on Facebook or sending and receiving text messages throughout the day.

Whether you're 20, 30, 50, or 80, if your friendship starts to feel more like it's a free substitute for paid professional therapy, or that you or your friends are doing "double duty" as surrogate parents, you might find that your emails or phone calls aren't returned as often, or that get-togethers become less and less frequent. Is your friend really busy, or is that an excuse because you're no longer fun to be with? Here are some tips for keeping the fun factor in your friendship.

Reviving the Fun Factor in Your Friendship

Going out for lunch or dinner is nice, but if you find you just fall into a pattern of talking about what's going on in your lives, you might want to add an activity to your get-together.

What about a concert? Pick a performer that you'll both like. It doesn't have to be someone for nostalgic reasons. Create new memories.

Start some rituals together if you don't have any yet. Are there favorite foods you can cook for each other if you visit each other's homes?

Take a class together. You'll be bonding over a new experience.

If you like movies, even though you can easily download lots of current or recent films, get out to the cinema again. Add a meal or a drink before or after the show.

Join discussion groups in your hometown. If you need some help finding some, check out your local Meetup chapters. If there aren't any activities offered that you and your friend enjoy, consider starting your own group.

Go to a comedy club.

Go on a trip together to a place neither of you has ever been to, even if it is just a day trip.

Do something physical like working out, taking a walk, going up in a hot air balloon, learning a new sport, or taking a dance or Zumba class together.

Think back to when you were a child or a teenager. What did you like to do for fun? Why did you stop doing it? Why not do it again if you can?

Next time you call each other, if you have a phone with video capabilities, use it. It's so much more fun to see your friend when you talk with each other than just to hear each other's voice!

Gift Giving

The greatest gift you can give your friend is your friendship, but many friends, especially close or best ones, exchange gifts, even token ones, as part of their friendship rituals. Birthdays and holidays are the most common times for exchanging gifts. Gift giving, however, should never be forced or expected. It should be mutual and reciprocal. The reciprocity should be in giving and receiving a gift, but also in the relative value of the gifts that are exchanged. Let's say one friend is having a great year financially, so getting a $100 necklace for a friend would not be out of the question. But he or she should think twice before doing it if the friend can't afford more than a $20 item.

In healing friendships, you also need to give a gift because it makes you feel good to give it. Be careful about what you expect in return, whether it's in terms of a material gift back or even in how your friend will make you feel about receiving your gift. Some people are actually shy about accepting gifts. It could be a self-esteem thing. It could be that they will feel pressured to reciprocate, and they may feel insecure about their ability to select a gift that will be appreciated and not ridiculed.

If you give a gift you also have to be careful that you're not sending a message to someone that your friendship is closer and more important to you than it really is.

Healing Friends Can Make Up for a Dysfunctional Childhood

Lizzie Z*. (not her real name) experienced emotional, physical, and sexual abuse as a child by her older sister. When she was 12, her older sister arranged for a boy have sex with Lizzie so she could have sex with the boy's friend. Around the same time, Lizzie met her best friend Rosemary* (not her real name). Although she did not tell her best friend about the abuse until after a suicide attempt and counseling in her early twenties, Lizzie found her friendship with Rosemary helped her see that the abuse she endured was not normal. Other families did not treat each other the way she had been treated.

Says Lizzie, who is in her early fifties now, "I think my friendships, especially with Rosemary, are what helped me learn about unconditional love. Our friendship is mutually beneficial, a partnership where you've both in it for what you can create together. There's also a beautiful balance of freedom and security, trust and courage." Friendship was a far cry from what Lizzie experienced in her home, which included her older sister bullying and trying to drown her more than once.

Being abused and neglected by her family—the ones who were supposed to love and protect—trust wasn't easy, but Rosemary made it easier to unlearn her patterns so she could let healthy friendships into her life. Says Lizzie about the reasons she didn't speak up about the abuse, "When the people you expect to protect you aren't there for you, when they're the ones harming you, why would I think that the world and anybody outside of my family would help me?"

Befriending Rosemary was a turning point for Lizzie. "I started to do sleepovers. I would go to my best friend's house and be with some of my classmates. That started to open me up to this idea that maybe the way my family operated wasn't the only way."

***

Now we will shift gears, from healing friendships to the opposite, friends that are really so-called frenemies—a negative force in your life—as well as the ultimate betrayal in friendship, what I call fatal friends. The challenges of work or business and friendship are nothing compared to the issues that we will probe in the next chapter, "Frenemies and Fatal Friends."

Chapter 6
Frenemies and Fatal Friends

"A college friend of Boston Marathon bomber Dzhokhar Tsarnaev was sentenced Tuesday to six years in prison after he apologized to the victims and their families for not calling police when he recognized photos of Tsarnaev as a suspect...."

—AP article posted at aol.com on June 2, 2015

This chapter is key to *Friendgevity* because recognizing a negative friendship, or what is now called a *frenemy*, and even preventing fatal friendships, are hard-hitting issues that I feel compelled to address in this book. Too many articles and books "sugar coat" friendship when it needs to be considered as the powerful relationship that it is: one that can improve your health and extend your life, but one that has the potential to make you emotionally distraught, sick, or even end your life or the life of a loved one.

Just as choosing the right friend can heal you, selecting the wrong friend could harm you. In this chapter, we'll delve into frenemies and fatal friends. Understanding and recognizing the dynamics of these kinds of destructive friendships can be critical to your life and the lives of those you care about.

Here are the traits of a negative or destructive friendship, or what is popularly known as a *frenemy*:

- Secrets are shared without permission.
- The friendship is unequal.
- The friendship is a low priority for your friend.
- Conversations are usually one-sided and strained.
- Promises are broken too often and without acceptable explanations.
- Even if you once had fun together, the friendship has become so stressful that it is not fun or pleasant anymore.
- Borrowed items or money are never returned.

- Your friend makes you feel like he or she is using you for the friendship. The relationship has opportunist motives behind it.
- There is excessive competitiveness.
- There is much too much jealousy on your friend's part.
- More than one other friend, relative, or business associate has made comments about this friend's character or behavior that are causing you to question whether you should continue this friendship.
- You are maintaining the friendship because of the past, not because of how you feel about your friend now.
- Your friend is getting you into something that is unhealthy such as nonmedical prescription drug use.
- Your friend is putting you at risk for getting issued a summons or even arrested such as being present when your friend engages in illegal behavior such as turnstile jumping (instead of paying for the subway) or shoplifting.

Unsure if you are in a relationship with a frenemy? Here is a self-quiz to help you identify the warning signs:

Self-Quiz:
Recognizing a Harmful Friendship or Frenemy

Is your friend untrustworthy?
Yes   No _____
Has more than one of your other friends or relatives warned you about this friend?
Yes   No _____
Does this friend engage in any behavior that puts you, your family, or your career in harm's way, such as out of control drinking, drug use, or any criminal activities?
Yes   No _____
Is this friend dishonest?
Yes   No _____
Are you afraid to trust this friend with your secrets?
Yes _____   No _____
Does this friend flirt with, or has this friend engaged in a sexual relationship with your current romantic partner? Yes   No

Is this friend disrespectful of your boundaries and your privacy?
Yes _____ No _____
Are you afraid of what your friend will say or do?
Yes _____No _____
Is your current friendship based on who you and your friend used to be rather than what he or she is like now, and if your friend has changed, it's not in a positive way?
Yes _____ No _____
Does your friend refuse to get the professional help that he or she seriously needs?
Yes   No _____

The above questions are all posed in such a way that if you answered yes to one or more of them, you need to seriously consider that you may be dealing with a frenemy. Frenemies are negative friends that you will want to fade or end your friendship with, or, if there is hope that your friend can change into a positive friend, to keep your distance from as that transformation is occurring.

Fatal Friends

In my research, I have been able to identify five types of frenemies. I will also share my suggestions about how to deal with each one:

The Toxic Frenemy

A toxic friend is someone who puts your career, reputation, or even your life at risk, or through their behavior causes you or your loved ones emotional or physical pain. This can manifest itself in many ways, some more obvious than others. They could be living an unhealthy lifestyle by smoking, taking drugs, or excessively drinking, all of which has an effect on you when you're with them. You do not have to follow your friend's lead just because of what she's doing.

However, if you feel you are in jeopardy because of how her drinking or smoking impacts on you when you are together, you need to tell her that. You also need to take care of yourself, choosing not to get together with this friend until she gets help for her excesses that are putting her and you at risk. You could choose to only get together during the day, for a cup of coffee, and spend your nights with other friends who do not indulge to excess. Or you can consider taking the radical step that an emergency room nurse was forced to take in just such a situation: end the friendship until her former friend cleaned up her act. It took a while, but her friend got the help she needed and down the road they resumed their friendship.

If you choose to keep your friendship going, however, let your friend know that you care, that you're worried about her, and that she needs to take a good look at what her behavior is doing to herself and to her friends. Most of all, make sure your friend is never allowed to drive when she or he is inebriated, and that you and others protect yourselves from the known hazards of secondhand smoke by avoiding putting yourself in situations where your friend's smoke, or the smoke of others, has to be inhaled for hours on end.

There are self-help support groups, books, rehab programs, and counselors available to help your friend; let her know how to find someone if she needs your assistance in finding help. You can also consider going to the self-help groups available to those who have a family member or friend with a drinking or drug problem to get support as you go through this challenging situation.

Another form of toxicity is the frenemy who crosses the line and makes a pass at, or acts upon romantic feelings for, your current partner. It's a gray area if a friend having a relationship with your "ex" would constitute being frenemies. He or she is your "ex," after all. But as one thirty-year-old married man, who considered it the most hurtful thing a friend had ever done to him, said, "[My friend] dated my ex-girlfriend, regardless of me voicing my disdain."

But if it's your current partner, and especially if you have children and you and your partner are trying to work things out, flirting with or, even worse, having a sexual interlude or affair with your romantic partner, is probably one of the ultimate acts of a frenemy. It gets complicated if you were trying to dissolve the romantic relationship and directly or indirectly see your friend's behavior as a welcome catalyst to ending it. But, in general, romantic partners are "off limits" to genuine friends.

Make sure your perception that a friend is flirting is an accurate one, however. A 49-year-old Dutch woman living in Amsterdam shared that the most hurtful thing a friend had ever done to her was "Accusing me of flirting with her boyfriend while she knows I will never do anything to hurt her. I always care for the feelings of others, which she knows very well."

The Too-Critical Frenemy

These people seem to revel in criticizing everything you say or do. If this is the kind of frenemy you're dealing with, and you want to try to save the friendship, start by pointing out to your friend how much her criticisms hurt you: "I value you and our friendship, and I know you like me, but when you criticize me, especially in front of others, it makes me feel bad about myself." She may tell you that it's all in your imagination, or that she's giving you these criticisms because "it's for your own good," but you have to help her to see that it's beyond "feedback." That it is painful and very negative, and that you're not being defensive but expressing how badly these putdowns make you feel.

One dramatic way of dealing with this frenemy, before winding down the friendship or ending it, is to start finding fault with your critical friend, showing her how it feels. This may not, however, sit well with you since those who are excessively critical often pick as their friend those who can't be critical. Or, as they say, opposites attract. But if you can be critical back, and your too-critical friend is upset, you could repeat that adage, "You can dish it out, but you can't take it."

You could also suggest a truce: "Let's stop criticizing each other so much, okay?" Since your friendship probably started out on a positive note, there is hope that it can return to the more positive relationship it used to be. In time, if this is not the case, you will have to decide whether there are enough positive traits to this too-critical friend that you want to keep the friendship going, or whether you just can't be friends with someone who is overly critical of you.

The Two-Faced Frenemy

You could start by asking her straightaway, "I've been hearing comments about me that you've been saying behind my back. What's going on?"

See what she has to say for herself before you throw in the towel on this friendship, especially if she has other redeeming traits. Maybe this is a negative trait that she could work on and change. Also take a look at the rest of her life. Does she have loyalty to anyone or anything so you can hope that, if she changes, your friendship could turn into a positive one? If not, wind this friendship down, pull away, and put your energy into other friends who don't put you down behind your back—and resist the temptation to put her down behind her back, or you could get a reputation for being two-faced as well.

It's not an excuse for what she does but do see if there is a family history of this kind of behavior. Perhaps she had a negative relationship with her mother, being positive to her mother's face but talking to everyone else, including her friends, about her true feelings about her mother. If that is what happened, see if pointing out that you're not her mother, and that she should share directly with you any negative feelings that she has. This might help to bring her feelings out into the open so you and she can handle things directly, rather than in the passive-aggressive way she's handling them now by going behind your back. Being two-faced—including being nice to you directly but writing negative things about you on social media, including Facebook—is definitely a negative trait in a friend. But it might be something that she is able to correct, especially if she gets to the root of why she does it and also understands the consequences it is having for your friendship.

The Well-Off Frenemy Who Lacks Empathy for Those Who Are In Need

A 27-year-old shared how when she and a group of 12 went on a road trip vacation for two weeks, her money challenges caused problems in their friendship, even though she had tried to make her money issues no one else's:

> Beforehand, I told my friend I saved up enough to make [the trip] but just enough to be spent in a way that suits me. I don't drink much, and I watch out. I don't order too expensive meals and one of our friends is really bad with money. So, he would order lots of beers and then split the bill. As I was not willing to pay for his insane drinking habit, I wanted to split the pot, and pay for my share. Then the first day, there was a small fight between our boyfriends. And her boyfriend was too afraid to say anything and she took it out on my boyfriend. And finished by taking me down in front of the whole group saying that it was cheap to pay just for me, that it was way too much of an effort and I was overreacting. After that vacation, we stopped the friendship. Well actually she did by not inviting me to come to her birthday a week later. At that time, I didn't have the courage to walk up to her and talk about it. I was still mad and disappointed.

If you have your own money challenges, and you find a particular friend is always relying on you to pay, even if they actually have the funds to cover things, you will need to be firm and consistent that you have your own money challenges. Even if you did it in the past, you have to explain that you no longer can pick up the tab for anyone else, including her. If you are clear within yourself that you are not responsible for your friend, including loaning your friend money or picking up the tab, and you don't waver about it, she will get the very clear hint and either cough up the money herself or tap someone else for help. (If your friend is truly in need, and you can afford to help her out on occasion, that is a different situation. You might, however, want to either consider any help you give your friend a gift that you are unlikely to ever get back to you could draw up more formal papers, even if it is just a letter agreement, clarifying the terms of repayment for any funds that you advance your friend.)

If you and your friend want to go out but she's down on funds, and you prefer to avoid picking up the tab for the both of you, suggest ways to spend time together that are less expensive or even free. If going out to eat is beyond her means, eat at home and do something else together. If you do want to go out to eat together, before you order, make it clear that you're going to split the check, or that you will each pay separately, so you don't get into a situation where you're picking up the tab because you've already ordered and it's too late to change your plans.

Foul-Weather Frenemy (or Pseudo-Friend)

This frenemy needs you to be in a foul mood or even in a foul state of things. It's the opposite of the fair-weather frenemy who needs you to always have things going your way and who disappears on you if things go badly. As a 35-year-old single mother of an 8-year-old put it, "[My friend is] not happy for me when something goes right."

You have to reconsider if this false or foul-weather friend is a friend at all since she or he truly personifies that saying, "With friends like these, who needs enemies?"

Be careful of this false friend; she could have power in your career to sabotage you in a really big way.

You may want to pull away from this false friend or frenemy in a way that doesn't fuel the situation and give him or her even more reasons to make life difficult for you, whether it's badmouthing you or ruining a career opportunity so she or he feels better about herself.

Ask yourself if there were any warning signs that you were dealing with a false friend or foul-weather friend from the get-go. Look back and see what it was about this false friend that attracted you to him or her in the first place so you can avoid getting yourself in situations like this again and again.

It is possible that this false friend was actually an okay friend when you first met, especially if things were not going as well for you then. But since you're doing really well now in your relationships or in your career, her inadequacies may be causing her to lash out against you, especially if things are not going that well for him or her. Since this false friend has to get help so she can deal with the way her feelings of inferiority cause her to act this way, you have to protect yourself in the meantime by recognizing the relationship for what it is, not by hoping it will get better because of the way it once was. You don't want to hold yourself back, and fail, so your false or foul-weather friend feels more comfortable!

If you feel there is truly a wonderful friend and person behind the false friend that she has become, you could try to discuss the change in her behavior as you've become more successful to see if she is willing to work on her behavior so your relationship can be salvaged. If you don't think she has that capability, or you think the situation is too far gone to salvage, avoid badmouthing your false friend in person or on social media, including Facebook. Doing so could fuel the situation even more since she will sabotage you even further if she feels you're turning on her. Don't be like the bug that is drawn toward the light that is going to do it in. Put your time and energy into your other positive friends.

Putting Yourself in Harm's Way

You have to be even more self-protective to avoid putting yourself or your loved ones in harm's way if you are in a fatal friend situation. Here are some examples of fatal friendships:

Lifelong friends, celebrating the New Jersey college basketball team's victory, participated in a prank that got out of hand. They set fire to a banner in a third-floor lounge in the six-story college dorm. The smoke quickly spread throughout the building, killing three freshmen who died from smoke inhalation. Several years later, when they were finally about to go on trial for murder, the friends took a guilty plea, each receiving a five-year prison sentence.

Thirteen-year-old Danny committed suicide; five days later, his best friend Michael shot himself as well. Considered model students by their teachers, were there any clues that parents or other friends missed that could have saved them both?

Four French teenagers, who are friends, were arrested for allegedly setting fire to an apartment house that resulted in several deaths. They were said to have been seeking revenge for a wrong done by rival teens.

A college student is arrest for shoplifting. Her parents hire a lawyer for thousands of dollars, and she is placed on probation, avoiding jail time.

She explains that she fell in with the wrong group of friends who were into shoplifting finding it exciting to avoid detection.

A 32-year-old was released from prison after serving ten years for his part in the felony murder of a robbery victim. He participated in the robbery; his friend at the time fired the fatal bullet. When asked what could have made the difference in what happened, the young man said he should have hung out with different friends.

One of the most infamous examples of a fatal friendship are the Columbine High School friends who, on April 20, 1999, shot and killed 13 classmates and one teacher before committing suicide. Fatal friends Eric Harris and Dylan Klebold committed their horrific acts of violence together.

As Heath Z. Mui, Paloma Sales, and Sheigla Murphy point out in their scholarly article, "Everybody's Doing It: Initiation to Prescription Drug Misuse," originally published in the *Journal of Drug Issues*, besides getting exposed to prescriptions by family members, the 120 interviewees with a median age of 21 in their study revealed that their misuse of nonmedical prescription drugs started because "peers often shared their legitimately prescribed drugs." According to the National Institute on Drug Abuse, in 2014, the year Mui et. al's article was first published, an estimated 1,700 young adults between the ages of 18 and 25 died from prescription drug overdoses. Most were opioids but ADHD stimulants and anti-anxiety drugs were also linked to those overdose deaths.

Naheed Rajwani, Julieta Chiquillo, and Claire Ballor reported in the *The Dallas Morning News* on February 12, 2018, that Rene Gamez, 30, was allegedly killed by a 26-year-old friend whom he had given a place to stay. Two police officers arrived at the apartment; a 37-year-old officer, who was married and the father of two, was allegedly shot and killed by Gamez's friend. The article states that the two friends "had been arguing before police were called."

The Ultimate Betrayal: Killing a Friend, Accidentally or On Purpose

Being killed by a friend or the case of the Columbine friends who became mass murderers are, fortunately, the exceptions rather than the rule. The more common kind of fatal friendship is when the actions of a friend lead to another friend's demise, even if it's unintentional, such as friends who are killed in a collision because they are the passenger in a car driven by a friend who was inebriated or was a bad or reckless driver. Or an accidental death, like when Kemp Powers accidentally shot and killed his best friend Henry when Powers was fourteen years old. (What a powerful description and discussion in *The Guardian* article, based on Kemp Powers' Moth talk, about what happened and how Powers, who got a year of counseling after the tragedy, continues to cope with what happened to his friend more than two decades later.)

Yes, fatal friends can unintentionally or deliberately put their friends in harm's way in all sorts of situations. For example, the shoplifting example mentioned above. Or the all-too-common circumstance of high school kids hanging out together and smoking pot in a state where it is still illegal rather than attending class and getting arrested together. Drag racing, bullying, and all sorts of dysfunctional or illegal acts which might not be tried alone but when a couple of friends agree to do it, it unfortunately seems less deviant, which it is not.

Columbine is extreme and you may think the shoplifting example is extreme as well, which, fortunately, it is. But vehicular homicide and even deaths related to drunk driving, careless driving, and distracted driving including texting while driving, are all too common. According to the National Highway and Transportation Safety Administration (NHTSA), there were 37,461 deaths because of auto accidents in 2016 compared to 32,999 in 2010, quite a dramatic increase. But the United States isn't alone in having this problem. The World Health Organization, in 2013, reported there were 1.25 million deaths on the road worldwide.

In America, that increase in the number of road deaths might be related to texting while driving, talking on the phone while driving, and even drowsy driving. But the lower price of gas may also be a factor because more people are driving than before, which opens up the potential for more accidents and fatalities.

However, we have to look at the role that friendship plays in these fatal friend driving-related situations. At the website for Mothers Against Drunk Driving (MADD), for example, is this sobering statistic: "Every day in America, another 27 people die as a result of drunk driving crashes." This is according to the National Highway Traffic Safety Administration report, "Traffic Safety Facts 2014: Alcohol-Impaired Driving."

But it's not just friends driving drunk that are killing friends. Friends who are bad drivers are doing it too! An example of this is a couple of teenagers who were stopped because when they went by the police, the police smelled alcohol in the car. They gave the driver, the designated driver, a sobriety test, and he passed. However, several hours later, at four in the morning, that sober designated driver unfortunately allegedly lost control of the car and crashed it. The driver and one other passenger died, two more were injured, and two more were okay. So, it wasn't the drinking that got these friends killed, but the driver's driving or some other factor that could include human error, falling asleep at the wheel, or even mechanical failure. I have not seen any follow-up reports related to that tragic crash, but the fact remains that, tragically, two teenagers are dead, two injured, and so many more loved ones in their immediate family as well as their friends are forever traumatized by this car accident.

Statistically, there is a greater likelihood of car accidents and deaths if there are passengers in the car, especially with younger drivers. This headline from the *Daily Mail* in the United Kingdom, attributed to a story from the Associated Press, emphasizes this reality: "Risk of Teen Drivers Dying in Crash DOUBLES if Friends Are in the Car." The article shares this astounding fact: "The risk is double when carrying two passengers younger than 21, and quadruples when carrying three or more passengers that age."

Those statistics bring up another issue: how much do you really know about the driver, the car, or the other passengers in a car that you or those you love get into to get a lift to the mall or to the movie theatre? What should be a benign car ride, unfortunately, can turn into a fatal one in the blink of an eye.

Although it is impossible to control everything in our lives, there are at least some steps we can all take to learn more about the things we do have some control over so that fewer tragedies occur. Before you or your loved one get into the car with a friend, ask yourself these questions about the driver. At least you will have as much information as possible so you can be more confident that you are not putting yourself or your child, teen, or other loved one in harm's way.

Self-Quiz:
Assessing Your Confidence Level in a Friend's Driving

Answer "yes," "no," or "don't know" to the questions that follow.

Is the driver over 21?
Is the driver over 18?
Will you or your loved one be the only friend in the car?
Will there be two or more other friends in the car?
Are you sure the driver is a designated driver who has not been drinking?

Will the other friends/passengers be drinking?
Does the driver ever text while driving?
Does the driver talk on the phone while driving?
Do you know the driver's driving history, e.g. if he or she has gotten into any accidents?
Does the driver stay within the speed limit consistently?
If you have previously taken a ride with this driver, did you feel comfortable and confident about his/her driving?
Is your friend's car reliable?

Look over your answers to the above self-quiz. For starters, any questions that you checked off "Don't know," take the time now to get the answers to those questions.

Now that you have either a "yes" or "no" answer to all 12 questions, review your answers. See where your answer indicates that you or your loved one need to do more research to make sure the situation, he or she (or you) are putting yourself in is safe. You might decide, after you have reviewed a specific situation, that it is better to drive yourself, take public transportation or find another alternative that you are confident will be a safer one.

Killed by a (Former) Friend

Between 35% and 45% of all homicides in recent decades are unsolved; we don't know the victim-offender relationship in those cold cases. But for those cases that are solved, the likelihood of being killed by a friend or former friend or acquaintance is 45%. By contrast, stranger killings account for only 12% to 16% in cases where investigators could figure out the relationship between the victim and the perpetrator. Those who were killed by family members accounted for 25% of homicide cases that were solved. That translates into this statistic: that of the 12,253 homicide victims in the U.S. in 2013, it's possible that 5,513 were killed by a friend, former friend or an acquaintance.

Here are some examples of real-life killings related to friendship.

- Specialist Kevin Shields, home from Iraq, was allegedly killed by three buddies with whom he had been hanging out at a nightclub where he overheard them making plans to commit several robberies. Shields was allegedly killed to silence him about the crimes. (Source: Dan Frosch, *New York Times*)
- 53-year-old Eleanor Jackson was stabbed to death and then dismembered as retaliation allegedly because of the advice she

gave to her friend that she should stay away from her ex-husband (the alleged murderer). (Source: Michael Wilson and Janon Fisher, *New York Times*.)

- At a school about 600 miles from Tokyo, during a lunch break, a 12-year-old girl was killed by her 11-year-old friend. Her friend allegedly slashed her throat with a knife because she was mad at her about a message that she posted on a website. (Source: Justin McCurry, *The Guardian*)

What are the main causes of homicides or involuntary manslaughter committed by fatal friends? Besides vehicular homicide, which is usually related to drinking and driving, or distracted driving, as discussed in the previous section, the common threads to these tragedies are as follows:

- Anger, jealousy, or blind rage (like the 12-year-old Japanese girl who was enraged by what her friend posted about her on the Internet). That anger can be related to a friendship that has ended. But it is the anger with the former friend that is at the core of the fatal encounter, not that they are former friends per se. That is what seems to have happened with two former friends who lived two doors away from each other in the same Brooklyn apartment house. One of the former friends, a 23-year-old, was arrested and accused of stabbing his 27- year-old former friend and neighbor. (Source: Michael Brick, "Cooled Friendship Recalled Between 2 in Fatal Stabbing," *New York Times*)
- Arguments that go too far.
- During the commission of another crime such as a robbery (see the story above about the friend allegedly killed to prevent him from telling on his friends who were planning to commit several robberies).
- Carelessness and failure to act in a timely fashion. You can put into this category situations like fraternity hazing that go too far, drug overdoses or medical emergencies that are mishandled, or pranks that go too far.
- Under the influence—alcohol, drugs (prescription of illegal) causing impaired judgment and/or altercations.

In a 2005 interview conducted by Eve Tahmincioglu of the *New York Times* in 2005 when Moglia was Chief Executive at Ameritrade Joe Moglia shared about what happened to his two best friends from elementary school. One died from an overdose. The other one was killed by the police when he was robbing a store. In that article/interview, Moglia explores why his fate might have been so different than what happened to his two best friends. His father owned a vegetable store and from the age of 10, Moglia was expected to work there. He notes, "I think that kept me from getting into trouble." (Source: "A Tale of Two Streets" *New York Times*.)

The key point I want to convey regarding fatal friendships is that you need to be very aware of who you are dealing with, especially if your friend has rage issues that could lead him or her to overreact if he or she feels threatened, as in the case of romantic jealousy. Although, as several of the above examples indicate, guns are not the only weapons used in such killings, a friend's access to guns is definitely something you should know about because of both the obvious and the not-so-clear potential hazards. In my Victimology course at John Jay College of Criminal Justice, each semester I show a powerful video about the forgotten victims of violence. It is the video story of several siblings who lost their brother or sister to a tragic killing. One of the stories is about a young girl of around 11 years old who goes to her friend's house to play as she has so many times before. Unfortunately, this time, her friend gets access to a firearm and she shoots and kills her friend by accident. (I just tried to find the video on YouTube, but unfortunately it seems to have vanished!) What is powerful about that short interview, several years later, with the victim's two siblings is that the loss of their sister to an accidental shooting still leaves a very deep and painful hole in their lives. Even though it was an accidental shooting rather than an intentional homicide, the loss and grief are strong as they share how the entire family's lives have been forever changed.

You or your loved ones have to be careful about getting, or staying, involved with any friends who exhibit criminal tendencies or behaviors. You or your loved ones don't want to be pulled into their criminal actions, even unwittingly, because you were in the wrong place at the wrong time.

Especially with friends you make online, or later in life, keep your eyes open for behavior patterns that indicate that you may be in jeopardy if that person should become enraged or if you end the friendship. We don't have the statistics on fatal friendships to know how common it is, and it certainly is not as typical a concept in pop culture as the fatal attraction of romantic interludes that become lethal. Romantic fatal attractions are the stuff of movies, like the classic 1987 movie *Fatal Attraction* starring Michael Douglas and Glenn Close. But fatal friends can still wreak havoc in your life. The John Lutz novel, *Single White Female*, and the movie based on it, starring Bridget Fonda, is a classic fictional tale about a friendship/ roommate situation that goes terribly wrong as the fatal friend tries to steal the identity and even the boyfriend of her roommate.

Fatal friendships are tied to assault and murder as well as bullying and cyberbullying (as discussed in Chapter 2, "The Impact of Social Media on Friendship" in the section entitled, "When Social Media Leads to Cyberbullying"), which, sadly, have been linked to suicide, especially among teenagers, too many times. Less fatal or dramatic, but still capable of causing emotional and even financial ruin, is if friends know your secrets and they want to hurt your reputation or upset your life. Fatal friends, unfortunately, can do so.

Suicide, the tenth leading cause of death, can be another form of fatal friendship if the person committing suicide takes a friend with them. While rare, this also does occur. Most murder-suicides, however, are situations where the perpetrator is male, and the victims are their romantic partners and possibly their children as well. Where we have information on the offender-victim relationship, friends are rarely the targets of murder-suicides, unless a friend happens to be present when the romantic partner commits the murder and the friend is killed as "collateral damage" before the perpetrator takes his own life.

When Friendship Heroism Leads to a Fatality

There are also situations when friendship leads to a fatality, though not for a vicious or malicious reason. Instead, it's for a heroic one. For example, back in 2007, Michael LaMaris Simms, an 18-year-old who had just returned from boot camp as a Marine reservist, became the 134th homicide victim in Baltimore that year when he heroically tried to stop an attack on his two friends. According to a *Baltimore Sun* article, it was 1:55 a.m. when two assailants armed with a knife and a shovel approached Simms and his friends. Simms interceded when the attackers stabbed his friends, only to be knifed in the left side of his chest. His friends were treated at the hospital and survived, but Simms died from his wounds.

Heroism by friends that led to a fatality is not just for adults. It is what seems to have happened to Purvis Parker, 11, and his friend, Quadrevion Hennin, 12, who were finally found a month after they disappeared. Originally the Milwaukee families of the two missing children suspected foul play. But after analyzing the park lagoon where their bodies were found, the new theory was that one of the boys may have fallen in and the other one jumped in to try to save his friend. (Source: Associated Press, "Two missing WI boys apparently drowned.")

Another brave and heroic friend, Rebecca Draper Townsend, and a couple of her friends had finished watching a fireworks display, and as she crossed the street with one of her friends, the newspaper account notes, "she pushed him out of the way from an approaching car, costing the 17-year-old her life." One of Rebecca's other friends and the friend she saved were quoted in Alexandra Zaslow's article about what happened as saying, "I'm not surprised that she would save him."

Because Rebecca was such a caring and giving person, her two sisters set up a Facebook page, Remembering Rebecca @rememberingrebecca16, as a place where visitors can share about the kindnesses that they do.

I recently revisited Rebecca's page on Facebook https://www.facebook.com/rememberingrebecca16/ . This is reprinted from the July 5, 2015 post:

> *Rebecca Draper Townsend was a beautiful, caring, brilliant 17-year-old girl who tragically died on July 2, 2015 while crossing the street after watching fireworks. Rebecca was passionate about service work and charities, constantly working to better the lives of others. For this reason, we have made this page where people can share a memory or document ways, they have kept Rebecca's spirit alive by showing kindness to others. Whether paying for a meal, volunteering time, or donating to a cause, we all have the opportunity to pay it forward every day, just as Rebecca strived to do. Please use the hashtag #RememberingRebecca when paying it forward or sharing a memory. Be sure to like and share this post to spread it around the world!...*

Michael LaMaris Simms, Purvis Parker, Quadrevion Hennin, and Rebecca Draper Townsend. Just four of the countless heroic fatal friendship that serve as reminders of the life and death positive power of friendship.

***

We will now move on from fatal friendships to Chapter 7, "Dealing with Friendship Conflicts," which deals with how to better handle conflicts.

Chapter 7
Dealing with Friendship Conflicts

"She heard a rumor from another friend that I said something about her. She never talked to me again, not even after I called her and cried my eyes out. So, I lost two friends that day."

—23-three-year-old single woman living in the Netherlands

"When I was 16, a friend of mine was sleeping with my girlfriend for many months. Most people knew, except for me. I found out during a party where they were both present and was crushed. More embarrassed that everybody else knew. "

—Joe, 37-year-old married fundraiser with two sons

My previous book, *When Friendship Hurts*, deals in much greater depth with conflict among friends since the entire book is about that issue. Rather than duplicate that entire book, in this chapter I will highlight how to deal with conflict in a friendship exploring these issues, namely

- how conflict in friendship impacts on our longevity or mortality
- how the handling of conflict in a friendship can cause it to end or flourish
- what to do if a friend is drifting away emotionally or physically moving

Conflict and Longevity

As I mentioned in Chapter 1, but it definitely bears repeating, research has discovered that arguing too often increases your risk of dying. What that means is being able to deal effectively with conflict in your friendships—without frequent arguments—is not just important in order to have healthy and nurturing friendships, but because it can impact your health and even how long you live.

In a University of Copenhagen study of 10,000 men and women between the ages of 36 and 52, reported on by Steven Reinberg at Health. com, researchers looked at arguing with family members as well as with friends. The result was the same in both cases: conflict shortened people's lives. The good news is that conflict with friends was reported to occur less frequently than it did with spouses or children and even other relatives: only 1% of the time, tying between friends and neighbors, compared to 6% with a spouse or children, and 2% with other relatives.

However, having frequent arguments with a friend (or a family member) was the strongest stressor, doubling or even tripling the risk of death from any cause.

Conflict as a Test

In *Friendshifts*, I shared my finding that it takes, on average, three years from when two people meet until they consider each other tried-and-true friends. Two people may feel like they are "fast friends," but it is those tests that happen during those first three years that will help a new connection or acquaintanceship move toward the status of being a true friend or fade away and end.

How friends deal with conflict is one of the determiners of whether a friendship will either thrive or end. Previously you were introduced to Annalisa and Landa who are best friends/healing friends. One of the many reasons that their friendship is so strong is because they can deal effectively with conflict. As Annalisa explains: "Yes, we have major disagreements. But we take our time and always come back to our friendship."

Few, however, are trained during our formative years in conflict resolution skills. Too many of us were raised by parents who practiced the rule that "It's my way or the highway," which, sadly, teaches children that they have to go along with what someone who means the world to them says or they may be punished. So too many children—and teens and then adults—keep their feelings to themselves. Or they go along with someone else's demands, in this case a friend's, but only for so long. Instead of negotiating or working through a conflict when there is a disagreement, they "throw in the towel" and either move on to another friend or simply avoid the friendship.

Sadly, just like the divorced man or woman who keeps making the same romantic relationship mistakes over and over again, until an individual learns what his or her role is in the conflicts, the outcome will be the same when it comes to friends. And they are doomed to continue having disappointing or failed relationships, or a shortened life, just because of constant arguing and an inability or an unwillingness to resolve conflict.

Why is it so hard for so many to speak up when the friend they care about does something to annoy them? We may have been told to express our feelings, but too often when we tried to do it, someone else's feelings got hurt, or, worse, we were cut off from or out of that relationship. Or the other person reacted with hurt and rejection when we did express our feelings, so the next time, we were less likely to do so. In the short run, it gets easier to keep those feelings to yourself, but in the long run, the friendship suffers because one or both of you pull away.

What if you and your best friend ran in the Boston Marathon together, and it turned out to be the marathon of 2013 where bombs were exploded near the finish line, people died, and hundreds were injured? What if your friend went home with his brother, leaving you behind, feeling abandoned and alone? Could your friendship survive such a situation? Here's how Tom Ingrassia explains what happened to him and his best friend, Jared, at the 2013 Boston Marathon:

> *Shortly after returning from running my first marathon in Atlantic City, Jared and I decided to run in the ultimate race—the 2013 Boston Marathon—as charity runners.*
>
> *Although we were on different charity teams (I ran for the Boys & Girls Club of Newton, MA; Jared ran for Wake Up Narcolepsy), we trained together for months—and Jared convinced me that I really could complete the Boston Marathon . . . Heartbreak Hill and all!*
>
> *We all know the tragedy that occurred at the finish line of the Boston Marathon on April 15, 2013. The day had dawned bright, clear and crisp—the perfect day for a marathon. Jared's brother, Jason, had flown in from Minneapolis to join us in the race. Running with my best friend and his brother boosted my confidence immeasurably—I was doing this with my adopted family. By Mile 10, Jared and Jason pulled ahead of me—they are, after all, better, faster and younger runners! That was OK with me, though. I was in the zone, as they say— savoring every moment of this biggest challenge of my life. I especially enjoyed high fiving all of the children along the race route who cheered me on. A friend watching from*

the crest of Heartbreak Hill told me that I had a huge grin on my face as I powered up that hill. I knew that Jared, Jason, and my wife, Barbara, would be waiting for me at the finish line. This was my moment. Nothing could stop me. Nothing ... . .

Then the unthinkable happened. Just beyond Mile 25, there were police barricades across the race route. Thousands of runners had been stopped, and we were milling around, not knowing what had happened. Cell phone service had been blocked, so I wasn't able to call or text out. But, for some reason, I was able to receive texts—and I was getting dozens of them from family and friends around the world asking if I was OK, and if Barbara was OK.

Panic set in when word started circulating through the runners that there had been a bombing at the finish line. My first concern was my wife, Barbara. I had scored a VIP pass for her to watch the race from the bleachers at the finish line. Was she there when the bombs went off?

I didn't know where Jared and Jason were. I just knew that they were somewhere ahead of me. Were they near the finish line?

After about 90 minutes of having no information and not knowing—my cell service was still blocked—Barbara's cousin in Texas was able to contact her and texted me that Barbara was OK. She had been delayed in traffic and had been about 10 minutes away from the finish line when the bombs went off.

Another friend was able to text me that Jared and Jason were OK, too—they had been stopped just 2/10 mile ahead of me. We were all safe! And I was so relieved!

Once the bomb site was cleared, and we runners were given the OK to make our way back to the family meeting area near the finish line in downtown Boston, cell service was restored. I was able to call Jared and found out that he had gone directly to his car, and that he and Jason were already out of the city and heading back home.

He had abandoned me. There I was, standing in a storefront in downtown Boston, wearing nothing but my running shorts, singlet and running shoes, exhausted, physically and emotionally, caked in salt from sweating,

and shivering as temperatures dropped. And he had left
without me . . .
I have never been so pissed at Jared. By 6:30 p.m., subway
service was restored, we made it back to our car. We arrived
home at about 9 p.m. I had been up since 5 a.m.

For many, this would have been the end of the story, and the end of
the friendship. With so few knowing how to handle conflict, the tendency
is to see situations like this in a "doer" and "done to" way. "Look what my
friend did to me!" is the mindset that so many of us get into when there is
a conflict. As each person dwells on what he or she is upset about, it gets
harder and harder to see what happened from the other person's point of
view. As Tom explains, he was definitely upset with how Jared acted after
the Boston Marathon tragedy:

This was the one and only time that Jared and I have been
estranged. I have never been so angry at him. I did truly
feel abandoned by the person I trusted more than anyone
else in my life. I felt that he had broken that trust . . .
Despite the fact that Jared tried to explain to me that the
battery in his cell phone had died and he had no way to
contact me, I refused to listen. He knew that he had let me
down.

How many times has someone tried to tell you that something
happened that made it impossible for them to come through for you, but
you refused to listen, the way Tom wouldn't listen to Jared's explanation?
What did you do after that? Did you make up and go forward, or did you
let the misunderstanding and disappointment derail your friendship?
Let's see what Tom decided to do:

It was at that point—about a week after the marathon—
that I finally realized that it was not Jared I was mad at
. . . it was the Marathon Bombers who had destroyed so
many lives and had robbed me of my "one moment in time"
experience. I couldn't lash out at the bombers—so I took out
my anger out at the person closest to me at the time. As the
old song says, "you always hurt the one you love."
I apologized to Jared for treating him so shabbily,
telling him that he had been the target of my venom simply

because he was there. He apologized for abandoning me. We both shed some tears. We were finally able to share with each other what we had experienced that day. Our bond became stronger than ever.

And we returned to Boston in 2014 to again run—and finish—the Boston Marathon. I know, beyond a doubt, that Jared has my back, and I have his.

Just Two Little Words That Go a Long Way to Resolving Many Conflicts

Tom shares, "I apologized to Jared for treating him so shabbily." That is such an important thing to do if you've had a disagreement with your friend. Whether you're the one apologizing, or your friend is, and you need to decide if you're going to accept the apology, there are two little words that can go a long way in resolving conflict: "I'm sorry."

Here are some ways to tell your friend you're sorry if you're the one who hurt your friend:

1. Pick up the phone, call, and say, "I'm sorry."
2. Send an email and say, "I'm sorry."
3. Pick out a really nice card, write inside "I'm sorry," and mail it to your friend or, if appropriate and comfortable, deliver it in person.
4. Ask your friend to get together and discuss what happened and let him or her know that you want to make amends for what you did and that you're really sorry.
5. Send flowers.
6. Send a fruit basket.
7. Write an "apology email" and send it.
8. Write an "apology letter" and send it.
9. Ask your friend how you could make it up to her or him.
10. Ask "What can I do to make things right?"
11. Take a cooling off period and try saying "I'm sorry" again in a day, a week, a month, or as long as it takes.
12. Ask your friend that you've wronged if she/he has ever done something to someone that she/he regretted and what she/he did to make it right.
13. Reaffirm how much your friend and your friendship means to you.

If you're the one who was wronged, and if you decide you are willing to accept your friend's apology, you need to train yourself not to go back again and again to the old wound of the conflict. But instead to go forward.

Dealing with Conflict More Effectively

Besides saying, "I'm sorry," friends can take other actions to get their friendship back on track. Here are some suggestions:

- Take some time to "cool off" and think long and hard about what happened, why it happened, what you learned from the falling out, and how one or both of you can behave differently so another falling out is less likely to happen.
- Write in a journal about your falling out and share about it so you can really understand this experience and use it as a positive learning experience about friendship in general and about this friend and this friendship in particular. You can write in a paper journal, on your smartphone, or on your computer. The key is to get your thoughts down. Writing everything down is the key, not whether you share what you write with your friend or anyone else.
- Depending upon what caused the falling out—who was at fault and what it was all about—decide if you want to ease back into the friendship, or if you're up for getting right back to the frequency of interaction and level of intimacy you had before. For some, a cup of coffee at a location that is easy for both of you to get to might be the right first step. For others, having a long lunch at a favorite restaurant might be better. For others, getting together in a group with other friends might be preferable so you can work up to a more intense one-on-one interaction again.
- Be positive and move forward with your friend and friendship. See getting through this falling out as a sign that your friendship is stronger and more enduring than either of you realized it could be. This has been a "test" on your friendship and, fortunately, your friendship passed, so pat yourselves on the backs for caring enough about each other to work through your conflict.
- Use "I" statements to express how you feel. Instead of reacting with accusations and angry words to what your friend said or did to upset you, try to express how you feel with an "I" statement. In this way, you are not faulting your friend, but you are sharing how his or her behavior made you feel. For example, "You have

the right to cancel our plans to accept a date, but are you aware that I felt like I'm not that important to you when you did that?"

- Try to put yourself in the other person's shoes. It is often very easy to judge others, and overreact to the hurts that they cause, while forgetting or ignoring similar behaviors in oneself. Without excusing the actions or words of others that upset you, it at least gives you a more realistic perspective if you consider whether you have ever done or said something similar.
- Perhaps you used to brag, the way your friend does now, and you figured out you did it because you were really insecure about yourself at that time in your life.
- Perhaps your friend is feeling insecure right now; if you put up with her bragging while she builds up her self-esteem, the bragging may cease or at least become less frequent. How did others deal with you when you tended to brag? Did they point it out to you, or ignore it till you curbed that tendency on your own?
- Take some time off from the friendship. Try taking a break from your relationship while you work out your angry feelings. Instead of saying things you will regret, put some distance between you and your friend and the incident as you try to gain some perspective on what occurred. That is what Tom and Jared did, and it worked for them. It could be a couple of hours or a day or two, or even a week. But if it becomes a couple of weeks or even months or longer, it's time to try another strategy. This one hasn't worked, and you may need to more actively work at repairing this relationship if it is to survive and thrive.
- Remind yourself and your friend how much you care about your friendship. Express to your friend how much you care about him or her and that you really want to clear the air and work out your conflicts. By validating your friendship and emphasizing how much your friend means to you, you can help him or her to see that you are motivated to preserve your relationship.
- Agree to disagree. Reminding your friend that you do not have to be carbon copies of each other and that you are both entitled to your unique opinions and ways of doing things can go a long way toward diffusing certain conflicts. You can both be "right" even if you see a situation in radically different ways.
- Learn to react without overreacting. Develop the ability to express how you feel without shouting, cursing, name calling, or, in extreme cases, hitting or throwing things.

Even the closest relationships can have incidents that could push you and your friend apart. But, if dealt with properly, it will just be another situation that you have to deal with as your friendship continues to grow and deepen.

Real Life Example: Admitting You Were Wrong

A few years ago, one of my friendship coaching clients uninvited her friend and her friend's family to an annual holiday party that my client had decided that particular year to cancel. (This was pre-pandemic so fear of catching the COVID-19 virus was not a factor.) Her friend and her friend's children, who had looked forward to this annual event, were hurt and angered by the cancelation, so the mother stopped talking to her friend [my client].

The other friends of the friend who canceled the party told her that she had every right to cancel the party. It was, after all, her house and she could do what she wanted. They said her friend was being selfish to hold a grudge and stop talking to her. But my client was bothered by the situation, and together we discussed what happened and looked at it in a more objective way. The end result was that my client sent her friend a card that apologized, and they went back to being friends. The friendship was not as close as it used to be because of that rift, but at least they were not frenemies anymore.

Six Tips for Renewing a Friendship After a Fight

1. Make sure you let this friend know that you appreciate her, and you value your friendship. She's not just one of hundreds of Facebook "friends," but a key friend who means a lot to you, and you will work hard to keep your friendship positive and current.
2. If there are any "big" events in your friend's life that you're invited to, even if it involves a commitment of time and money to get there, make the extra effort to show your friend you care.
3. Do something unexpected and endearing so you show through your actions that you care about your friend and your friendship, especially if you were the one who caused the falling out. Donate to her favorite charity. Track down and mail her a copy of one of her favorite books from childhood that you know she'd appreciate having in her library again.
4. Change the way you communicate so you are connecting in a multiplicity of ways. If you always text, give a call. If you've

mostly been posting on Facebook lately, set up a get- together in person at a time and place that's convenient for your friend.

5. Have fun with each other, but do it in a friendly and caring way, not in a way that makes either of you feel like it's an obligation. Remember that the strength of friendship is that it's an optional relationship and that you choose each other, so reinforce that choice.

6. Most of all, learn from the big fight or falling out. What caused it? How did you or your friend handle it? What did you learn that might help you to avoid a similar conflict in the future? Do you need to work on your friendship skills independent of this particular friend so you're more likely to have a smoother time of it now and down the road?

Forgiveness

Tom and Jared had to practice forgiveness. I'm not talking about a really horrific "crossing the line" type of action that is so over-the-top that almost everyone would understand if you did get upset and find it hard to forgive. Like helping your friend plan her wedding but being left off the guest list. Or being used by your friend for opportunistic reasons—what your friend can get out of your friendship – rather than just for the sake of being each other's friends. Or flirting or, worse yet, having an affair with, the person you are dating or your spouse. Most would agree that those are "crossing the line" situations—all situations I've learned about through my research.

Forgiveness in those situations is certainly possible, but that's asking a lot. I'm suggesting, for starters, that you begin forgiving yourself or your friend for the little annoyances that can eat away at a friendship. The phone call that doesn't get returned right away. It turns out your friend was out of town and did not remember to tell you. The birthday that is missed this year. Your friend is preoccupied with lots of career and personal challenges and it slipped her mind. Letting too much time pass between phone calls or get-togethers. You or your friend are plain overwhelmed by everyone and everything you have to do. Fitting in your friendship just doesn't seem feasible for now.

If you are lucky enough to have a close or best friend that goes back to your school days or even your childhood, you are fortunate indeed. That friendship is what I call a "nostalgic" friendship, meaning that you have a shared history together, and that is a very precious part of what makes you value each other as well. Because of that shared history, something you have to cut those nostalgic friends the most slack, slack you might not grant a more recent friend, because they have known you in a way that no one else could ever know you again. They knew you at five or ten or in your teen years. If you grew up together, and your parents are all gone now, they remember your parents, and you can recall theirs. You can relate to the street you grew up on, or the town where you both went out on your first date.

Even the newer friends you meet at work or through your Mom activities may become nostalgia friends before you know it. They might not date as far back to your formative school years, but those newer friends have been there for you at another time in your life when you needed them, and they needed you. I feel that way about Elizabeth and Linda. I consider them my Nashville friends during the year-and-a-half that my husband and I lived in Nashville even though Elizabeth and Linda now live in Florida and Fred and I are back in Connecticut. Coincidentally, Elizabeth recently sent me a message on Facebook suggesting that we all try to have a reunion in Nashville one of these days soon!

Friendship requires two people who are equally committed to making this unique and powerful relationship last. It is based on trust, honesty, mutual liking, and sometimes even shared activities, but most of all shared values. One of those shared values that will take you very far with each and every friendship, including the friendship with yourself, is recognizing and agreeing on the value of forgiveness. That doesn't mean you let a friend walk all over you if they are mistreating you or ignoring you to the point that is unacceptable. But the next time you want to criticize or express your condemnation of your friend because she let you down, at least try to find out just what was going on in her life that was behind her actions and see if you can forgive her. So many today have to put up with bosses or co-workers they would prefer to leave behind, but the tough job market and economy cause them to have to stay put for longer than they would like. Friends and friendship, more than ever, needs to be that safe place where we can be ourselves. Where we are appreciated and understood, and we are cut some slack.

Fighting Fair

Friendship is an intimate relationship and it is rare that close connections, whether with a family member or your romantic partner, don't have at least an occasional conflict. But the key point is to fight fair and for conflict to be a rare or occasional occurrence, not a constant problem.

What does it mean to "fight fair?" Here are some rules that will help you and your friend to handle your conflict in a way that will not sabotage your friendship and might even strengthen it:

1. No name calling to each other's face or on social media.
2. Avoid gossiping about each other and your fight with others, especially on social media sites that one or both of you regularly post on, such as Facebook, LinkedIn, Twitter, or Instagram.
3. Do not take down photographs on social media, drawing attention to the fight you're having with your friend. Keep your fight private.
4. No hitting or physical violence of any kind, not even pushing.
5. No weapons of any kind, not even for "dramatic effect."
6. Use the "I" approach: "What you said hurt me because . . ." or "I feel as if you're . . ." The point is to emphasize that this is your reaction, and your feeling, not "the" only explanation of why this conflict is happening.
7. No spitting or hair pulling either.
8. Be direct. Avoid sarcasm.
9. Listen to what your friend has to say, do not just talk.
10. Keeping confidences, even if you are tempted to blurt out or put in writing on any of the social media sites, you're on, any of your friend's entrusted secrets because you're annoyed with your friend.
11. Remind yourself and your friend that conflict is a natural part of any relationship. It does not mean that your friendship is doomed.
12. Conflict offers an opportunity to test and grow your friendship. Through this conflict, you might even be able to get to know each other even better and to forge a stronger and deeper friendship that lasts the test of time and occasional conflict.

Crossing the Line

You have to ask yourself if your friend's words or actions "crossed the line" and you feel like there's no going back (or at least that's how you feel right now). If you think about the situation that occurred that makes you want to end your friendship, you might realize that it was actually something that was building up and not really this one "crossing the line" incident.

If it is something your friend said, maybe you just need to explain to your friend that her/his words hurt you.

Words are an action.

Some words, especially those that criticize, can make you feel like you've been slapped across the face by your friend. Some words or comments can really hurt.

There are actions that can be considered "crossing the line" behaviors; it can be hard to salvage the friendship when those types of situations occur. Everything from flirting with a significant other, to having an affair, to borrowing something that doesn't get returned. What matters, however, is what you and your friend work out with each other. What may seem like a "crossing the line" comment or action to one friend might be tossed off and taken in stride by someone else.

Should You Continue Your Friendship or End It?

You have tried everything, but the friendship is still not going the way you want it to go. How do you know if you should throw in the towel or keep trying to make it work? Take this self-quiz to see if this friendship is even good for you. That will help you to know if you should continue to put in all the effort to work things out.

Self-Quiz:
Is Your Friend Good for You?

Take the following quiz and discover if your friendship is a positive one or if it's time to say goodbye.

True or False
1. My friend always tells me the truth, although she/he might try to be tactful and say it in a nice, not a cruel, way.
True_____False _____
2. If something comes up, my friend and I can deal with it without theatrics or name calling. True__False __
3. It is great to have a shoulder to cry on, but my friend and I also have fun times together. True_____False __
4. Through thick and thin, my friend and I come through for each other. True__False __
5. My friends want to share with me, but this friend always listens to what I have to say. True_False __

6. We are both busy, but we find time for each other even if we only have time to send emails or just phone each other. But we

also try to get together in person as often as possible.
True_____False ___

7. My friend cancels on me at the last minute too many times and without really good reasons. True___False___

8. I listen to my friend, but when I start to talk about myself, it's always, "Sorry, I have to run now."
True_____False ___

9. My friend's a promise-breaker, disappointing me on a regular basis, always having an excuse for not coming through for me.
True_____False_____

10. I realize my friend's changed in a negative way, and I really don't like my friend that much anymore.
True_____False ___

Look over your answers. How many questions did you write True for and how many were False? Ideally, for a positive friendship, you checked off True as your answer for questions 1–6 and False for questions 7–10.

Don't let conflict end a friendship if your friendship is worth saving. Here are some tips to try to make that happen.

5 Steps to Try to Salvage a Friendship When There Is Conflict*

This is an edited version of an original list that is posted at the website whenfriendshiphurts.com and is reprinted with permission.

- Ask yourself, "Do I want to—am I committed to—investing the time and energy that may be necessary to try to turn this friendship around?"
- Assess whether you've gotten indications from your friend that he or she is also willing to work through your conflict(s).
- Will you discuss the situation with your friend right now, or is it better to take some time to let things ride for a while—cool off—as you figure out what ways you will try to work out your differences?
- If and when you do decide to try to work out your conflicts,

here are some conflict resolution techniques to consider using (explained in greater detail in *When Friendship Hurts*).

- Strive to understand the words or actions that caused the conflict. Try to understand what happened *from your friend's point of view*, not just your own.
- Listen carefully and thoughtfully to each other. *Really listen* with an open and nonjudgmental mind.
- *Agree to disagree.* Remind each other that it's okay to have unique views.
- *Validate your friendship.* Reinforce how much you cherish your friend. Let her know that you really want to work out your conflict(s) so you may remain friends.
- *Make amends.* If appropriate, say, "I'm sorry." If your friend apologizes, accept it graciously.
- If you are able to save your friendship, *avoid dwelling on the resolved rift.* Instead, emphasize what's positive about your friendship. Put your energy into creating new fun memories together by sharing activities and experiences that move your friendship forward in a positive way.

Even though initially it may be tough and challenging to work through conflicts in a friendship, rather than just walking away and ending it, if you do work out your disagreements or disappointments, you may find that your salvaged and repaired friendship is now even stronger and more resilient than it was before the conflicts emerged and were resolved.

When Friends Move Away—Physically or Emotionally

What can you do when you or your friend moves away physically or, even more challenging today since social media makes staying in communication despite distance so much easier, when you or your friend pulls away emotionally?

Before the invention of social media, keeping up with your friends who moved away physically, especially if it was far away and you didn't have free long-distance on your phone, it was a big deal to stay in communication. You could write a letter, but it could take a week or two to get delivered and it was decidedly one-way.

Fast-forward to the 1990s when communicating through email

became feasible. Then, in the 2000s, social media sites popped up—with the grand version of it all, Facebook, founded in 2004, largely for personal communications, followed by LinkedIn, founded in 2003, largely for business connections—and you now have easier, and usually free, ways to connect with your old friends and people from your personal life or from work.

So why do so many friends use the excuse of moving away physically as the reason their friendship has wound down or even dissolved?

Here is a phenomenon I discovered. It's the ones who move away who think they should be pursued, but it's actually the ones who are left behind who need to be comforted. It's not logical or rational but on some deep, psychological level, the friend who is left behind feels, "Wasn't I enough to keep my friend here?"

This makes absolutely no sense since the move has little if anything to do with the friendship. Moves are for jobs, for a climate change, to be closer to family members, because the new destination offers opportunities that are not available in the current place, or maybe even just because the friend wants to move "on a whim."

That is the thing about this optional thing called friendship. You don't have to explain yourself to your friends. They have to adapt to you and your choices. So, if you want to keep a friendship going, and you're the one who moved away, make the overture. Don't stand on ceremony.

And if you want to keep your friendship going, and you're the one left behind, and you're feeling rejected, and hurt, and even jealous of your friend's move, have the courage to be magnanimous and reach out to your friend. Scrape together the money and go visit even before you are given a royal invitation. Find some excuse for having to be "in the neighborhood" even if it is 2,000 miles away. You can tell your friend you miss her and you want to visit, and if there's no room for you to stay at their new place, stay at a motel or hotel, or maybe your friend even has relatives nearby who have room for you.

But now that we have social media as a way to easily stayed connected, or to reconnect, if someone has physically moved away, distance alone is no longer a reason for a friendship to end. With that in mind, list below the friends you care about who you have lost touch with because one or both of you moved away.

Friends Who Have Moved Away That I've

Lost Touch With

1. _____
2. _____
3. _____
4. _____
5. _____
6. _____
7. _____
8. _____
9. _____
10. _____

Now think about each of those friends. In a new list, make a note about whether or not you'd actually want to reconnect if you could find him/her.

Reconnect?

Friend That I Lost Touch with Because One of Us Moved Away

Look over all those friends for which distance has been the main reason that you are no longer in each other's lives. How many have a Yes next to their name? How many have a No? Consider all your yeses. If you have a yes that you'd like to start the friendship up with again, what's stopping you? Use social media, including Google as a way to search for people, to start looking for that friend if the only reason you stopped the friendship was physical distance.

For those friends that have a *No* next to their names, if you've been dwelling on wanting to have those friends in your life again, you can see from this exercise that you really don't want them or you'd have check off *Yes*. Distance was the excuse, not the reason, that you stopped being friends.

Those friends are probably in the category of friends that you lost touch with because of emotional moving away. That's usually a lot harder situation to turn around than when the reason for the friendship fading or ending was physical distance.

Try not to be too quick to pass judgment if your friend moves away from you emotionally.

Gather as much information as you can about what's going on

with your friend, directly or indirectly. That's one of the advantages of Facebook and other social media. You can find out things about your friends, especially if they've stopped communicating with you because you've had a disagreement, or they are busy or any number of other reasons.

***

In the next chapter I will address 14 challenging friendship situations with suggestions about how to deal with each one.

Chapter 8
14 Tough Friendship Situations and How to Handle Each One

"One of my best friends romantically pursued every woman in which I expressed interest"

—24-year-old single male living in Texas

Here are 14 friendship situations that you, or someone close to you, might have to deal with, along with possible solutions. Remember that every friendship is unique. Scenarios and solutions are only generalizations meant to provide overall information, not direct calls to action. You need to weigh the circumstances of every friendship challenge you're personally dealing with and, if necessary, seek the help of a professional. This chapter is not a substitute for individual help or therapy.

1. My spouse or romantic partner does not like my best friend. What do I do?

Unfortunately, too many people take the easy way out and they just cut the best friend out of their life. That may work in the short term, but in the long term you're going to miss your best friend, and you're unnecessarily burning a bridge that you might want to cross at some point.

An alternative way of handling this situation is to get together with your best friend without your spouse. If you work in the same city, you might be able to meet for lunch. If you don't live nearby, you might have to keep the friendship going through Facebook postings, emails, text messages, or occasional phone calls, preferably when your spouse is not around so he or she will not potentially become jealous or annoyed by the situation.

You also want to avoid discussing this best friend too often, if at all, if you know your spouse does not like him/her. Why fan the flames of the situation? Without being too direct or confrontational, do try to figure out what might be behind this negative attitude toward your best friend. Is it something someone did or said, or is it jealousy that someone else is close to you who might even pre-date your relationship with your spouse by years or even decades? Once you figure out what might be behind this negative feeling about your best friend, you might be able to help your spouse sort it out.

2. My best friend is childless and doesn't want to be around my children.

You and your children need not be a package deal. Get together without your children and avoid talking about them to your childless friend unless she asks. There are some childless friends who actually like to be around their friends' children. It helps them to feel as if they are not missing out on as much that way.

But what if your friend does not seem to feel that way? He or she might change, in time. Perhaps your friend does not like to be around babies or young children but, as your child becomes a teenager, your friend might enjoy being included again. You can also invite your friend to events with your children and let your friend decide if he or she wants to join in. Sometimes people like to be invited even if they turn down the invitation.

3. My dear friend shared a confidence with someone else. Can our friendship survive?

It depends on what the confidence was, and also if you told your friend that what was being shared in confidence could not be repeated to anyone. Your friend might not have realized that. What you thought was so secret may not have been a big deal to your friend. It also depends on whether the confidence was shared out of ignorance about the delicate nature of the information or out of a malicious wish to hurt you. You could mention to your friend what happened, that it hurt your feelings, and that you would like to be reassured that something like that won't happen again. You might try to figure out why it happened so you are confident that your confidences will be kept private in the future.

4. My friend wants to share a secret with me, but I can't share it with

anyone, including my spouse. How do I say that I can't agree to her terms?

Be clear about your approach to secrets and secrecy when it comes to your spouse or significant other. If that condition is not comfortable for your friend, that's fine with you. But you will then have to decide if you will break your rule, even once, or if you will refuse to hear the secret. This interesting challenge is included in the Friendship Oath (in the Appendix).

5. My friend moved far away, and we rarely get together or communicate except by email. How do I get the friendship back on track in a closer way?

The first step is to be aware of what is happening, so you're off to an excellent start. The second step is to figure out if the decline in the frequency of your get-togethers is related to time and being busy, or if something else is going on with your friendship. Is your friend pulling away—or are you pulling away—and that is why you're not getting together in person as often, if at all? If it is because one or both of you are pulling away, you're going to have to work on reestablishing or improving your closeness before you worry about when you next get together. Start by sharing more, even if it's through email, or direct messages through Facebook, or an occasional phone call, and see if you friend shares back or if it's one-way.

Just reaching out more and sharing more with your friend may be all that is needed to get things back on track. Sharing on Facebook, Pinterest, Instagram, or LinkedIn are ways to communicate through social media. But that might backfire if you're not sharing first or exclusively with your friend. You want her or him to feel special. Take the time to private message (PM) your friend on Facebook *before* you make an announcement to your "group" about some event or news. Pick up the phone and call your friend now and then even if you "hate the phone," as so many say these days. But it's still a wonderful two-way communication tool. Throw in FaceTime and you are as close to being in person as you can get.

If things are back on track, take the initiative to set up getting together. If you live close by, schedule breakfast, lunch, a cup of coffee, dinner, or a weekend outing that is mutually convenient. If your friend lives farther away, figure out how you can get together soon. Perhaps you want to meet halfway between your two homes, or you may want to schedule a trip that includes a visit with your friend for some or all your time away.

If communicating more with your friend didn't bring back the closeness that you used to have, decide if you want to let things go for a while and see if things get better in time without any direct intervention, or if it's time to ask your friend, in a conversational rather than a confrontational way, if something's wrong with your friend or with your friendship. You can say something like, "I noticed we're communicating a lot less frequently and I can't remember the last time we got together in person. Is there something going on with our friendship or with you that I should know about?"

I used to be part of a friendship network but now I seem to be left out of get-togethers. Should I say something or just take it in **stride?**

Has this been a recent or a more ongoing situation? If it's just happened recently, you might want to make sure you don't have an email problem or that you didn't unwittingly set yourself up for being left out by saying something like, "I'm going to be away for two weeks next month," which turns out to be the very time that they're planning their next get-together. So, you weren't invited because everyone knew you would be away.

But if it is an ongoing situation, you can certainly say something to one of the members of the friendship network if you feel comfortable enough with that person to ask what's going on. This friend may volunteer some feedback right away, she or he may deny that there's any overt reason you're being left out and suggest it's all in your mind or may even thank you for pointing it out and say it was an oversight (or an email problem or because someone was using an old phone number).

Friendship networks can be challenging friendship relationships to maintain because so many friends within the network have a unique connection to one or more of the friends. You may have once been very connected to one or all the participants in this particular friendship network, but, in time, they may have become more intimate with others. You may have started to feel left out and, in time, whether consciously or unconsciously, some or all the group has started to leave you out from their plans.

The sad truth is that if nothing concrete happened to turn one or more of the friends in the network off, they just may not like you anymore. You can't force people to like you and to include you, as much as we all wish we could do that. But if something specific happened, if you do find out what it was and you feel an apology or an explanation is in order, it could turn the situation around. You could also decide that there are other friendship networks you either already belong to or that you'd rather be part of and use this pulling away as a chance to forge ahead with different or new friendship networks.

Whatever you do, although it's useful to try to learn from what happened, and why, don't put yourself down because this friendship network has started to ignore you. Remind yourself that you are a wonderful person worthy of positive friends. Seek out those friendship networks that do embrace having you in their group and enjoy those friendships.

If you have traditions with the old friendship network, like celebrating birthdays together by going out on the town, if it's not too painful to participate in those rituals without being invited to more frequent, ongoing events, then keep up with those celebrations. This friendship network probably falls into the category of a nostalgic friendship: it's hard to replace, so it may be worth the effort to maintain this network even if the way it has evolved is less than ideal.

6. My friend had an affair with my romantic partner. Is this friendship salvageable?

Generally, the answer is no. This is, for most, the ultimate betrayal. However, I interviewed an Australian woman when I was working on the Australia/New Zealand edition of *When Friendship Hurts*. She shared with me that she arrived home one night and discovered her roommate, who was also her friend and a business colleague, kissing her then-boyfriend. Was that the end of the friendship, I wondered? She explained that she got rid of the boyfriend, but she kept the friend, at least for another seven years, when the friendship ended over a work- related issue.

The more typical response to this type of situation was shared with me by Carol Gee, a retired Air Force Non-Commissioned Officer and college administrator, and author of *Random Notes*. When she and her husband were stationed at a military base together, they befriended another couple. The husband was in the military; the wife was working on the base as a civilian. For several years, Carol had a friendship with the wife, and they also went out together as two couples.

Suddenly, her friend showed up at Carol's place of work and declared that she was in love with Carol's husband. "Does he feel the same way?" Carol asked, shocked by this disclosure since she had never seen any signs of what this friend was stating. "Yes," her friend answered.

Carol said she was going to call her husband and ask him to come over, which he immediately did, so she could confront him directly herself, with their friend still present.

As soon as he arrived, she repeated to her husband what her friend had said and asked if he felt the same way. He denied having any feelings for Carol's friend.

"Screaming and crying, she left…," explains Carol. "That feeling of betrayal was not like anything I had ever felt before. It made me afraid to trust other women."

Not only was that the end of their friendship, but Carol shared that this incident, which happened more than 30 years ago, impacted her friendships with other women. "To this day," notes Carol, "while I have a couple of loving women friends, I find myself holding something back in our relationships. I have always valued relationships and could never imagine hurting a friend like that. I don't know whatever happened to her and her husband. We received military orders soon after and left."

What about Carol's marriage? Carol shared, "This past March my husband and I celebrated 43 years together, and our marriage is stronger today than ever."

I asked Carol if she ever wanted to work things out with that friend, and she answered with a very clear "No." So, going back to the original question about whether or not it's possible to salvage a friendship if your friend makes a romantic pass at, or even consummates a romantic or sexual relationship with, your significant other, perhaps the alternate question is "Why would you want to?

7. My friend dominates our conversations or makes all the choices in our friendship. How can I get our relationship to be more equitable?

Reciprocity in a friendship is usually one of the conditions for a connection growing and lasting. However, what is shared need not be equal. So, you can try to get this friend to let you talk the same amount as she or he does, or to pick the restaurant you're going to next time, but will she or he really change? Being too dominant a person or always needing to be in control are deep-seated traits that may not be that easy to correct, especially if those qualities have been engrained in your friend for years or even decades.

While it's worth a try, another approach is to look at your friendship and consider where your friend defers to you. Maybe your friend picked the last movie that you went to see, but you got to decide if you'd even get together or not. Or maybe every single time you call or send a text, your friend *always* takes your call and talks, or always texts back within seconds or minutes, no matter what she's doing, except driving. So, what must change if you want to keep your friendship going, and without as much angst, may just be you and your attitude about your friend and your friendship, rather than your pal.

8. I have messed up and done something I'm not proud of to my friend. What can I do to prevent our friendship from ending?

The first step is to admit you did something that you now regret. Ask your friend for forgiveness. As you know from the example in number 7, above, about the friend wanting to have an affair with her friend's husband, some behavior may be too hard to forgive. What was missing in the scenario related to Carol Gee's former friend is her friend's expression of remorse, although we don't know if she might have expressed regret if Carol had given her the chance to do so.

The second step, if you express remorse and your friend is okay with accepting your remorse or apology, is to try to avoid dwelling on what happened and bringing it up over and over again. It's tempting to do that because, for many of us, talking about a trauma or a situation that is complicated can feel good as you try to work it all through verbally. But that can just rub salt in the wounds of those who were hurt, for starters, and it also makes it harder for the wound to heal, like picking at a scab.

The third step, and this is something you have to do on your own or through talking with others (probably everyone but the friend you hurt), or maybe even talking with a coach or a therapist, is to figure out why you were compelled to hurt your friend in that way. Was it jealousy? A misunderstanding that got out of control? To avoid hurting this friend or another friend in the future, you will want to understand the dynamics of the action or words so you can avoid duplicating that annoying behavior.

Finally, here is a possible fourth step. Let your friend know that health expert and bestselling author Jonny Bowden, Ph.D., author of *The Most Effective Ways to Live Longer*, considers forgiveness to be the key to happiness and longevity. So, if your friend wants to be happier, and to live longer, why not forgive you? It's in your friend's best interest to do so!

9. I can't get to my friend's big event. How can I deal with this situation, so it does not end **the** friendship?

I learned the hard way that telling people who share with you that they can't attend your big event that they'll be missed and that you're disappointed, can backfire. In the cases where I told that to people, thinking that they would be flattered that I was trying to show that I actually cared if they attended or not, my expressions were seen as pressure and it led to several rifts.

The mistake I made is the error that can lead to a lot of friendship misunderstandings, namely, putting myself in the other person's shoes and thinking, "What would I like someone to say to me in this situation?"

Unfortunately, what you might like may be the exact opposite of what this friend prefers.

You might want someone to tell you how much you will be missed, so you'll try even harder to be able to get there or, if you still can't attend, so at least you'll know that you matter. But someone else might see it as being insensitive to the reasons that he or she is unable to get there. So, my suggestion is to find out what your friend might feel best hearing from you.

And if you are the one who can't attend an event, if possible, share a specific reason rather than just saying in a vague way, "Sorry, I have a previous commitment." Sharing what that scheduling conflict is will help the friend whom you must disappoint know that you're not just making up a lame excuse to get out of an obligation.

But do express genuine regret that you're unable to attend. Without belaboring the point, just show that you feel conflicted and disappointed that you must let your friend down.

Sharing in a heartfelt way will go a long way toward helping your friend feel that your absence is not a reflection of how you really feel about your friend and your friendship, but rather is just a matter of extenuating circumstances that are preventing you from being in two places at once.

Depending on the situation, if you really care about this friend and whatever event it is that you're missing, send a gift anyway. Most people will do this when it comes to something huge, like a wedding, but you might not be as quick to do it for a birthday or anniversary party or another kind of celebration. If this friend is special to you, your failure to attend the big event should not be the reason you fail to provide a present to mark the importance of the special event, whether that present is something tangible for the person being celebrated, or even a donation to a favorite charity of theirs.

Next, ask about the event even though you were unable to attend. Show an interest in hearing about it and even seeing photos or videos. Just because you were not able to be part of the event, don't shut yourself out of this important event in your friend's life, or you may find that a gap starts to form between you that in time just gets bigger and bigger.

10. My friend has stopped talking to me and I do not know why. She will not discuss what is going on with me either. What do I do?

When I was a little kid, and even at times when I was a grown woman, my mother would use the "silent treatment" on me. It was torturous! In my friendship research, I have found that having a friend that pulled away and who will not discuss what happened, leaving the abandoned friend clueless and frustrated, is one of the more sobering and challenging situations to cope with.

Atlanta-based Carol Gee shared with me about a situation like that. She had a friend in college who suddenly stopped talking to her. It bothered Carol for years, but her friend would not take her phone calls or have anything to do with her. After ten years, Carol asked her former friend's husband, who was still a casual friend of Carol's—they had all served in the military together—why his wife wouldn't talk to Carol. Her friend replied that it was because Carol had borrowed a slip and never returned it. (FYI: A slip is that garment that women used to put under their dresses.)

Carol did not even remember borrowing or failing to return the slip, although she took her friend and his wife's word for it. It solved the mystery, but it did not make Carol feel any better about the situation. She was still frustrated that her friend had simply cut her out of her life and that there did not seem to be a chance to resolve their conflict.

In *When Friendship Hurts,* I share the powerful anecdote about a woman I call Dolores. She shares how two different friends, within a short period of time, ended their friendship by not talking to her ever again. She even shared a therapist with one of the former friends. She asked the therapist to tell her patient that Dolores wanted to talk with her and work out their differences. The therapist told Dolores that her former friend refused to discuss things with her. In Dolores's case, since it was clear that neither friend would discuss matters with her, she decided to use it as a catalyst to see what might be going on. She analyzed the dynamics of both friendships with the two different women that had the same outcome: termination and silence.

What were the common denominators? What Dolores realized was that she was a married woman with a son with learning disabilities. A big part of her friendship with those two women was complaining about her marriage and her son's situation. Both women were younger and single.

They just wanted a friend to hang out with and have a good time. Since they were both single and childless, they couldn't relate to the traumas that Dolores was dealing with, nor did they want to.

Dolores learned a valuable lesson from that self-analysis. The next time she befriended someone, and with the other friends she still had, she was much more careful to avoid dwelling on what was wrong in her life. After that, friends did not drop her anymore.

So please do the same thing. Without self-blaming, consider the dynamics of the friendship with the friend who is now refusing to speak to you. What can you learn from this self-analysis about this friendship, if anything? Perhaps it will help you in other situations.

Finally, if all else fails, remember that it might be about your friend and not you. The cutting off may be tied to something going on in his or her life. Someday, your friend might seek you out and explain to you what happened, and maybe even apologize. In the meantime, move on and strengthen your connections to other friends. Avoid dwelling on this disappointing situation. Always remember that you're worthy of one or more positive, healthy, nurturing friendships.

11. I feel jealous of my friend. Does that mean I'm a bad friend?

A little bit of envy or jealousy is normal. It's human nature. But if it becomes excessive, then you need to consider what's going on in your own life that you're so focused on what others have.

Studies by University of Houston psychologist Dr. Mai-Ly N. Steers and her colleagues on the link between Facebook usage and depressive symptoms isolated what they call "Seeing Everyone Else's Highlight Reels," in which people make "social comparison to peers through computer-mediated interactions on Facebook." Or, to put it another way, comparing what you're doing, and what you have, to others can make you feel more jealous.

There are individual differences in how these Facebook (social media) comparisons impact someone. You must know yourself. If you're the type who gets upset, or depressed, when you make these comparisons, maybe you should be spending less time on Facebook, since the amount of time spent on Facebook was a factor for both genders in the prevalence of depressive symptoms. You don't have to totally cut out Facebook, unless you want to, but at least cut down on the time you spend on it.

Also, catch yourself and talk to yourself if you find yourself feeling jealous. Here is affirmation #344 from my book, *365 Daily Affirmations for Healthy and Nurturing Relationships*, that you might find useful:

> *I know there will always be someone who has more than me,*
> *or someone who has less than me, but there is only one me*
> *and I am appreciative of who I am and what I have.*

12. I accepted a "friend" request on Facebook from someone, but now I regret that we are Facebook friends.

You may unfriend that person or block him/her. Here is some more information about either of these ways of handling the situation—if you prefer not to just ignore him/her.

At the Facebook Help Center, you will find this question: "If I unfriend someone, will they be notified?"

Here is the official Facebook answer: "No, but you'll be removed as a friend from their friend list as well."

You can also "block" someone so that you won't see his or her post and yours will be off- limits to them as well. To do this, put in the name or email address of the person you want to block and hit "block."

As with unfriending, the person you are blocking will not be notified.

In the future, obviously you may want to be more careful about who you grant access to your Facebook and other social media profiles. Take the time to go through the privacy settings on each of the sites that you belong to and make sure you have the privacy settings that match your personal and professional needs.

Remember that Facebook and the other sites may be suggesting people for you to "friend" or connect with based on a site algorithm that uses the data in your profile, such as your hometown, age, schools you attended, places you worked, and other factors. It's up to you to decide if you want to pursue a recommendation for connecting, whether from the site or from an individual.

You are in control. Social media is supposed to be a positive tool for personal and professional socializing, not a source of anguish, cyberbullying, or cyberstalking. Unfriend them.

13. I do not like my child's friend. What can I do?

It depends on your child's age and on whether the friend is someone you just don't particularly like, or whether there's something truly negative or nefarious going on. Is your 15-year-old hanging out with a friend who is a bully, someone who is cruel to animals, or who engages in criminal behavior or self-destructive habits that are putting your child in jeopardy? Or is it just that you would prefer that your child picked someone else to be a friend, but this friend is perfectly okay?

With younger children, since they are usually dependent on you to facilitate their interactions, such as through playdates, you can try to shift your child toward getting together with other children, especially if you're the one making the phone calls and organizing the playdates.

If it's an older child, you may have to have a dialogue about why you object to a friend. Once again, trying to shift your older child or teen toward other choices may work better than making definitive pronouncements like, "I forbid you from hanging out with so-and-so," especially since older children or teens, unless they understand and agree with what a parent wants, may find a way to go around you anyway.

If it's a life or death situation, however, you might have to put your foot down, or even move. If your child's or teen's friend is involved in such risky behavior that it threatens your child or teen, or even others, don't be shy about proactively intervening to save your child (or to get your child or teen the help that he/she needs).

In the more run-of-the-mill situations where you just think your child can "do better," use his or her friendship choices as a learning experience for all of you. What are these friendship choices saying about your child? Are they reflective of low self-esteem or wanting to fit in with a crowd?

Making friendship choices, and learning from those choices, is one of the jobs of growing up. Taking away that experience from your child or teen will not help him or her to develop the friendship skills that will help them to sort these interpersonal relationship issues out on their own in the years ahead.

You can certainly have a dialogue about a friend. You might also consider finding books, TV shows, or movies that you and your child or teen can read or watch together to prompt discussion of some of the issues behind your negative feelings about a friend. It's possible, with some outside input, that your child or teen will figure out on his or her own what better friendship choices he or she could be making.

***

In the next chapter we will look at friendship at work and in business, such a key place for new friendships to form after the school years.

Chapter 9
Making Meaningful Connections at Work and in Business

"We work at the same office, but not together. ...Since we have mutual interest in each other's company and we have lots of fun together, I think we are friends. We communicate pretty much every day while we are both in Australia, and much less frequently (maybe once a week) when one of us is traveling for work. We have a similar sense of humor, both read a lot, and like to discuss the books we read together."

—24-year-old describing her opposite-sex friendship
that started two years ago at the office
when she moved to Melbourne

Practically everyone is so busy today that, after the school years, it is at work that new friendships are most likely to form. Research supports the benefits of friendship at work in terms of increased productivity and worker satisfaction; it is more pleasant to work with friends than strangers. But work-related friendships are not without their potential challenges, as explored in this chapter.

In my snowball sample of 178 men and women, when asked the question, "How did you meet your most recent friend?" 37% wrote that it was through work. In addition to meeting friends through work, there are a lot more friends working together as well as those who met through work. Here are the results of several SurveyMonkey Audience surveys on that question:

Q3 Do you have any friends at work or that you met through work?

82% of the 51 surveyed from the United Kingdom answered "yes"
81% of the 58 surveyed from Australia answered "yes"
83% of the 339 surveyed from America answered "yes"

Working with or For a Friend

- Ben and Jerry, the co-founders of Ben and Jerry's ice cream, were friends going back to their meeting in gym class in seventh grade on Long Island, where they grew up.
- Hewlett and Packard were college buddies, and so were the founders of Starbucks.
- Bill Gates and Paul Allen, cofounders in 1975 of Microsoft, were childhood friends.
- Hayley Barna and Katia Beauchamp became friends at Harvard Business School in 2010. A few years later, they launched their business, Birchbox.com, a monthly subscription service of beauty samples. They now have more than 100 employees as well as offices in New York City, the U.K., France, Spain, and Belgium.
- Google cofounders and billionaires Sergey Brin and Larry Page became friends when they were both Ph.D. students at Stanford University.

As these examples attest, friends can and do successfully work together and cofound companies. But is it for you? Still unsure if you can work with a friend or not? Take the following quiz, reprinted with permission from my book, *Productive Relationships: 57 Strategies for Building Stronger Business Connections*. This self-quiz should help you decide if you could work for or with a friend.

Self-Quiz:
Should You Work for, or With, a Friend?

1. Have you picked the friend with whom you wish to work very carefully? Not all friendships, or business situations, are equal.
2. Do you and this friend share the same values, such as honesty, loyalty, trust, a similar work ethic, or family priorities?
3. Is there a way to divide the responsibilities so that you are in complementary rather than competitive roles?
4. If you will be reporting to your friend, are you able to take orders from your friend, separating the friendship from his or her supervisory role?
5. If your friend will report to you, are you able to do the same?
6. Are you able to be objective at work or in your business despite

your emotional attachment to your friend?

7. If the arrangement does not work out, are you or your friend prepared to leave the job?

8. If you are not at the same level, are you still able to work well together despite your different status or roles?

9. If you are in business together, even though you are friends, do you have a legal document that you are relying on as well as an exit strategy for the business if the arrangement does not work out?

10. Are you willing to make a choice if you must between saving your job and saving your friendship?

If you answered *yes* to all ten questions, working with or for your friend has a better chance of a positive outcome. If you answered no to one or more questions, you should seriously consider if this is an arrangement that is in your best interest. If you answered no to three or more questions, especially to question 10, "Are you willing to make a choice if you have to between saving your job and saving your friendship?" you may be better off having a "no friends" policy at work or in business that you strictly enforce.

Larry Winget, an international speaker and author, and his four friends write a weekly blog called Five Friends, and it's working out! Why does it work? First, the friendship part came first. Second, they are at a similar place in their careers and their skills sets are comparable. I asked Larry to share about his unique Five Friends blog. He explained in an email reprinted here how the blog happened and why he thinks it's successful:

> *The whole Five Friends thing came about mainly out of my laziness. I didn't like writing a weekly blog, so I asked my four best friends to write guest blogs for me. Then it hit me that we should do a joint blog where we all contributed 200 words each to address an issue about business or life.*
>
> *We all operate at the same level in the industry, all have unique points of view, and all have great respect for each other's work. It was fun and easy and smart business as well. Our individual work got exposure to the following of the others. That's good marketing.*
>
> *It works because of friendship. Friendship based in trust and respect. We all know that the others are going to*

say something smart and we will never be embarrassed by them. We don't talk about what the other one is going to say in advance, we just pose the issue and contribute our 200 words. Recently, we changed to video blogs with a one-minute limit each. It's fun for us to see what the others will say.

Bottom line for all of us is that we have been friends for over 25 years. We like each other, trust each other, and respect each other. We are all respected by our audiences and followers. We get to bounce great ideas around and know that at least one of us will resonate with the folks who read or watch what we've done.

Coworker, Workship, or Friendship?

In my book, *Who's That Sitting at My Desk? Workship, Friendship, or Foe?*, I introduced the concept of a *workship*. That's a work-related relationship that is more than a coworker but less than a friend. I pointed out the benefits of a strong relationship in work or business that is not as committed as a friendship, since friendship may bring challenges such as how to supervise your friend or how to have a friendship without others feeling jealous or at a disadvantage.

In time, as you get to know your coworkers, service providers, employees, or even your boss better, you can decide if you want to open more and turn the workship into a friendship. If you do move the relationship along to a friendship, start with a casual one where less of your personal life is shared but you still feel the bond of friendship.

There are lots of journal articles, as well as my own books, that caution about having friends at work. Here is a cautionary tale of a friendship at work that soured to keep in mind. A 50-year-old single woman, who asked to remain anonymous, shared what happened with me. This woman, whom I'll call Kate, worked at a company where part of her job involved gaining access to personnel files and such information as what employees earned. She was required to keep that information confidential. She befriended a woman at work, and during their three-year friendship she revealed the salary information about one of their fellow employees. Probably nothing would have happened from that indiscretion, but she and her friend went bowling with her friend's son and granddaughter. The granddaughter, who was around ten years old, was acting up. Kate said something to her friend about her granddaughter's behavior. Kate's friend was offended and said, in words to this effect, "I don't think we can be friends anymore."

Almost immediately, she went to Human Resources and reported that Kate had shared salary information with her. Even though it had been a while since Kate shared that information, she was instantly fired.

Her friendship and her job ended, and, at the time of our phone interview, she was still struggling to get a new job after a few years. In addition to a tough job market, being fired for cause certainly makes the job search a lot more challenging.

In addition to the potential negatives of having a friendship at work noted above, there are also the possible complications of an opposite-sex work friendship becoming romantic, the unwitting disclosure of privileged information (because of the friendship) compromising one or both friends at work, and others in the workplace feeling jealous of the friendship.

On the plus side, we know that those who work with friends tend to enjoy their jobs more and feel like work is more than just a job. Their work friends become a second family. The groundbreaking book by Tom Rath, *Vital Friends*, included the results of a March 2005 Gallup poll in which 1,009 people were surveyed about friendships and other topics including their health, life satisfaction, and workplace attitudes. Rath notes in the Appendix that data was also analyzed from 2002, 2003, and 2004 which represented 4.51 million respondents. The findings from all that data that relate specifically to having a best friend at work discovered that those with a best friend had "better safety records."

Rath sums it up this way: "When people have a best friend at work, they simply achieve more."

In addition, employees with a best friend at work are "21% more likely to report that at work, they have the opportunity do what they do best every day."

Rath regrets that, in the millions of people polled, only 3 out of 10 indicated that they have a best friend at work.

The conclusion is that a *well-managed* work friendship is possible. Also, with more and more individuals working from home or telecommuting, as well as the growth of solopreneurs and entrepreneurs, being able to have friendships through business—which might mean you meet and connect through a non-traditional shared outside workspace or at a conference or through an association—is more important than ever in reducing the potential isolation of working alone.

But what does a well-managed friendship at work or in business mean? Here are some rules:

- Whether the friendship started at work, or you were friends before you started working together, you agree to discuss how your relationship will be handled on the job or in business.
- If you are coworkers, you discuss what would happen if one of you got promoted and you had to report to the other. Could you supervise your friend? If the answer is no, how will you both handle that situation? Would one ask for a transfer? If yes, which one?
- How will you handle at work the privileged information you have about each other because of your friendship?
- What about communicating through social media and over the Internet? Are there company rules about that which you need to consider? Are you allowed to communicate on your personal phone with another employee who happens to be a friend, or would that be considered a sticky wicket situation?
- Will you avoid using nicknames at work as well as having too many public displays of affection (PDAs), such as hugs or kisses on the cheek, that could make others uncomfortable?
- What will you say if coworkers, vendors, or others ask, "Are you friends?"
- Are you prepared to end the friendship if it becomes necessary to choose between your friendship and your job?

There are wide ranges of situations when it comes to friendship, work, and business. Some companies are so excited by the improvements in productivity and morale that having friends working together can bring that they offer financial incentives to current employees whose recommendation of a friend for employment leads to a hiring. Other companies frown on it. So, consider your personality, your friend's temperament, as well as the industry you're in and the policies at the company where you work when deciding if friendship at work or in business is the right approach for you.

In General, When Starting a New Job Be Cautious About Making New Friends

When you start a new job and someone who works with you wants to become your friend, some caution is usually warranted. When deciding if a potential new friend connection is "safe" for you and your job, you need to be careful. Close or best friendships are all about opening and self-disclosures, so you need to be especially wary about making intimate friendships too soon after starting a new job. The stakes are very high at a job if you share too many of your professional or personal details and it turns out that you spilled your guts to the wrong person. If you share about your family or professional challenges with someone in your department who wants to advance at your expense, whatever you share, especially if it is of a sensitive nature, could be used against you.

How Much Information You Will Share at Work, and That Includes on Facebook, Instagram, and LinkedIn

A good rule of thumb is that anything you share that you would not want reprinted on the front page of the *New York Times* is personal or professional information that you should not be voluntarily sharing with your coworkers. If something comes up, you can comment on it, but you do not have to go out of your way to volunteer it.

Some examples? It's okay to share that your spouse's sister, husband, and children are visiting from out of town for a few days, but you don't have to go into details about the history of messy conflicts your spouse has been having with extended family over the last ten years. Or you might mention that you're going to a college alumni gala Saturday night that you're looking forward to, but you don't have to add that you bought $350 tickets to attend the event.

Is It a Good Idea to Make New Friends at Work? Why or Why Not?

If you take your time to get to know someone at work really well, testing out the new relationship over months or even years and in a variety of work and outside-of-work situations, making a new friend at work can be a good idea. For example, have lunch together and see how much gossiping your potential new friend does about the job and others at work. Is it malicious? Do you fear, especially if your relationship goes sour, that you might be the subject of similar gossip down the road? Or do you and your new potential friend have enough shared interests outside of the current job that you can keep the conversation going without everything revolving around work? Perhaps you both like sports activities, going to the movies, or reading novels? Do you genuinely like this coworker?

Another important consideration is whether you are at the same level at work: stronger connections, or *workships*, and even friendships between peers are less fraught with potential conflicts than if one of you is reporting to the other. Some companies may even have policies against friendships between those who are in a supervisory/subordinate relationship.

Where Do You Draw the Line Between Friendly Coworkers and Coworkers Who Are Friends?

Drawing the line between friendly coworkers and coworkers who are friends is an important if you feel that a friendship can compromise you and your job in any way. Years ago, I interviewed a woman who shared with me that if she had a friend at work and anything happened at the job that made it necessary to choose between the job and her friend, she would choose her friend.

What would you do in that situation? If you must honestly answer that you would choose your job, you should probably err on the side of caution and stick with being friendly to your coworkers but avoid becoming friends.

When Having Friends at Work Can Backfire

Here is a situation where becoming friends at work can backfire. You and your coworker started at the company together, and you've become friends. But you, or your friend, just got promoted, so one will be reporting to the other. How do you and your friend handle this change in status without either ruining the friendship or jeopardizing your jobs?

The most important step you and your friend can take to avoid this new situation becoming a problem for either your jobs or your friendship is to discuss this change and

But you should also not minimize the value of having friendly coworkers. Even having coworkers who know you name and who smile and say, "How are you? How are things going?" when they see you during the day, or first thing Monday morning, can add to the workplace in a positive way.

It is How You Handle A Work or Business Friendship

By being proactive about possible situations that might occur and what strategies you will use to deal with them, you're more likely to save your jobs and your friendship. For example, you might have to be strict about avoiding references to your personal lives or activities you do together outside of the company. You might have to develop some rules or even decide that now that you are a subordinate and not a coworker, your friendship needs to be put on hold temporarily. You might even decide that you should put in for a transfer to another department or even company. Or that if your friend-turned-boss must criticize you because of any job-related situations, you will agree not to take it personally and to realize that, for both your sakes, the job has to come first. Communicate about this change and what it might mean. Even simply agreeing to deal with any issues that arise in a way that is in the best interest of both your jobs and your friendship can help both of you to feel less worried that you won't be able to deal with any friendship-related challenges that the promotion might bring.

A second situation is staying at a job too long because you have friends there. If it is time to move on for the sake of your career, you should make that your priority. If your friendships are genuine, it will last even after you no longer work together.

A third situation when having a friendship at work can backfire is if the friendship is with your boss. What do you do if your boss/friend has to reprimand you? What if your boss/friend knows things about you, and that knowledge stands in the way of your advancement at work?

Here is an example. You have shared with your boss/friend that you and your teenagers are having some issues and being around more is proving a useful way to improve the situation. An office for the corporation in another country needs an employee to be sent there for a few weeks to help train the local employees on a skill that you've mastered. Much to your disappointment your boss/friend chooses a coworker for this plum career-advancing assignment. You find out privately that your boss/friend feared that being away from home for a few weeks might make the situation with your teenager worse. You assure your boss/friend that your teenager will do just fine even if you're away for a few weeks.

Unfortunately, it is too late to change the boss's decision about who will go on this international assignment. You regret that you shared that personal detail with your boss/friend because you know that without that information about your home-life challenges, information you shared because your friends, you would have been the first choice for this exciting assignment.

See if you can adapt or adjust your privacy settings on Facebook so some or all your posts are concealed unless someone is actually one of your FBFs. How to handle defriending work or business connections that you realize, in hindsight, you never should have allowed to friend you in the first place can be complicated.

Defriending them could really backfire, as they might get offended and take it out on you and your career. Rather than defriending them, it might be best to just be more careful about what you post and when you post it, as well as the photographs that you share.

Slowing Down the Pace of a Relationship if Your Workship Wants to Move It to a Friendship

A coworker wants to get together with you and your spouse on a Saturday night for dinner. You can tell this is an effort to move your relationship from coworker to friend. You prefer to keep your relationships at work very professional and outside of the friend category. Do you tell your coworker that, or just say you're busy and hope he or she gets the hint and doesn't ask again?

You have to figure out what to do based on the personality of the coworker and also how often he or she keeps asking you to get together. Some people will "get the hint" when you say you're too busy to get together even once especially if you do not offer an alternate time. Others may continue to be persistent in their request. If your co-worker is insistent in asking you to get together outside of work, if you don't think it will be taken the wrong way, and if you don't think it will backfire if there is another employee down the road that you want to cultivate an outside-of-work friendship with, you can state, in as nice a way as possible, that you have a "no socializing outside of work" policy and that she or he shouldn't take it personally. Once again, be careful about stating that you have a "policy" in case you will want to violate that policy at some point and get together with someone else outside of work. So perhaps part of this is being clear with yourself about whether you do indeed want to avoid getting together because of your "no socializing with coworkers outside of work" policy, or if it's just this particular coworker and their particular romantic partner or spouse that you don't want to socialize with.

You can also suggest a modified alternative. You could say that you'd rather not get together as two couples because you don't want to expand your work relationship in that way, but you would like to get together for a cup of coffee or tea or lunch with your coworker. Getting to know your coworker better in a way that will help you both to improve your jobs performance is a different circumstance than getting together outside of work with other family members in the hope of developing an outside-of-work friendship, which it seems you fear will backfire.

Until your relationship with this co-worker is tested out enough times that you feel you can trust him or her, or you have even elevated the relationship to the level of friend, rather than co- worker or what I call a *workship*, it goes without saying that you will need to watch everything you share about yourself and your opinions during your get together. Most of all, avoid badmouthing the boss or other employees, or criticizing the company or agency, even if your co- worker does it.

Developing a Friendship from an Online Business Networking Site

There are currently an estimated 500 million—that's half a billion!—LinkedIn users throughout the United States and internationally. I'm sure by the time you are reading this book, there will be even more. I won't be surprised when the number hits and exceeds one billion. LinkedIn is an amazing site that has become so much more than just a database of information about its members or subscribers. It has become a news portal, it has become a place where subscribers post articles that are often read by thousands, it has become a job search engine, and lots more.

A LinkedIn member begins by writing his or her profile, so you have to be cautious about accepting at face value what someone says in his or her profile. It should all be accurate, but it may not be.

But let's say you like the way someone's profile reads, and you think this is someone you might want to get to know better. Remember that most people are using LinkedIn for their career, business, or job hunting. They are *not* searching for friends. I have termed these relationships LIFs—LinkedIn Friends or, more accurately, LICs—LinkedIn Connections—in a similar vein to FBFs (Facebook Friends) and SMFs (Social Media Friends). Developing a friendship on LinkedIn, especially initially when you first make a connection, is probably the furthest thing from everyone's minds. So, if you are *too* direct with anyone you connect with about wanting a friendship, not only might they wonder what's wrong with you that you are misusing the basic intention of LinkedIn in that way, but they might not even want to do business with you!

You have to be subtle, *and* let the friendship evolve naturally if it's meant to be. Just like a potential friendship starting in any other place in your life, whether it was at school, or at camp, or through work, watch for the body language and the subtle and not so subtle clues that someone likes you and wants to get to know you better. Remember that friendship is a two-way relationship, so make sure you're learning more and more about this LinkedIn buddy or the person you've met through another online business networking site. Take it slow. The stakes are high in any situation where you are potentially combining business with your personal life.

But you also want to make it easy to be "found" on LinkedIn. So, when you set up your profile, when you are asked for contact info, if you really want to make it easier for potential connections (and possible future friends) to be able to communicate with you, try to have an email address that you are comfortable sharing in this public way. If necessary, create an email that you use just for these types of situations. Many put their website URL or their Twitter "handle" as the way to contact them. Unfortunately, that can put someone into a very time- consuming loop of not really getting to you directly.

You might also include a mailing address, which will help someone know where in the universe you are in case, they prefer to put their time and energy into new connections nearby, as well as a phone number.

You want to make it as easy to contact you as you are comfortable sharing in that way with strangers. For instance, if you work from home you might have a mailing address, like a UPS store or a post office box where you get business mail, so you are still keeping your personal information private.

Be cautious about moving the relationship from online to in-person. Take as many steps as you need to feel confident about doing that. Talk on the phone a few times. If you feel at all uneasy about someone, or you don't have enough contacts in common to informally or more formally find out more about this potential new friend, you can always do a Google search on him or her or even a more formal background check.

Just like meeting someone for a date through anything online, you do not want to have that first meeting in private. Keep it in a public place.

Also, if you are at all uneasy, invite other people along. You could also plan to meet at a business-related conference or event so there's not as much pressure on both of you in case either of you prefers to keep the connection totally focused on business.

If and when you do meet, if you both want to get together again for coffee, lunch, or dinner, this friendship that started online and through work will evolve according to the same rules as any other friendship. Namely, you will both test each other out, directly or indirectly, to see if your first impressions of each other, assuming they were positive, were justified. You will take it slowly, but you will also watch for cues from your new potential friend. Is he or she continuing to move forward, wanting to get together again, or backing off? If he or she is backing off, is it because there's no shared wish to become friends, or is it that he or she is truly busy, and you should cut him or her some slack?

Remember that this new friend, even though your connection started online, will expect you to be as responsive and caring as any other friend who he or she met in more conventional ways. That means providing the emotional support and putting in the time if and when major events happen in your new friend's life, such as if he or she has to deal with the death of a loved one, which is discussed in Chapter 10, "Coping With Illness, Dying, Death, and Grief."

The First Step Is Getting on LinkedIn in the First Place

There are countless examples of careers that have been launched, jobs that have been found, not to mention friendships that have been made, because of LinkedIn. What my survey discovered, however, is that there is a disparity in participation on LinkedIn based on gender.

In my snowball sample of 178 men and women, of those who answered the question about what social media platforms they were on, a whopping 91.43% of the men noted they are on LinkedIn, compared to only 60.36% of the women. That is more than a 30% difference! According to those results, more men are using LinkedIn, meaning that they have an advantage when it comes to making connections, getting job referrals, and starting the process that can lead to more friendships at work and in business. In my snowball sample, more women are participating in Pinterest than the men: 46.85% of the women compared to 28.57% of the men.

It is possible that Pinterest could be a way to form friendships, find new jobs, and strengthen your connections, but I haven't heard about it as much in that regard compared to the powerhouse of LinkedIn.

Hopefully, these findings will be a wake-up call to women reading this book who would like to give their work relationships and their career a boost. LinkedIn is definitely a place to start, with its close to half a billion users around the world. Friendship, or a new job, are not guaranteed just because you participate in LinkedIn. But creating your profile, putting in the time and effort to connect with current work friends, and asking for introductions to friends of friends, is a place to begin making those connections that might lead to a business relationship which could become a friendship.

Developing Friendships Through Associations

It is possible to start a friendship through an online service like LinkedIn, but it's a lot harder than it is if you belong to the same association. That is because most associations, by their very natures, structures, and mandates, have face-to-face meetings, something that has to be orchestrated if you meet through an online service. Especially if you belong to the local chapter of a national or international association or organization, you are more likely to meet in person at a meeting because you are within a certain geographical area. By contrast, when you meet someone online, he or she could live halfway around the world, and meeting in person could be a lot more expensive and time-consuming to make happen.

It may sound simplistic, but if you want to use associations for developing friendships, it requires that you show up. Preferably you should show up consistently and often. And volunteer for a committee and participate in the committee eagerly and regularly.

Too many people, I've observed, pay their dues but rarely, if ever, show up for a meeting. Yet they bemoan, "Why isn't this association working for me?" or "I haven't made any friends from being a member of this association. Why not?"

The main reason is that if you fail to go to the meetings, and by that I mean both the local chapter get-togethers and the annual meeting, you are seen as someone who is unreliable and not a "team player." Failing to go to the meetings is consciously or unconsciously seen as a rejection of that group and your fellow members.

Let us say you went one year, two years, or even three years in a row, but you still didn't get any friends. So, disgusted, you skipped a year. But then you decide you still like the group and what it could offer you professionally, and you like a whole bunch of people who you hope will want you as a friend, so you go back to the annual meeting the next year.

Guess what? It's like starting all over! You have to slowly rebuild everyone's trust in you. That you can be counted on. That you are reliable. That you are one of them. That you won't reject them and fail to participate in the next meeting.

If you want to make friends through an association, you need to be active.

Now you may not want to put the time and effort into associations in this way. You could pick up the phone and try calling members instead.

You could even try to get together with selected members outside of the meetings. But you will have to take the initiative and doing this involves a much bigger risk than meeting at a local chapter or annual convention. After all, if you bump into someone in the hall, and you grab a cup of coffee, and a good conversation ensues, it's a lot less of a risk and a commitment than setting up a meeting at the local coffee shop or at a restaurant for a meal and finding yourself wondering, "Does this person like me?" or "Why did I set this thing up in the first place? I feel so awkward!"

You may just want to remain a member of various associations because it's prestigious, or you need to be a member for the sake of your career, or you just like reading their newsletters or using their job sites. That's fine. But don't get frustrated if you haven't made any friendships from these associations. It is possible to make friendships from associations. I know. I've been blessed with a couple of really strong, positive friendships that started from meeting through an association. But it happened at a time in my life when I did all the things that I suggested at the beginning of this section: consistently attending meetings and annual conferences, and even getting together between meetings. When I'm inconsistent about doing those things, it just doesn't "work" to lead to friendships the way it could and, in theory, should.

Developing Friendships from Meeting at a Conference or Convention

Linda Swindling, a speaker and author, initiated her most recent friendship two years ago with someone she met at a convention. She considers that new friend a close one. "When she comes to town, she visits me," notes Linda, adding, "I help her. She helps me. [We] think alike."

The rules I shared in Chapter 4, "Making Friends," about meeting through an online site, or through being members in the same association, are similar for meeting through a convention or conference. It's great you have this initial shared positive connection to each other, but you have to accept that from that point on, you will be testing each other out to see if a friendship should and can ensue. The courageous part was the reaching out. The miraculous part was that you and this other person, out of the more than seven billion people in the world, have "clicked." There is enough of a spark, of an appreciation, of a connection, that you both want to see each other again.

Using Work Trips to Keep Up with Your Personal Friendships

Everyone's busy these days and so many are trying to make money go further, so why not consider reconnecting with a friend if you happen to be attending a business conference or having a business meeting, and your friend lives nearby? It might take some coordination, but with a little bit of advance planning, it's a way to keep those long-distance friendships from languishing on the Internet. Or, if you have friendships that have yet to become in-person ones, it might be a way to move those relationships along.

Twenty-three years ago, my sons were at an age that made it hard to get away for an entire day to visit my best friend, Joyce, in her New Jersey town almost four hours away. But I knew I was going to Philadelphia as part of my author tour for *Friendshifts*, and Joyce lives only about 40 minutes away. It was wonderful to get to see her in between television and radio interviews! I went out of my way to meet with Joyce during that trip and on many trips since. Now that my sons are grown, I am even able to get to New Jersey and back just for the day without a work- related reason!

But you can't force it. It has to be a natural occurrence. If a friend is coming to town for business and she or he simply can't handle anything else in her or his schedule, you have to respect that. It may not be a reflection on your friendship, but rather what the other person is able to handle. If there are other signs that your friend is pulling away, that's a different story. But don't automatically assume that a reluctance to combine business with pleasure rules out your personal friendship.

Considering Befriending the Competition Instead of Trying to Sabotage It

If you're old enough, you will remember a scandal that broke a few years ago about a competitor posting negative reviews and comments about another company, calling into question the reputation of the rival firm. When it was revealed that it was actually the competing company's CEO who had been trying to poison the well of public opinion, it backfired big-time as the evil naysayer became the object of ridicule and scorn.

That type of negative behavior is the opposite of what Brian Scudamore is advocating in his Forbes.com article with the apt title, "Make Friends with the Competition and Win Big in Business." Scudamore, founder and CEO of 02E Brands, the umbrella company for 1-800-GOT- JUNK?

and other companies, begins his short but eye-opening article with a courageous confession. When his top employee advised him that he was leaving the firm to start a competing service, Scudamore tried whatever he could to stop that new company from succeeding. The end result, however, was that his own company floundered as his former employee's venture soared.

That taught Scudamore a valuable lesson that he shares with his readers: competition, or what he notes Martin Zwilling calls "coopetition," can actually help to grow both businesses. (Zwilling, the founder and CEO of Startup Professionals, used the term in his article in the *Harvard Business Review*, "Make Your Competition Work for You.")

Here are the three reasons Scudamore shares that support his current approach to competitors, namely, to turn them into friends:

1. "Let's get real: There are no secrets anymore."
2. Scudamore contends that if a business is strong in its everyday practices, it doesn't have to worry about idea theft since it's the execution of ideas that counts. (In Zwilling's article, he suggests you still "take precautions" to protect yourself and your company by having a "good joint non-disclosure and non-compete agreement.")
3. "Building bridges will get you further."
4. "Competition makes you stronger."

Don't we all wish some of our competitors that we reach out to would read the articles by Scudamore and Zwilling and return our emails and phone calls and even want to "take a meeting? But, as Scudamore notes, "not everybody is going to be your BFF."

Still, friendship at work and in business, in general, will take you a lot further than rivalry and the business version of being frenemies. If you want to foster those friendships rather than stop anything positive from happening, avoid the following seven behaviors.

Seven Unfriendly Things That Will Stop a Work or Business Friendship In its Tracks

If you want to make, and keep, your work or business friendships, here are some cardinal behaviors *to avoid* doing:

1. Taking credit where credit is not due, especially if you're taking credit for your friend's idea or accomplishment.

2. Outright stealing your friend's ideas.
3. Sharing privileged information, you know because of your friendship before your friend is ready to release that information at his or her company or in his or her career.
4. Bragging about your friendship, especially if your friend is someone who is famous or a person of influence, in a way that could be construed as being opportunistic.
5. Failing to show up for important events in your friend's career, such as a launch party or a celebration of his or her accomplishments, wrongly assuming that since "that's business" your friend will understand your absence (without a really good reason for it).
6. Ignoring the gift giving or receiving policies at your friend's company, which could put him or her in jeopardy (e.g. unwittingly exposing him/her to accusations of influence peddling or even corruption).
7. Pushing to get partners together as an expansion of your friendship when having a friendship between just the two of you is fine for your friend and all he or she can handle right now.

Keeping Up Your Friendship After One or Both of You Leaves the Job or Company

This is actually a timely topic to discuss at this point, because the process that you will need to go through if one or both of you leaves the company is similar to what you will find yourself doing if you meet initially at a conference, through an association, or online.

Unless you work together, or live together as roommates, keeping up with a new or established friend takes effort. Working together made it convenient. Sitting next to each other at a conference day after day and going out to dinner in the evenings made it easy.

But will you or your friend take the time to get together once you're no longer working together? Once you're no longer at the same conference in the same city?

We all have to filter relationships in our lives, or we simply would not be able to handle absolutely everyone that we have connected to. So, if you or your friend pull away once you no longer work together, that is okay. Do not be too hard on yourself or your friend if it turns out it was work, after all, that was the glue that held your friendship together.

If your work friendship helped you both to enjoy work more, or even to be more productive, that is great. If you are no longer BFFs in the "real world" outside of work, no big deal. Maybe you will be casual friends who get together for a work reunion every couple of months, or once a year, or if you happen to go to the same work convention.

If, without forcing it, you and your friend want to keep up your friendship with the same intensity that you had when you worked side by side, or in the same department or company, that's fine too.

If you want to get even closer now that you can share more openly and you do not have to worry as much about what coworkers will think of your friendship, that's also okay.

No longer working together is one of the biggest friendshifts for work friendships. The other ones are when two friends find that one has become the other friend's boss, or if a friend doesn't just leave the company but goes into another field altogether.

You can keep your friendship going after you no longer work together as long as you both want to.

***

In Chapter 10, "Dealing with Illness, Dying, Death, and Grief," we will look at two of the hardest situation friends have to cope with: illness and death.

Chapter 10
Coping with Illness, Dying, Death, and Grief

"[A year ago] a close elderly lady friend died within two weeks of being diagnosed with colon cancer. We met in church and became good buddies, going to events in the community together and having good talks and also good laughs. I could confide in her. We enjoyed each other's friendship in spite of our 20 plus year age difference. I was shocked and saddened to lose her. It has left a void. I don't really have any close friends now except relatives."

—62-year-old married Kansas woman with five grown children

Dealing with illness and death is a concern that we associate with aging but, unfortunately, there are too many examples of sickness and even death afflicting our friends or our loved ones at any age, whether it's a friend in her early forties who is dealing with a miscarriage, or a friend in the senior year of high school dying from an overdose. Coping with the illness or death of a friend may even happen in childhood.

But it is also true that sickness, especially terminal illness, and death will happen more often as we age. Baby Boomers are facing the inevitable deaths of their friends as they mature into their 60s, 70s, and older years. Is there anything that can be done to help sick friends when they are dying? What would minimize the immediate or long-term consequences to the surviving friend when a friendship ends because of death? Death, including the death of a friend, may be inevitable, but there are ways to try to cope better with these unavoidable life events.

When a Friend Becomes Ill

Fortunately, not all illnesses will lead to death. Yet even if a friend is recovering from cancer treatments, surgery, or a stroke, few of us are trained in how to cope with a sick friend.

It is certainly true that illness can be a big "test" on a friendship, but it's also important not to overreact if you or your friends don't suddenly stop everything that you're doing and rush to the hospital or to a sick friend's side. That is because everyone reacts to illness differently. Some may want to be surrounded by their friends and family. Others may actually prefer just to have their close family nearby and to keep their friends, even their close or best buddies, at a distance.

If it's your friend who is sick or going through surgery, you need to know your friend's personality and how he or she wants to be treated. If you're the one who's sick, let your feelings and needs be known. If you want visitors, your friends aren't mind readers. Let them know that. If you prefer to deal with your illness in a more private way, thank your friends for whatever they want to do on your behalf, but let them know that you prefer to heal with the help of your family or even a professional caregiver.

There are exceptions. If a friend is either not getting along with their family, or their family lives far away, friends may be seen as a substitute, offering the care during illness that is more typically provided by family members. I met a woman in Honolulu who, when I was speaking at a bookstore about *Friendshifts*, shared with me that she took a few months off to return home to the Midwest to take care of her friend who was gravely ill. She had to take time off from work, and she was willing to do it whether or not her boss was okay with the idea. (Fortunately, her boss understood and approved.) She was a single woman without dependents. But I wonder if she would have made the same decision, risking her job and losing that income, if she was married with children and the sole provider for her family.

There's no doubt that how you handle a friend's illness—or how your friends react when you become ill—can either help a friendship to become stronger or weaken it to the point that it fades or even ends. Lynn Rosenberg shared with me about a week after her best friend, Pam Lane, had a stroke just how much her friend's surprise attack impacted her and their friendship. Lynn says Pam's stroke definitely made them closer: "We were close before but if there's any possibility of getting closer, we are."

Lynn has three words to sum up what friends who are sick need from their friends: "Support, support, support."

When I interviewed her best friend, Pam, and I asked her how important Lynn's visits were to her when she had her stroke, she replied, with conviction, "She has come and spent the better part of a day with me. She's just been so true blue."

Here are some of the many ways you can show support for a sick friend:

Ways to Show Support for a Sick Friend

- Visit
- Send flowers
- Send a fruit basket
- Call
- Text
- Send an email
- Visit
- Send a traditional paper card through the mail
- Send an ecard
- Send a "Get well" balloon
- Send or bring a newspaper
- Send or bring a book
- Send or bring a magazine
- Send an audiobook or a way to download it
- Send or bring a token gift
- Write and mail a letter to your friend
- Ask if there are any chores you could help with, like making sure bills get paid, especially if a friend is single without relatives or other friends nearby

When Illness Becomes Terminal

Witnessing someone who has the skills to be there for a sick friend can provide a lifelong lesson in compassion. In their fascinating book, *Final Gifts*, hospice nurses Maggie Callanan and Patricia Kelley point out that the stages of grief, as described by physician Elisabeth Kübler-Ross and others, that apply to how you react to the death of a friend—shock, denial, disbelief, apathy alternating with anger, bargaining, and resolution—also apply to how friends (and family) deal with a friend's terminal illness and impending death. The advice they share with friends from their first-hand experiences is that listening is what those who are dying need most.

Interestingly, all the skills that contribute to being a better friend, as discussed throughout this book but especially in Chapter 3, "Assessing Your Friendship Skills, and Current Network" as well as in Chapter 5, "Healing Friends," will serve you and your terminally ill friend especially well at this stressful and emotionally draining time.

Unfortunately, as Callanan and Kelley point out in their powerful book, too often friends are in denial about their buddy's terminal illness, and they avoid visiting their friend because they cannot—do not—want to deal with their friend's condition. Or they are afraid of saying or doing the "wrong thing." If they do visit, they often think it's best to try to cheer up their friend with such well-meaning but hollow phrases as, "I'm sure you'll get better soon."

These experienced hospice nurses, however, think the dying need understanding and empathy from their friends to approach death as peacefully and comfortably as possible. They discuss the phenomenon that they observed in the terminally ill, what they call "Nearing Death Awareness." The key points that apply to friends are that you need to listen to your dying friend's needs and try to be there for your friend as much as you can manage emotionally and timewise.

In the section entitled, "Talking about Death," they write:

> *Show that you're willing to talk, then let the conversation develop. You might begin with a simple comment: "I'm sorry to hear that you're so ill," or "I really feel sad when I think about what's happening to you." Wait for a response. Listen. There is no one right thing to say, although it's never wrong to speak of our love and concern. Don't worry about saying or doing the "wrong" thing ...*
>
> *What's often harder to forgive—whether for the dying person or in one's self—is the failure to do or say anything ...*

I found *Final Gifts* an incredibly useful book to read back in 1996 when my father was dying from an inoperable brain tumor at the age of 80. I had never personally had to deal with a situation like that—someone close to me dying from a terminal illness over several months—before. (It is true my maternal grandmother was ill when I was in my mid-30s but my mother, who visited often, didn't share much information about her condition with my sister or me.)

My father was diagnosed in February. By April, things were getting bad, but no one was really talking about the situation. Then, one day I visited my father by myself at the hospital. Out of the blue, during my visit, my father said, "You know I'm dying." If I hadn't read *Final Gifts*, my response would have been to say, "Oh, no, you'll be fine." Instead, I let him share how he was feeling.

It was a particularly important moment that my father and I had together, because by the next visit he was basically in a coma and, till he died a week or so later, he would not regain consciousness.

But there is another part of my Dad's death and the denial of impending death as it relates to friendship that I want to share because it might be helpful to others. My Dad had one close friend throughout his life. They met when they were kindergarteners at age five in Brooklyn, New York, and they remained best friends till the end. I know his best friend, Dave Schaeffer, had a lot of other friends—he was much more gregarious than my Dad and I seem to recall that he was even a salesman, compared to my Dad who was a solo practitioner dentist. But my Dad just had his one friend, Dave, who had relocated to California from Queens, New York a decade before.

I do not know why I didn't pick up the phone the night my father said to me "I'm dying." I am sure I was probably hoping it wasn't true even though intellectually I knew it was. But I should have called Dave, because if I had called that night it's possible Dave would have gotten on the first red-eye flight and he could have spoken to his best friend one more time.

Instead I waited. Finally, when it became clear that my Dad was right and the inevitable was going to happen. So, I did call Dave, and he did get on the next plane. Alas, my father died while Dave was making that cross-country flight. He was able to attend his best friend's funeral a few days later, but Dave and I were both heartbroken that he did not get to see his best friend before he died so that could have that one final conversation. It might have been a one-way exchange since my Dad was basically unconscious at that point. Much to his credit, Dave, whom I always called "Uncle Dave," never admonished me for not calling sooner, and that was very kind of him.

A woman I will call Maja recently shared with me about how she is coping with the terminal illness of her friend Claudia:

> *I have a close friend who is in the process of dying of cancer. She is a friend I went to high school with and although she is living in Frankfurt, I am in close contact with her since we are texting and chatting through WhatsApp almost every day. And while [my casual friend] Christina's passing was terribly sad for me and I cried for her, and the loss of her life, and for her 12-year-old daughter who now has to grow up without a mother, and for the general heartbreak of it all—I am actually really terrified of losing my friend Claudia. It will happen soon. I am aware of that. It is just so heartbreaking when you think of it—she is 46 years old!*

> . . . *Before she became sick, she was an academic and professor at a renowned German university and her career had just started to soar and then she got the diagnosis. It is all such a tragedy, really. She studied all her life for this moment of becoming a tenured professor and then her sickness started and now in her mid-forties she is looking at the end of her life. I am trying to keep our conversations interesting and fun and I tell her about my lectures and my audiences and the questions that my audience members ask, and she is very interested in all of that.*
>
> *Right now, she is in the hospital and she said that she probably won't be able to go home anymore. It really sounds like she does not have too much time left. I am experiencing all kinds of feelings when it comes to her and her impending death: I am first of all terribly sad that I will lose her as a friend. She will not be there anymore—that will be so odd and weird. To not receive any messages anymore and to not be able to talk to her anymore. I mean, yes, I have had friendships end and people chose to not want to be a part of my life any longer and all that—but I have never had a friendship ended by the death of my friend.*

Some efforts to help terminally ill friends have become more formal. I recently reread the powerful article originally published in Parade about how 12 friends got together. This was not your typical get-together. They didn't start a book club. They didn't have a cooking club. No, this group, for the next 3¹/² years, took care of their friend, Susan Farrow, who was dying of a brain tumor. The group, which included Susan's two daughters, came to be known as Susan's Funny Family.

To share what they did with others, best friends Sheila Warnock and Cappy Capossela, as well as two of those original 12 women, co-authored a book, *Share the Care: How to Organize a Group to Care for Someone Who Is Seriously Ill.* Susan's psychotherapist, Sukie Miller, Ph.D., who helped bring together all the women in the original group, wrote the foreword to the book. This comprehensive book has chapters such as "Going With Your Friend to the Doctor," "Ten Steps to Making a Hospital Stay as Painless as Possible," "Making the Home Safe and Comfortable," and "Being With Someone Who is Seriously Ill."

The first edition of the book was published in December 1995. In 2002, coauthor Cappy Capossela was diagnosed with a brain tumor.

Sheila Warnock organized a group to help Cappy through her illness. Then, after Cappy's death, Sheila created a Share the Care website and a nonprofit organization to help get the Share the Care model out to a wider circle of caregivers.

Another model for helping out when a friend is ill is the site What Friends Do. Founded by Aimee Kandrac and her mother, Fran, this free site is an outgrowth of a site that Aimee had created to coordinate information and help for her sister Stephanie's best friend, Laura, who had been diagnosed with a terminal brain tumor. The site offers assistance to countless friends on how to provide help to a friend in need.

When a Friend Dies*

Portions of this chapter about coping with death, are edited and updated, with permission, from Friendshifts by Jan Yager, Ph.D.

The death of a friend is a different kind of ending to deal with than an ending that comes about because of conflicts or unmet expectations. Just as a child often harbors the fantasy that divorced parents will someday remarry, friends with ruptured relationships have the possibility of reconnecting in the future, even if it is a remote one. Not so if a friendship ends because of death.

For previous generations, wars and a shorter life expectancy were reasons they might have had to cope with the death of a friend. Today, car accidents, cancer, heart attacks, and even homicide are, tragically, increasing the likelihood that you may lose a friend at a younger age than you might have expected. Furthermore, as you age, with life expectancy, on average, at 78.8 years in the United States, the older you get, and the longer you live, the more likely you will mourn the death of one or more of your friends. In addition, whatever your age, you may need to be there for a friend who has been touched by the loss of a loved one, whatever the cause of death or the age of their dearly departed. Learning how to cope as effectively as possible with these predictable, but challenging, friendship issues will help you to be as much of a source of comfort to your friends as possible.

When Your Friend Loses a Friend or Someone Close to Them

I am going to create a sympathy card that others can use, if Hallmark doesn't beat me to it. It will say "Sympathy on the Loss of Your Friend." I haven't seen such a card yet, although there may be some out there that I have not found yet, and there are also more generic cards that you could use that are for situations where you have lost someone "special." Until a card is available specifically for the loss of a friend, just send a general sympathy card or even a blank card or a note. You can send an email as well, but your grieving friend might prefer to get an old-fashioned letter or card through the mail.

Back in September 1994, when I was just 46 and 73 seemed so much older, I reached out to my friend, noted writer Lucy Freeman, soon after I read the obituary in the *New York Times* announcing the death of her friend, fellow writer Thomas Chastain. Lucy and I had become friends after meeting through the ASJA (American Society of Journalists and Authors). We were friends despite an age difference of several decades. Lucy wrote me such a thoughtful letter thanking me for expressing my sympathy that her friend had died. Here is the last paragraph from the letter Lucy wrote back to me:

> *Yes, as you put it, friends grieve just like family members and relatives. I have felt deep grief about Tom. For the past 20 or 30 years, I have played poker practically every other week with Tom, his wife and several other players and Tom's wife called me and said we would still continue this without him. They never had children; poker was their only relief from working hard.*
>
> *Again, thank you for writing me. I miss Tom more than I can say and for many reasons, which I will tell you about when I see you. ...*

Coping with Grief When Your Friend Dies

Losing a close or best friend through death can result in the same kind of loneliness and need for emotional support that is experienced by those who lose any meaningful intimate relationship. Kübler-Ross' stages of grief will now come into play upon the death of a friend: shock, denial, disbelief, apathy alternating with anger, bargaining, and resolution.

How long bereaved friends remain at any stage of mourning, or even how many stages you or other friends who have lost a friend go through, is an individual matter that may have as much to do with each person's psychological makeup, as well as how many other intimate relationships you may now turn to for support, as it does with the closeness or value of the friendship that death just ended.

It is pivotal that others recognize that you are in mourning for your departed friend, and that you are entitled to feeling grief and sadness in the same way as those who lose a spouse, parent, grandparent, or any other close relative. Friends grieve just like family members and relatives. As the sixteenth-century philosopher Michel de Montaigne wrote in his essay, "Of Friendship," about the death of his best friend, Étienne de la Boétie: "There is no action or thought in which I do not miss him, as indeed he would have missed me. For just as he surpassed me in every other ability and virtue, so he did in the duty of friendship."

The unexpected death of a friend may result in the "if onlys"—regrets and remorse that you lost the chance to tell your friend how much he or she meant to you.

Another way that death affects a friendship is when someone close to you or to your friend dies—a parent, sibling, grandparent, child, a miscarriage, or even a cherished pet. Does your friend come through for you? Do you come through for your friend? If you are unable to attend the funeral, do you at least phone, visit, or somehow express your sincere condolences?

Some may find it hard to share their feelings in such situations, but friends need to get beyond those excuses and be there for each other. Just how important is it to come through for your friends at these times? As a 33-year-old New Jersey woman writes: "I sincerely believe my friends are more dependable than my relatives. I discovered this when my mother died. I felt the support from my friends and sorority sisters at that time."

I remember calling the widow of a writer I considered a friend to express my remorse as soon as I belatedly heard that my friend had died the week before. I asked if she wanted me to stop by or if there was anything I could do to help. She replied, expressing this thought, even if not in these exact words, "Call me in a year, when no one's remembering me anymore. Right now, I'm overwhelmed with visitors and attention."

In *Women Make the Best Friends*, Lois Wyse expresses a similar thought when she writes about how friends are the ones that come through in widowhood: "I know that Liz's friends were on call when her husband became ill. Friends were there through the terrible times. And I'm sure she has a houseful now. But the ones who are still there after the last casserole disappears are the stayers; the others are the goers, off to the next event. Staying is what separates acquaintances from friends."

For me, coming through for a friend when someone he or she loves has died is the definition of a tried-and-true close or best friend. I learned that the hard way when I was 20 and my older brother died tragically at the age of 23. The stupidest comment I heard at that time was from a former friend who, in explaining why she was not going to his funeral, said, "After all, I didn't know your brother."

I wish I had been able to blurt out what I must have been thinking at the time: "But you know *me!*" Instead, I just went numb.

You attend a funeral for the living probably more than for the person who died.

But now that I am older and supposedly wiser, I realize that maybe saying she didn't know my brother was the excuse she told herself that gave her permission to avoid the funeral. Maybe she couldn't emotionally handle going to a funeral, or she had something to do that day that she didn't feel comfortable sharing with me. There could have been a million reasons that she couldn't be at that funeral and, fortunately, over time I have learned that life is a lot more complicated than putting people into simple boxes: Yes, you do this and you're "on my side," or no, you don't do this and that means you're not "with me." I hope I am teaching others to be more flexible as well.

In general, however, when someone close to a friend dies, you attend the funeral to support that person and their family, and to help them feel your concern at this difficult time.

What I learned from my brother's funeral and how much those who were able to show up and lend their support meant to me was a lesson that I have applied since that time. Peers less experienced in these matters have thanked me for steering them in the direction of coming through for their friends in their darkest hours.

There are numerous ways you might want your friend to be there for you at your own time of need. Some friends you might expect, or want, to be at the wake, viewing, or calling hours, and to attend the funeral, go to the cemetery, or pay a Shiva call if you are Jewish and are observing the custom of visiting the bereaved to pay condolences for as few as three days or as many as seven days.

But since funerals are rarely planned far in advance, there may be some friends who are unable to attend because they live too far away, are away on trips, are too ill themselves, or have their own obligations that they cannot set aside. They may have a family wedding or a graduation to attend, they may be emotionally unable to deal with death, or they can't go to a funeral because it's just not in their DNA to do that. As you know from reading *Friendgevity*, one of the key ways to develop and maintain your friendships is, as much as possible, not to take a friend's behavior that hurts your feelings personally, especially if their explanation is a reasonable one.

A new trend is videotaping a funeral and offering it to friends and relatives who could not attend so they can see the service, at their convenience, on their computer. If you are offered such an option, even if you are unsure if you want to view the service, accept your friend's offer for the file. You can always decide later if you want to view the service or not, but at least you won't have had a confrontation with your friend at this emotional time.

What Not to Say

Try not to make a general statement to someone who has just lost a loved one, such as "Tell me what you need." Because those who are dealing with loss just might not know what they need at that moment, or, if they do figure it out, they may not know how to ask for it.

Carole Thomas Copeland, a Boston-based speaker, author, and travel organizer, shared about what happened right after her 17-year-old son was killed in a car accident 20 years ago. He had been drinking at a birthday party for a 21-year-old and, unbeknownst to anyone, grabbed the keys to someone's car and took it for a joyride, unfortunately crashing it soon afterwards. He died within five minutes from his injuries. There are many positive things that her friends did and said when they all came over to comfort her upon learning about her son's tragic death, as well as at the funeral. But there were also some very painful ones. As Carole explains:

> I always try to encourage people that if you haven't lost a child, it is best, when you're greeting someone who has experienced that loss, not to say, "I understand how you feel," because your words can be completely turned against you. Because you cannot understand how I feel unless you have also lost a child. It's better to say, "I am deeply sorry for your loss," and use that kind of language in the company of someone who has lost a child. It is equally as hurtful to say, "I know how you feel. I understand how you feel because I just lost my mother or my uncle or my . . ." But not *your* child. I'm very adamant about that.

Immortalizing Your Friend

Friends offer each other a kind of immortality when they name their child after a friend or organize a memorial at the time of death or even a year or two or a decade later. Writing down your feelings about a friend who has died in a diary for yourself, or in a letter to a mutual friend or to your family, is a way of sharing your feelings. You might even put those thoughts and feelings down and get them published so many other people may share in them. These are all ways of granting your friend immortality and trying to work through the intense emotions and void conjured by death.

I am reminded of the gathering of her daughter's friends organized by the mother of a high school senior who had been senselessly murdered in Central Park by a young boy who stole her bicycle. At that assembly, which was a celebration of her daughter's life and friendships, music was played, and selections of her daughter's diary were read, thereby sharing her intimate feelings in a way that granted her a kind of immortality.

You can consider setting up an award in your friend's name or, if there's an award or charity that was important to your friend, you can donate to it in your friend's name.

Fundraising races are another popular way to memorialize a friend who has died.

Writing a song, a poem, or even rewriting a song in tribute to a friend that has died, the way songwriter and performer Elton John did when he rewrote the words to "Candle in the Wind" when his good friend Princess Diana died, are other ways to let the world know that you cared about your friend and you will not forget him or her. Dedicating a film or a book to a friend is another way.

Friends matter, and if we take the time to remember our parents, grandparents, and other loved ones who pass on, why not our friends? But that doesn't mean that you don't force yourself to move on after a friend is gone.

Moving On

We have to eventually move on after a friend dies. That does not mean that we try to replace that departed friend with other friends. Each friend is unique, and no one can take that friend's place. But living in the past, dwelling on the past, is unproductive. A man I'll call Dean, who is 67 and married without children, shared with me how challenging it's been to move on since his best friend's wife died. That's because the two couples were as close as two couples can get. The four of them did everything together. Vacations. Trips. Barbecues. As Dean explains:

She died last year. Everything changes. You have a whole new dynamic. He actually was over last night for dinner.

It's very tough and we're all seeking the new relationship. We don't know where it's going but we're all trying. We're not speaking about it. First of all, it's not his style anyway. There's nothing to say. He's hurting. We don't know what it's like for him. The other thing, it's still so raw. No kids. That was one of the things why it was such a close friendship. [Neither couple had kids.] We introduced them. We met through work.

In time, when Dean's friend starts dating again and he brings a date to their couple activities, things may go to a new state of normal. But till then, they have moved on to this new interim state, putting up with the awkwardness they all feel. At least Dean and his wife are not abandoning their friend in his time of need as others may have done.

What can you do if you are hurting because you have a friend who died? Instead of leaving a big hole in your life that your friend used to fill, find other friends to hang out with. If you already have other positive friends, spend more time with them. If you don't feel your other friends want to hear about your friend who died, join a support group for dealing with grief. It's okay if the other support group members have lost a family member. You have a right to be there so you can get help with grieving for your friend.

When a Workship or Friendship at Work or in Business is Impacted by Death*

(This section is reprinted, with permission, from Who's That Sitting at My Desk? Workship, Friendship, or Foe? by Jan Yager, Ph.D., from Chapter 9, "Coping with Endings," pages 127-130.)

Tens of thousands of coworkers, friends, and family from throughout the United States, especially on the East Coast, as well as from more than 100 countries around the world, had to deal with loss and grief because of colleagues who died in the September 11, 2001 terrorist attacks in Washington, D.C. and Manhattan. Some also had to deal with "survivor guilt" because they survived, and their coworkers or bosses did not.

Death is less of a taboo subject in the United States since those tragic terrorist attacks on 9/11 forced the entire country to cope with such horrific loss. Coworkers lost dozens, even hundreds, of men and women who had become members of a corporate family. The youth of the victims, so many in the prime of their lives and with so much to live for and look forward to, highlighted the tragedy of the loss.

Fast forward to 2020 in the United States and throughout the world when the COVID-19 pandemic led to the death of hundreds of thousands of adult men and women, especially seniors and those with underlying medical conditions, and even teens and children, although in smaller numbers. As of October 24, 2020, according to the Johns Hopkins University and Medical Center Coronavirus Resource Center, there were 1,147,020 globally. On December 21, 2020, that same website noted there were 318,782 reported deaths in the U.S. from COVID-19.

Grief is, ultimately, a private emotion that is handled by each individual in his or her own way. There is no right or wrong way when it comes to grieving. To cry, to write a poem, to erect a memorial, or to set up a scholarship in the name of the deceased friend—these are all options.

But what unites those who lose someone they currently work with every day or someone they used to work with, is that they may have shared hours, weeks, months, or years of their lives, and now that person is gone, though not forgotten. Certainly, the grief of the immediate family members is paramount when a coworker, boss, or business associate dies, but the sadness of those who worked with and also liked and loved the deceased should not be diminished or ignored. It is a loss for them, too, and the healing process will take time and they will deal with it in a unique way.

When a workplace or business *workship* or friend dies, there is a loss, but the depth of the loss is usually tied to how close you felt to your deceased friend beyond your roles of coworker, boss, or business associate. It may also be tied to your previous experiences coping with the death of a peer. For example, Martin met his best friend, Jim, when they were both in sixth grade. "At the time our school district was growing so fast it had to rent churches, so all of the sixth grade was put into one church," says Martin, who is now 42 and working in the West as an educator. Martin and Jim remained friends all though middle school and high school.

"After I graduated from college, I went to the same town where he was going to pre- seminary school," Martin explains. "That year the friendship was cultivated. We had always been in contact through letters and telephone calls. One time he lost his sight temporarily [Jim developed cancer behind his eye] and we were in contact by tape. They didn't have email at that time."

Jim died at the age of 28 from a heart attack related to his cancer. Martin still misses his best friend, but he says, without bitterness, "He lived a good life."

Martin also shared with me the following story about how two coworkers handled it when their beloved coworker died:

> *I worked in a nursing home in the kitchen. I was a food service worker and I was around 21 and in college at the time. They were all food service workers.*
>
> *Soon after I was hired, someone suddenly died. It was a woman who was going to retire. She became ill. She was in her early 60s. It was a sudden death.*
>
> *After she died, they discovered she had left her sweater at work. They never returned it to her husband for the longest time. They kept it for two years and every time they went into the cooler or walked into the refrigerator, they would put it on. It seemed that each time they put it on, they would remember that woman.*
>
> *Then, shortly before the nursing home closed, they gave [her sweater] back to her husband.*

Tips for Coping with Death in Work-Related Situations

Here are some tips for coping with the death of a *workship* or friend at work, as well as friends you met through work, including in the military, even if you no longer work together:

- There is no right or wrong way to express your grief or sadness to other coworkers or to the family and other friends of the deceased. If it is comfortable, express your feelings in whatever way suits you: sending a card, sending flowers, donating to a favorite charity, or writing in a journal.
- Your everyday routine will be different without your *workship* or friend. Give yourself time to adjust to the changes. Give yourself time to mourn.
- If you need time off, or to see a counselor or therapist, do what you have to do. Don't minimize what you're going through and what your needs are because it was "just a friend" rather than a family member who passed away.

- Create a memory book and compile some of the work-related memories, photographs, or memorabilia of your *workship* or friend who died. It could just be from you or you could ask others at the office to contribute. Give it to his or her family as a source of comfort.
- Here are some suggestions for offering comfort to your *workships* or friends at work if they have lost a loved one.
- Express your sympathy to a coworker or friend at work upon the loss of a loved one in the immediate family, in the extended family (including parents, siblings, aunts, uncles, or first cousins), as well as friends, *workships*, or pets.
- Ask if there are any tasks related to the funeral that you could help out with, such as taking care of children, making any phone calls on behalf of the family, ordering flowers, setting up at the house after the wake, funeral, or trip to the cemetery, and so forth.
- If your help is not required, consider sending a card expressing your condolences even though you did not know or have a relationship with the deceased. By sending a card to your *workship* or friend, you are showing support for what he or she is going through.
- If you say, "Is there anything I can do to help?" make sure you really mean it. If it is feasible and reasonable, be prepared to actually do whatever it is your *workship* or friend asks of you.
- If appropriate and allowed at your company, offer to take on some of the workload of your *workship* or friend until the funeral or grieving period for their loved one is over. Jewish coworkers, bosses, or subordinates may want to be out one week if they are sitting Shiva, the mourning period which traditionally lasts five to seven days but is sometimes shorter.

***

In the Conclusion which follows, I will share some tips for global friendships, among other issues.

Chapter 11
Conclusion

"There are two elements that go into the composition of friendship, each so sovereign that I can detect no superiority in either, no reason why either should be first named. One is Truth. The other . . . is Tenderness."

—Ralph Waldo Emerson, "Friendship," Essay VI (1841)

Social media has made friendship international for more and more people. Here are some suggestions to help those friendships across borders to go smoothly:

Rules for Global Friendships

1. Every culture, every country has its strengths and weaknesses. There is no one culture or country that is better than any other. This is not a competition.
2. Avoid polarizing discussions about religion, politics, and current events unless you want to learn about your friend's values. In that case it's okay to get into heated discussions with the full awareness that it might strain your relationship.
3. Be aware of, and respect, the values and customs of your friend's country. But that doesn't mean you have to approve of everything they practice.
4. Be especially aware if friendships between males and females is permissible in a particular culture. If it is not, avoid offending people of that culture with a request for a platonic opposite-sex friendship.
5. Despite the distance, try to arrange a face-to-face get-together. Tie it to a family vacation or a business trip or, if necessary, see if you can meet halfway so you share the expense and inconvenience of a visit.
6. Ask for suggestions on articles, books, and movies you can read or view to learn more about your friend's culture and country.

Offer to provide her or him with readings and visual material about your culture as well.

7. As you know, friendship takes time to develop. It may take even longer across cultures because of the differences that have to be understood and worked out. Be patient.

8. Use social media to facilitate your friendship, including posting on Facebook and using Facebook's direct messaging feature, which is instant and free but also private.

Summing Up

Thank you, dear reader, for going on this journey with me in *Friendgevity*. I hope you have learned a few things about friendship that you didn't know before.

Friendship is not a static relationship, I have discovered. Social media has definitely had an impact on how we connect to our friends and even on how many people we consider friends. But the comforting thought is that that is okay. There are some abuses that we need to address, such as cyberbullying, cyberstalking, badmouthing people online, or spending too much time online; we need to continue working on these issues. But we also have to relish the delightful benefits of social media, as long as it is used in the service of the human touch and is a complement to getting together with our friends in person or talking over the phone.

For example, two years ago I reconnected by phone with a classmate from high school, Valerie First, whom I had not spoken to for 51 years. We had connected a few years ago through Facebook and we have been staying up on each other's lives through our posts. When we finally talked on the phone, because of all those posts and occasional private messages, it was not an awkward conversation the way it might have been with someone I had called out of the blue after 51 years! But neither Facebook nor that phone call are substitutes for moving our friendship along even more by meeting in person. However, Valerie lives in Florida and I am up North in Connecticut. Hopefully, we can arrange a reunion soon.

So, it's okay to have 100 or even 300 casual friends, I've discovered, as long as your one or two best friends or four to six close friends are not getting ignored or pushed aside by all those other friendships that maybe largely social media based. Ditto for the family and romantic partners in your life. We need to make the time for all our meaningful relationships, including the friendship with ourselves, that make life so exciting and worthwhile.

So what makes for a good friend that lasts but also adds to your life, a friendship that has *friendgevity*? We have discussed that concept in various places in this book, but here are concepts related to each letter in *friendgevity* to remind you of how to be a better friend:

F – Forgiving
R – Reliable
I – Insightful
E – Enjoyable
N – Nice
D – Dependable
G – Growing your friendship at a mutually-agreeable pace
E – Enduring
V – Values that are shared or at least respected
I – Interested in your friend and their significant others
T – Truthful
Y – Yield and compromise

Here is a reminder of a few key ways to become a better friend (or to expect these positive ways of interacting from your friends with you):

1. Really listen to your friend. Whether it's over the phone, in person, via a Zoom videoconferencing call, in a text message or e-mail, do not just jump to share about yourself. Absorb and think about, and then respond, to what your friend is sharing with you.
2. Sometimes your friend just wants to vent or tell you something. You do not always have to give advice. Sometimes it's better to wait for your friend to ask for advice. You are her friend. Not her parent or her therapist.
3. Make time for each other. Not just reading each other's posts on Facebook but getting together in person even if that means taking a train, and a bus, or even flying to another state or half-way around the world. If that is impossible because of the pandemic, time, or money constraints, talk to each other over the phone, or via Zoom or another videoconferencing service. Your friendship needs you and your friend to spend quality time together now, building on your memories and shared experiences, not just living on the past.

Friendship is a unique, voluntary relationship that affirms us and applauds us. I hope *Friendgevity* has opened your eyes to its many benefits, taught you some of the potential negatives to watch out for, given you the courage to start a new friendship and strengthen the ones you already have, given you some useful tips for dealing more effectively with conflict, and, if necessary, helped you to have the courage to fade or end any destructive ones. I also hope *Friendgevity* has inspired you to reach across the globe for friends since social media, especially Facebook and LinkedIn, has made it so much more likely those international connections can happen. But please also consider picking up the phone and calling your friends or, most important of all, for those friends who live nearby or at least within the same state or country, work on arranging a get together in person so you can laugh together and give each other those endorphin-producing hugs that we all need.

Feel free to join my Twitter feed @drjanyager or write to me at jyager@aol.com. I also invite you to sign up for the mailing list at my website, shttps://www.drjanyager.com, or visit my alternative friendship site, http://www.whenfriendshiphurts.com.

The key idea that I want to emphasize from all the research I have done into friendship, and a key idea to *Friendgevity,* is this: since having at least one positive friend can increase your life by as much as 10 years, along with smoking, obesity, substance abuse, and inactivity, we need to add loneliness to that list as a preventable cause of death.

Glossary

acquaintance – more than a stranger but not a friend, an acquaintance is someone that you know and who knows you. Other terms for an acquaintance might be "contact" or "connection."

best friend – a primary friend, a confidant with whom you have a very intimate friendship based on trust, shared confidences, and the feeling that you're completely and selflessly concerned about each other's well-being.

BFF – slang for "best friends forever."

bullying – taunting someone verbally or physically in a menacing way, with the aggressor perceiving himself or herself as having more power than the person they are mistreating.

casual friend – more than an acquaintance but not as intimate as a close or best friend. You can therefore have many casual friends because you don't invest that much emotionally into the relationships. But it is still a genuine friendship requiring you to adhere to the "rules" of friendship as described in the Friendship Oath, although not to the high degree that close or best friendships require.

clique – a closed group of friends that excludes others and is not receptive to new members.

close friend – not as exclusive or as intimate as a best friend, but a big jump up from a casual one. You feel like you can trust a close friend with your secrets. As with a best friend, you must be there for your close friend, so you can't have too many close friends because it's expected that you attend major life events and listen as much as you talk, which takes up time.

cyberbullying – bullying that takes place over social media and the Internet rather than in the schoolyard or in the neighborhood or at work.

dyad – a two-person relationship usually referring to a two-person friendship or a romantic couple.

fair-weather frenemy – a pseudo-friend; someone who professes to be a friend but is only there for you when things are going fine, disappearing or being unavailable when things are challenging.

family – those you are related to by blood or legally through marriage. Some also use the term in a looser way to describe any group with whom one feels a close bond, such as those who work together and feel close referring to themselves as a "corporate family."

family of origin – the family you are born into or that you enter at a young age, and that you are raised in till adulthood. Also called a nuclear family, usually includes your parents and siblings and can be adoptive, foster, stepfamily, or single parent family.

FBF – Facebook Friend (Jan Yager term/a term created by the author)

foul-weather frenemy – a pseudo friend; someone who seems to need you to be having rough times or foul weather. When things start to go well for you, this person is unavailable to you or ends the relationship.

frenemy – someone who used to be your friend but is now your enemy.

friendly relation – family member with whom you feel close and that you would choose to spend time with even if you were not related.

friendgevity – a word that emphasizes the way that friendship can extend, or shorten, your life (Jan Yager term)

friendshifts – the way that friendships and friends may change over time; also the title of the book, *Friendshifts*. (Jan Yager term)

gang – a group of non-related individuals of any age who are bound together and derive strength from the group. Although the word has gotten a negative connotation because of its association with gang violence and gangs that commit crime, gangs can also band together for positive change.

LIC – LinkedIn Connection (JY term)

LIF – LinkedIn Friend (JY term)

loner – someone who gets used to being without friends and either chooses or is forced to be by themselves all the time.

network – four of more friends who band together but, unlike a clique, is open to new friends joining at any time. The only criteria to join the network is that everyone in the network must agree to accept the new member.

opposite-sex friend – a platonic friendship with someone of the opposite sex. Though not usually a romantic relationship, there is a phenomenon known as "friends with benefits" (i.e. friends who have sex with no strings attached). Also known as a cross-sex friend.

same-sex friend – friendship with someone of the same sex or gender.

shyness – feeling shy, apprehensive, or awkward around others that sometimes makes those who are shy reluctant to initiate a friendship.

significant other – the romantic partner in one's life, whether dating steadily, living together, or married.

SMF – social media friend (Jan Yager term)

Survey Monkey – online research site for sending, receiving, and analyzing questionnaires.

SurveyMonkey Audience – part of Survey Monkey that enables subscribers to buy responses from throughout the U.S. and selected other countries to anonymously complete short surveys.

stalking – repeated unwanted expressions of interest, harassment, or intimidation in person or over the Internet.

stranger – someone you meet that you have no known relationship to. It could be a stranger you meet on a train, over the Internet, or on the street.

triad – a three-way friendship.

trust – the feeling that someone won't intentionally or unintentionally hurt you emotionally or betray your confidences.

workship – a relationship that develops in the workplace or through business, including coworkers or business associates who are less than friends but more than acquaintances. (Jan Yager term)

Bibliography
Including Cited Works*

Please note: Most online links are not hot links to avoid readers finding too many links that are no longer valid. Instead, if you want to follow-up on any of the listings that are posted online, do a search on title and/or author, such as through Google, and you should be able to locate that original source material.

Adams, Rebecca G. "The Demise of Territorial Determinism: Online Friendships," in *Placing Friendship in Context*, Rebecca A. Adams and Graham Allan, eds. London: Cambridge University Press, 1998, pp. 153- 182.

Adelson, Rachel. "Buddy system eases stress, study suggests." APA Online, Vol. 35, No. 8, September 2004, posted at http://www. apa.org

Afifi, Walid A. and Sandra L. Faulkner. "On being 'just friends': The frequency and impact of sexual activity in cross-sex friendships." *Journal of Social and Personal Relationships*, Vol. 17 (2): 205-222.

Agence France-Presse in Washington. "Loneliness can kill you, and scientists think they have worked out why." Posted at scmp. com, November 24, 2015.

Allan, G. A. *Friendship: Developing a Sociological Perspective.* Boulder, CO: Westview, 1989.

AOL.com. "Boston Marathon Bomber's College Pal Gets 6 Years in Prison." Posted at aol.com n.d. Downloaded June 2, 2015.

Aristotle, Aristotle in Twenty-Three Volumes/Vol. 1, *The Nicomachean Ethics*. Translated by H. Rackham. Books 8 & 9. Cambridge, MA: Harvard University Press, 1968.

Associated Press. As quoted in the *New York Times*, March 6, 2002, page A19.

_____. As reported in the Daily Mail UK). "Risk of teen drivers dying in a crash DOUBLES if friends are in the car." May 8, 2012. Posted online.

_____. "Two missing Wi. boys apparently drowned."

Updated 4/16/2006. Posted at NBCnews.com.

Bacon, Sir Francis. "Of Friendship" (1625), in *Classic Essays in English*, Josephine Mile, ed. Boston: Little, Brown, 1965.

Banks, Amy. *Wired to Connect: The Surprising Link Between Brain Science and Strong, Healthy Relationships*. Foreword by Daniel J. Siegel. New York: Tarcher/Penguin Random House, 2016.

Barkas, J. L. (Janet Lee). See also Yager, Jan.

Barkas, J. L. (a/k/a Jan Yager) *Friendship: A Selected, Annotated Bibliography*, New York: Garland, 1985.

_____. (a/k/a/ Jan Yager) "Friendship Patterns Among Young Urban Single Women." City University of New York, Sociology Department, Sociology Dissertation, New York City, 1983.

_____. "How to Stay Connected with Your College Crowd." *Wall Street Journal*'s Collegejournal.com released February 14, 2001 (Part 2).

_____. "Wise College Students Find Friends for Life." *Wall Street* Journal's Collegejournal.com released February 14, 2001 (Part 1).

Bayum, Nancy K. *Personal Connections in the Digital Age*. Cambridge, UK and Malden, MA: Polity Press, 2010.

Beaumont, Karen. *Being Friends*. Illustrated by Joy Allen. New York: Dial Books, 2002.

Beckes, Lane; James A. Coan; and Karen Hasselmo. "Familiarity Promotes the Blurring of Self and Other in the Neural Representation of Threat." SCAN (Oxford University Press), 2013 page 670-677. Posted online.

Bell, Robert R. *Worlds of Friendship*. Beverly Hills, CA: Sage, 1981.

Benenson, Joyce F. and Athena Christakos. "The Greater Fragility of Females' Versus Males' Closest Same-Sex Friendships." *Child Development*. July/August 2003. Volume 74, pages 1123-1129.

Bergland, Christopher. "Having social bonds is the no. 1 way to optimize your health." Psychologytoday.com blog. Posted January 14, 2016.

_____. "The Neuroscience of Empathizing With Another Person's Pain" *Psychology Today* blog, June 19, 2016.

Berkman, Lisa. F; Linda Leo-Summers, and Ralph I. Horwitz. "Emotional Support and Survival after Myocardial Infarction: A Prospective, Population-based Study of the Elderly." *Annals of Internal Medicine*, 1992, Volume 117: 1003-1009.

Berkman, Lisa F. and Teresa Seeman. "The Influence of

Social Relationships on Aging and the Development of Cardiovascular Disease—A Review." *Postgraduate Medical Journal* (1986): 62, 805-807.

Berkman, Lisa F. and Leonard Syme. "Social Networks, Host Resistance and Morality: A Nine-Year Follow-up Study of Alameda County Residents. *American Journal of Epidemiology* 109 (1979): 186–204.

Berndt, Thomas J. "Friendship and Friends' Influence in Adolescence." *Current Directions in Psychological Science.* Volume 1. October 1992. Pages 156-159.

Bernstein, Elizabeth. "How Facebook Ruins Friendships." August 25, 2009, posted at the *Wall Street Journal* online.

Bernstein, Russell. *Doodles Lanhorn and the Quest to Save Inner Earth.* (middle school novel) Stamford, CT: Hannacroix Creek Books, Inc., 2016.

"Best friends commit suicide." *The Evening Bulletin* (Gladstone, Missouri) (AP). March 26, 1980, page C- 4.

Blieszner, Rosemary. "The Worth of Friendship: Can Friends Keep Us Happy and Healthy?" *Generations: Journal of the American Society on Aging.* Spring 2014, Volume 38, pages 38-30.

Blieszner, Rosemary, and Rebecca G. Adams. *Adult Friendship.* Thousand Oaks, CA: Sage Publications, 1992.

Bowden, Jonny. *The Most Effective Ways to Live Longer.* Beverly, MA: Fair Winds Press, 2010.

Brick, Michael. "Cooled Friendship Recalled Between 2 in Fatal Stabbing," *New York Times,* October 24, 2004, page 37.

Bucholz, Emily M., et al. "Effect of Low Perceived Social Support on Health Outcomes in Young Patients with Acute Myocardial Infarction: Results from the VIRGO (Variation in Recovery: Role of Gender on Outcomes of Young AMI Patients) Study," *Journal of the American Heart Association,* 2014.

Cacioppo, Stephanie; John P. Capitanio; John T. Cacioppo. "Toward a Neurology of Loneliness." *Psychological Bulletin,* 2014, Vol. 140, No., 6, 1464-1504.

Cacioppo, John T., Louise C. Hawkley, L. Elizabeth Crawford, John M. Ernst, Mary H. Burleson, Ray B. KJowalewski, William B. Malarkey, Eve Van Cauter, and Gary G. Bernstein. "Loneliness and Health: Potential Mechanisms." *Psychosomatic Medicine,* May-June 2002, Volume 64, Issue 3, pages 407-417.

California Department of Mental Health. *Friends Can Be Good*

Medicine. Sand Francisco: Pacificon Productions, 1981.

Callanan, Maggie and Patricia Kelley. *Final Gifts: Understanding the Special Awareness, Needs, and Communications of the Dying.* New York: Bantam Books, 1992.

Carey, Benedict. "Is the Pandemic Sparking Suicide?" *The New York Times*, May 19, 2020. Posted online.

Carnegie, Dale. *How to Win Friends and Influence People.* New York: Pocket Books, 1940 (1936).

Carroll, Melissa. "UH Study Links Facebook Use to Depressive Symptoms." April 6, 2015. University of Houston press release.

CDC (Center for Disease Control and Prevention) "NCHS - Death rates and life expectancy at birth," Updated June 4, 2018.

Caposella, Cappy and Shelia Warnock. *Share the Care: How to Organize a Group to Care for Someone Who Is Seriously Ill.* New York: Simon & Schuster/Fireside, 2nd edition, 2004.

Chatterjee, Camille. "Can Men and Women Be Friends?" *Psychology Today.* Posted at psychologytoday.com, Published September/October 2001, last reviewed August 30, 2004.

Chen, Angus. "Loneliness May Warp Our Genes, And Our Immune Systems." NPR, November 29, 2015. Posted online.

Chiang, Jessica J., Naomi I. Eisenberger, Teresa E. Seeman, and Shelley E. Taylor. "Negative and competitive social interactions are related to heightened proinflammatory cytokine activity." Proceedings of the National Academy of Sciences of the United States of America. PNAS January 23, 2012. 201120972; published ahead of print January 23, 2012.

Chopik, William J. "Associations among relational values, support, health, and well-being across the adult lifespan." *Personal Relationships*, Volume 24, Issue 2, April 19, 2017.

Cicero. *On Old Age and On Friendship.* Translated by Frank O. Copley. Anne Arbor: University of Michigan Press, 1967.

Cohen, Sheldon. "Social Relationships and Health." *American Psychologist*, November 2004, pages 676-684.

Cohen-Posey, Kate. *How to Handle Bullies, Teasers and Other Meanies.* Illustrated by Betsy A. Lampe. Highland City, FL: Rainbow Books, Inc., 1995.

Cole, Steven W. John P. Capitanio, Katie Chun, Jesusa M.G. Arevalo, Jeffray Ma, and John T. Cacioppo. "Myeloid differentiation architecture of leukocyte transcriptome dynamics in perceived social isolation." *PNAS (Proceedings of the National Academy of Sciences*), published in print, November 23, 2015 and posted online.

Collins, Clare, "Friendships Built on Bytes and Fibers." *New York Times*, Jan. 5, 1992, p. 32.

Consumersadvocate.org, "Top 10 Best Background Check Services [2018 Buyer's Guide]," updated November 21, 2018.

Cook, Julia. *Making Friends Is an Art*. Illustrated by Bridget Barnes. Boys Town, NE: Boys Town Press, 2012.

Cooper, A. and E. Smith. "Homicide Trends in the United States, 1980-2008." Bureau of Justice Statistics. Washington, D.C.: U.S. Department of Justice, 2011.

Crittenden, C.N, MLM Murphy, and S. Cohen. "Social integration and age-related decline in lung function." *Health Psychology*, May 2018 pages 472-480.

Czeisler, Mark E., et. al. "Morbidity and Mortality: Weekly Report. August 14, 2020. CDC (Center for Disease Control and Prevention). (14 pages, posted online)

Dahl, Melissa. "A bad friend—or lousy roomie—can really make you sick." NBC News, October 14, 2016.

David, Sampson; George Jenkins; Rameck Hunt; with Lisa Frazier Page. *The Pact*. New York: Riverhead Books, reissue edition, 2003.

Davis, Murray S. *Intimate Relations*. New York: Free Press, 1973.

Delaney, Tim and Tim Madigan. *Friendship and Happiness and the Connection Between the Two*. Jefferson, NC: McFarland, 2017.

Demir, Meliksah and Lesley A. Weitekamp. "I am so Happy Cause Today I Found My Friend: Friendship and Personality as Predictors of Happiness." *Journal of Happiness Studies*, 2007. Pages 181-211.

Derrick, Matthew. "She Was Robbed By a Good Friend, But What Happened Next is Even More Disturbing." Posted at Viralnova. com. February 16, 2017.

Deresiewicz, William. "A Man. A Woman. Just Friends?" *The New York Times*, April 8, 2012. Page 4.

Dickens, C.M., et al. "Lack of a close confidant, but not depression, predicts further cardiac events after myocardial infarction," *Heart*, 2004, Volume 90, pages 518-522.

Dickens, Wenda J., and Daniel Perlman. "Friendship Over the Life-Cycle," In *Developing Personal Relationships*, S. Duck and R. Gilmour, eds. New York: Academic Press, 1981.

Diep, Francie. "Confronting MyCyberbully, 13 Years Later." *The Atlantic*, September 30, 2014, published   in *The Atlantic* online.

Doheny, Kathleen. "Facebook Feelings Are Contagious, Study Says." March 13, 2014.

Doyle, M.E. and Smith, M.K. "Friendship Theory and Experience." Entry in *The Encyclopedia of Informal Education*. 2002.

Droze, Kim. "Why Friendship Matters More Than Ever as We Age." Lifescript.com, February 3, 2014.

Durkheim, Emile. *Suicide: A Study in Sociology*. Translated by John A. Spauldin and George Simpson. Edited by George Simpson. London: Routledge & Kegan Paul, 1952.

Duck, Steve. *Friends for Life: The Psychology of Close Relationships*. Brighton, England: The Harvester Press. 1983.

Emerson, Ralph Waldo. "Friendship," in *Essays by Ralph Waldo Emerson*, New York: Harper and Row. 1951, pp. 121–156.

Enright, D.J., and David Rawlinson, eds. *The Oxford Book of Friendship*. New York: Oxford University Press, 1992.

Essex, Marilyn and Sunghee Nam. "Marital Status and Loneliness among Older Women: The Differential Importance of Close Family and Friends." *Journal of Marriage and the Family*, Volume 49, February 1987, pages 93-106.

Farrington, David. "Understanding and Preventing Bullying." *Crime and Justice*, Vol. 17, 1993, pages 381- 458.

Fehr, Beverley. *Friendship Processes*. Thousand Oaks, CA: SAGE, 1995.

Fischer, Claude S. *To Dwell Among Friends: Personal Networks in Town and City*. Chicago, IL: University of Chicago Press, 1982.

Fischer, Claude S., and Stacey J. Oliker, "Friendship, Sex, and the Life Cycle." Berkeley: Institute of Urban and Regional Development, University of California, March 1980.

Flora, Carlin. *Friendfluence: The Surprising Ways Friends Make Us Who We Are*. New York: Doubleday, 2013.

Fradkin, Lori. "An Unfinished Friendship." Published in "Huff Post Women," at the Huffington Post online, September 13, 2012.

Frasure-Smith, Nancy; Francois Lesperance; Ginette Gravel; Aline Masson; Martin Juneau; Mario Talajic; and Martial G. Bourassa. "Social Support, Depression, and Mortality During the First Year After Myocardial Infarction." Published in *Circulation*; 2000; 101; 1919-1924, based on a paper presented in part at the American Psychosomatic Society Meeting, Vancouver, Canada, March 1999.

Friday, Nancy. *My Mother/Myself.* New York: Delacorte Press, 1977.

Friedman, Ann. "The Social Sex: A History of Female Friendship." *New York Times Book Review,* September 18, 2015.

Frosch, Dan. "3 Buddies Home from Iraq Are Charged With Murdering a 4th," *New York Times,* January 12, 2008, page A13.

Garfield, Robert. *Breaking the Male Code.* New York: Avery, 2015.

Gee, Carol. *Random Notes.* Charleston, SC: Createspace, 2016.

Gholipour, Bahar. "Frequent Family Spats Linked to Risk of Early Death." Live Science, May 8, 2014.

Gibbs, Nancy and Timothy Roche. "The Columbine Tapes." Monday, December 20, 199, Time.com.

Gilbert, Susan. "Social Ties Reduce Risk of a Cold." *New York Times,* June 25, 1997.

Giles, Lynne C.; G. F.V. Gloneck; M. A. Luszcz; and G. R. Andrews. "Effect of SocialNetworks on 10 Year Survival in Very Old Australians: the Australian Longitudinal Study of Aging." *Journal of Epidemiology & Community Health.* 2005, Volume 59, pages 574-579.

Glantz, Jen. "I Hired a Friendship Coach to Help Me Make Friends. Here's What Happened." Posted at NBCNews.com. February 24, 2020.

Glass, Thomas A.; David B. Matchar; Michael Belyea; and John R. Feussner. "Impact of Social Support on Outcome in First Stroke." *Stroke,* January 1993, Vol. 24, Number 1, pages 64-70.

Goleman, Daniel. "Stress and Isolation Tied to a Reduced Life Span." *New York Times,* Dec. 7. 1993. p. C5.

_____. "Therapy Groups Yield Surprising Benefits for Cancer Patients." *New York Times,* Nov. 23, 1989, p. B15.

Gompers, Paul; Vladimir Mukharlyamov; and Yuhai Quan. "The Cost of Friendship." Working Paper 18141, Natural Bureau of Economic Research, Cambridge, MA, June 2012, 46 pages.

Gormly, Kellie B. "Friends Forever." *Pittsurgh Tribune-Review,* December 12, 2006.

Gove, Walter R. "Sex, Marital Status, and Mortality." *American Journal of Sociology* 79 (July 1973): 45– 67.

Greif, Gregory. *The Buddy System.* New York: Oxford University Press, 2008.

Guilley, Edith, Stephanie Pin, Dario Spini, Christian Lalive

192 | Jan Yager, Ph.D.

d'Epinay, Fancois Herrmann, and Jean-Piere Michel. "Association between social relationships and survival of Swiss octogenarians. A five-year prospective, population-based study." *Aging Clinical and Experimental Research*, pages 419-425, published 2005.

Haberman, Clyde. "Mob Shaming: The Pillory at the Center of the Global Village." *New York Times*, June 19, 2016.

Hampton, Keith, Lauren Sessions, Eun Ja Her, and Lee Rainie. "Social Isolation and New Technology." Pew Research Center, November 4, 2009.

Harris, Misty. "Friendship Don't Last Like They Used to." *Edmonton Journal* (CanWest News Service), June 12, 2006, pages A3.

Hartup, Willard W. and N.L. Stevens. "Friendship and Adaptation in the Life Course." *Psychological Bulletin*. May 1997. Pages 355-370.

Hawkley, Louise C.; Ronald A. Thisted; Christopher M. Masi; and John T. Cacioppo. "Loneliness Predicts Increased Blood Pressure: Five-Year Cross-Lagged Analyses in Middle- Aged and Older Adults." *Psychol. Aging*, March 2010, Volume 25 (1): 132-141.

Hawthorne, Graeme. "Measuring Social Isolation in Older Adults: Development and Initial Validation of the Friendship Scale." *Social Indictors Research*, 2006, Vol. 77, pages 521-548.

Helfinstein, Sarah M., Jeanette A. Mumford, and Russell A. Poldrack. "If All Your Friends Jumped Off a Bridge: The Effect of Others' Actions on Engagement in and Recommendation of Risky Behaviors." *Journal of Experimental Psychology*. 2015. Vol. 144. Pages 12-17.

Hess, Beth B. "Friendship and Gender Roles over the Life Course," in *Single Life*, Peter J. Stein, ed. New York: St Martin's Press, 1981, pp. 104–115.

Hoffer, William. "Friends in High Places." *Writer's Digest*, October 1986, pp. 42–44. Holt-Lunstad, Julianne. "The Potential Public Health Relevance of Social Isolation and Loneliness: Prevalence, Epidemiology, and Risk Factors." *Public Policy & Aging Report*, Volume 27 issue 4, December 30, 2017, pages 127-130.

Holt-Lunstad, Julianne, Timothy B. Smith, and J. Bradley Layton. "Social Relationships and Mortality Risk: A Meta-analytic Review." *PLoS Medicine*, Volume 7, July 2010.

Hope, Jenny. "Why Facebook friends don't count: People are happier and laugh 50% more when talking face-to-face." *Daily Mail* (UK), April 9, 2013, posted online.

House, James S. "Social Support and Social Structure." *Sociological Forum*, Volume 2, Winter, 1987, pages 135-146.

House, James S., Karl R. Landis, and Debra Umberson. "Social Relationships and Health." *Science*, Volume 241, July 29, 1988, pages 540-545.

Hruschka, Daniel J. *Friendship: Development, Ecology, and Evolution of a Relationship.* Berkeley, CA: University of California Press, 2010.

Hughes, Michael, and Walter R. Gove. "Living Alone, Social Integration, and Mental Health." *American Journal of Sociology* 87 (July 1981): 48–74.

Inderbitzen, Michelle, Kristin A. Bates, and Randy R. Gainey (editors). *Deviance and Social Control: A Sociological Perspective.* 2nd edition. CA: SAGE Publications, 2017.

Isaacs, Florence. *Toxic Friends/True Friends: How Your Friends Can Make or Break Your Health, Happiness, Family, and Career.* New York: Morrow, 1997.

Jacobs, Andrew. "Where 80 Is Young, All Friends Are Old Friends." *The New York Times*, September 8 2005, page B2.

Johnson, Katerina V.A. and Robin I.M. Dunbar. "Pain tolerance predicts human social network size." *Scientific Reports*, Published April 28, 2016 published online at www.nature.com.

Johnson, Kristine. "Study: Toxic Friends Can Lead to Serious Health Problems." April 22, 2016. Posted at CBSLocal.com (New York)

Karmen, Andrew. *Crime Victims: An Introduction to Victimology.* 9th edition. Cengage, 2016.

Keller, Monika. "A Cross-Cultural Perspective on Friendship Research." Mx Planck Institute for Human Development, Berlin, Germany. In ISBBD Newsletter, Serial No. 46, pages 10-11, 13.

Kenyon, Mary Potter and Mary Jedlicka Humston. *Mary & Me: A Lasting Link Through Ink.* Familius, 2015.

Kim, Leland. "Loneliness Linked to Serious Health Problems and Death Among Elderly." Published at the University of California, San Francisco website as a press release, June 18, 2012 (regarding study published in *Archives of Internal*

Medicine by UCSF researchers).

Kleinhubbart, Guido and Antje Windmann. "Isolation Crisis Threatens German Seniors." Published at the online version of *Der Spiegel* magazine, January 2013.

Konnikova, Maria. "The Limits of Friendship." *The New Yorker*, October 7, 2014.

Kroenke, Candyce, Laura D. Kubzansky, Eva S. Schernhammer, Michelle D. Holmes, and Ichiro Kawachi. "Social Networks, Social Support, and Survival After Breast Cancer Diagnosis." *Journal of Clinical Oncology,* 2006, 24:7, 1105-1111

Kübler-Ross, Elisabeth. *On Death and Dying.* New York: Macmillan, 1969.

Lazarsfeld, Paul F., and Robert K. Merton. "Friendship as Social Process: A Substantive and Methodological Analysis," in *Freedom and Control in Modern Society*, M. Berger, T. Abel, and C. Page, eds. New York: Van Nostrand, 1954, pp. 18–66.

Levine, Irene S. *Best Friends Forever.* New York: Overlook, 2009.

Lewis, Robert A. "Emotional Intimacy Among Men." *Journal of Social Issues* 34 (1978); 108– 121.

Liao, Jing, et al., "Negative Aspects of Close Relationships as Risk Factors for Cognitive Aging," *American Journal of Epidemiology*, October 22, 2014, Vol. 180, No. 11.

Lindsey, Karen. *Friends as Family.* Boston: Beacon Press, 1981.

Litwin, Howard and Sharon Shiovitz-Ezra. "Network Type and Mortality Risk in Later Life." *The Gerontologist.* Vol. 46, No., 6, 2006, pages 735-743.

Lutz, John. *Single White Female* (originally titled *SWF Seeks Same*), New York: Pocket Books, 1990.

Lynch, James J. *The Broken Heart: The Medical Consequences of Loneliness.* New York: Basic Books, 1979.

MacMillan, Amanda. "5 Types of Friends You Need to Avoid." April 2, 2015, posted at Time.com.

Marsden, Rhodri. "Pplkpr: If real friendship makes your heart beat faster, this absurdly-named app isn't for you." *The Independent*, January 29, 2015.

Marver, Julia A., Hanga C. Galfalvy, Ainsley K. Burke, M. Elizabeth Sublette, Maria A. Oquerndo, J. John Mann, and Michael F. Grunebaum. *Suicide and Life-Threatening Behavior*, Vol. 27, Issue, 6. Posted at Wiley Online Library.

Mather, Mark. "Narrowing Old-Age Gender Gap in U.S. Linked to

Smoking Trends." Population Reference Bureau (PRB), July 13, 2015.

Mayo Clinic. "Friendships: Enrich your life and improve your health." N.d.

McCurry, Justin. "Schoolgirl, 11, stabs classmate to death in Japan." *The Guardian*. June 2, 2004.

Mendes de Leon, Carlos. "Why Do Friendships Matter for Survival?" *Journal of Epidemiology and Community Health*, Vol. 59, No. 7, July 2005, pages 538-539.

Mental Health Screening (SMH). "How Friendship Affects Your Physical & Mental Health." Blog. January 20, 2015.

Mills, Eleanor. "Facebook's friendship trap." The *Sunday Times* (UK), published May 30, 2010 and posted online.

Moglia, Joe. "A Tale of Two Streets." As told to Eve Tahmincioglu. *New York Times*, December 11, 2005, page BU 11.

Montaigne. "Of Friendship," in *The Complete Essays of Montaigne, edited and translated* by Donald M. Frame. Stanford, CA: Stanford University Press, 1958, pp. 135–144.

Morrison, Rachel and Terry Nolan. "Too Much of a Good Thing? Difficulties with Workplace Friendships." *University of Auckland [Australia] Business Review*, Vol. 9, No. 2, 2007, pages 33-41.

Mui, Heather Z., Paloma Sales, and Sheigla Murphy. "Everybody's Doing It: Initiation to Prescription Drug Misuse." Journal of Drug Issues. Volume 44. Pages 236-253. Reprinted in *Deviance and Social Control: A Sociological Perspective*. 2nd edition. Edited by Michelle Inderbitzen, Kristin A. Bates, and Randy R. Gainey. Thousand Oaks, CA: SAGE Publications, 2017.

National Institute on Drug Abuse. "Abuse of Prescription (Rx) Drugs Affects Young Adults Most." February 8, 2016. Natinoal Institutes of Health. Posted at drugabuse.gov.

Nelson, Shasta. *Friendtimacy*. New York: Seal Press, 2016.

_____. *The Business of Friendship*. New York: HarperCollins, 2020.

_____. *Friendships Don't Just Happen!* Nashville, TN: Turner, 2013.

Olds, Dorri. "Defriending My Rapist," January 13, 2012, in the "Townies" section of the *New York Times*.

Pahl, Ray. *On Friendship*. Cambridge UK and Boston, MA: Polity, 2000.

Park, Alice. "Feeling Alone Together: How Loneliness Spreads." *Time*, December 01, 2009.

Parker, Fiona and Alex Wellman. "Scientists reveal why being lonely increases your chances of dying early." Published by the online *Mirror* (UK), November 23, 2015.

Paul, Marla. *The Friendship Crisis.* Emmaus, PA: Rodale Press, 2005.

Peer, Basharat. "A Friendship, a Pandemic and a Death Beside the Highway." *The New York Times*, July 31, 2020.

Peralta, Eyder. "Boston Marathon Bomber's Friend Sentenced to Six Years in Prison." June 2, 2015, posted at the NPR (National Public Radio) site.

Perissinotto, Carla M., Irena Stijacic Cenzer, and Kenneth E. Covinsky. "Loneliness in Older Persons: A Predictor of Functional Decline and Death." *Archives of Internal Medicine*, Vol. 172, No. 14, published online July 23, 2012.

Perlman, Dan, and Letitia Anne Peplau, eds. *Loneliness*, New York: Wiley-Interscience, 1982.

Pope, Elizabeth. "A Longer Life is Lived with Company." *The New York Times*, September 11, 2012, published in print on page F5 and then posted online.

Pothukuchi, Madhavi. "In a Horrific Case of Honour Killing, Father Slits Throat of Daughter for Befriending Local Boy." March 12, 2018.

Potarazu, Dr. Sreedhar. "Addicted to Facebook? Study shows users are lonelier." January 24, 2014, FoxNews.com, posted at http://www.foxnews.com/health/2013/01/24/addicted-to- facebook-study- shows-users-are-lonelier.print.html#

Pothukucki, Madhavi. "In a Horrific Case of Honour Killing, Father Slits Throat of Daughter for Befriending Local Boy." Vagabomb, March 12, 2018.

Potts, Marilyn K. "Social Support and Depression Among Adults Living Alone: The Importance of Friends Within and Outside of a Retirement Community." *Social Work*, Vol. 42, July 1997, pages 348-362.

Powers, Kemp. "How I Accidentally Shot and Killed My Best Friend." The Moth: Storytelling Special. Published in *The Guardian* online, August 9, 2014.

Pratt, David. *Nobel Laureates: The Secrets to Their Success.* Wellesley, MA: Branden Press, 2016.

Pryor, Liz. *What Did I Do Wrong?* New York: Simon & Schuster/

Atria, 2011.

Putnam, Robert D. *Bowling Alone: The Collapse and Revival of American Community*. New York: Simon and Schuster, 2000.

Rajwani, Naheed, Julieta Chiquillo, and Claire Ballor. "Before Being Charged in Richardson cop's death, gunman and 2nd victim were roommates, friends." *The Dallas Morning News*, online version, February 12, 2018.

Rath, Tom. *Vital Friends*. New York: Gallup Press, 2006.

Raymond, Natasha. "Friendship: The Hug Drug," *Psychology Today*. December 1999, page 17.

Roberts, Sam. "John Cacioppo, Who Studied Effects of Loneliness, Is Dead at 66." *New York Times*, March 26, 2018, posted online.

Rimer, Sara. "Ecstasy Overdose Kills. Who Should Be Held to Account?" *New York Times*, February 12, 2002.

Roig-DeBellis, Kaitlin with Robin Gay Fisher. *Choosing Hope*. 2015. New York: G.P. Putnam's Sons, 2015.

Rosenberg, Lynn Brown. *My Sexual Awakening at 70*. Published by Lynn Brown Rosenberg. 2013.

Rosenblatt, Roger. "Friends and Countrymen." Time Essay. *Time* magazine, July 21, 1980.

Rubin, Lillian Breslow. *Just Friends*. New York: Harper and Row, 1985.

Rubin, Zick, et al. *Children's Friendships*. Cambridge, MA: Harvard University Press, 1980.

Ruff, Rachel. *Defriending Facebook: How I Deactivated My Account & Re-Activated My Life*. self-published, 2014.

Schumann, Karina and Michael Ross. "Why Women Apologize More Than Men: Gender Differences in Thresholds for Perceiving Offensive Behavior." *Psychological Science*, Vol. 21, November 2010, pages 1649-1655.

Science Daily. "Feeling lonely linked to increased risk of dementia in later life." December 10, 2012. Source: *BMJ (British Medical Journal)*.

_____. "Social networks as important as exercise, diet across the span of our lives." *Science Daily*, January 4, 2016.

Scudamore, Brian. "Make Friends with the Competition and Win Big in Business," April 13, 2016, Forbes.com.

Secunda, Victoria. *Women and Their Fathers*. New York: Dell, 1992.

Shalaraoff, Sara. "E-mail Nation." *U.S. News & World Report*, March 22, 1999, p. 54.

Shor, Eran and David J. Roeifs. "Social contact frequency and all-cause mortality: A meta- analysis and meta-regression." *Social Science & Medicine*, 2015, pages 76-86. Available online.

Silverstein, Merrill and Vern L. Bengtson. "Do Close Parent-Child Relations Reduce the Mortality Risk of Older Parents?" *Journal of Health and Social Behavior*, 1991, Vol. 32, December, pages 382-395.

Simmel, Georg. "The Sociology of Secrecy and of Secret Societies." *American Journal of Sociology*. Volume 11. January 1906. Pages 441-498.

Simon, Adam. "How Friendship Affects Your Health: Stress, Sharing & Good Habits." December 18, 2017.Published online at Push Doctor.

Singletary, Michelle. "Don't Trash Friendship When Pal Fails to Repay Loan." *The Advocate* (Stamford), October 31, 2004, pages F1, F2.

Slater, Philip E "On Social Regression." *American Sociological Review*. June 1963. Volume 28. Pages 339-364.

Smith, Kirsten P. and Nicholas A. Christakis. "Social Networks and Health." *Annual Review of Sociology 2008*, pages 405-429. Published online March 24, 2008.

Spiegel, David, Helena C. Kraemer, Joan R. Bloom, and Ellen Gottheil. "Effect of Psychosocial Treatment on Survival of Patients with Metastatic Breast Cancer." *The Lancet*, Volume 334, Issue 8668, October 14, 1989, pages 888-891.

Spitz, Rene A. "Hospitalism." *The Psychoanalytic Study of the Child*, (1945) 1:1, 53-74 Steers, Mai-Ly N. "'It's complicated': Facebook's Relationship with the Need to Belong and Depression." Current Opinion in Psychology, 2016, volume 9, pages 22-26.

Steers, Mai-Ly N.; Robert E. Wickham; and Linda K. Acitelli. "Seeing Everyone Else's Highlight Reels: How Facebook Usage Is Linked to Depressive Symptoms." *Journal of Social and Clinical Psychology*, Vol. 33, No. 8, 2014, pages 701-731.

Stein, Joel. "You are Not My Friend." *Time*, October 15, 2007.

Steptoe, Andrew; Aparna Shankar; Panayotes Demakakos; and Jane Wardle. "Social isolation, loneliness, and all-cause mortality in older men and women." *PNAS (Proceedings of the National Academy of Sciences of the United States of America)*. April 9, 2013, Vol. 110, pages 5797-5801.

Stevens, Heidi. "What Do You Two Battling Friends Have in Common? You." Posted at the *Chicago Tribune* online site. July 9, 2013.

Stier, Catherine. "15 Ways to Celebrate Friendship." *Woman's Day*, February 19, 2002, pages 28, 30.

Szalavitz, Maia. "Friends with Benefits: Being Highly Social Cuts Dementia Risk by 70%" Time.com, May 02, 2011.

Taylor, Shelley. "Tend and Befriend: Biobehavioral Bases of Affiliation under Stress." *Current Directions in Psychological Science*, Vol. 15, No. 6, December 2006, pages 273-277.

The Tending Instinct: How Nurturing Is Essential to Who We Are and How We Live. New York: Times Books, 2002.

Tjalling, Jan Holwerda; Dorly J.H. Deeg; Aartjan T.F. Beekman; Theo G. Van Tilburg; Max L. Stek; Cees Jonker; Robert Schoevers. "Feelings of Loneliness, but not social isolation, predict dementia onset: results from the Amsterdam Study of the Elderly (AMSTEL)." *Journal of Neurology Neurosurgery and Psychiatry*, 2012 DOI: 10.1136/jnnp-2012-302755.

Traister, Rebecca. "What Women Find in Friends That They May Not Get from Love." *The New York Times*, February 27, 2016. Sunday Review, "Opinion." Online version. A print version was published on February 26, 2016 on page SR4 with the headline, "What Women Find in Friendship That They May Not in Love."

Umberson, Debra and Jennifer Karas Montez. "Social Relationships and Health: A Flashpoint for Health Policy." *Journal of Health and Social Behavior*, 2010, Vol. 51, pages. S54-S66.

University of Oxford. "Friends 'better than morphine.'" Posted at http://www.ox.ac.uk/news/2016- 04-28-friends-better-morphine

Valtorta, Nicole K.; Mona Kanaan; Simon Gilbody; Sara Ronzi; and Barbara Hanratty. "Loneliness and Social Isolation as Risk Factors for Coronary Heart Disease and Stroke: Systematic Review and Meta-analysis of Longitudinal Observational Studies." *Heart*, 2016, Vol. 102: 1009-1016.

van Niekerk, Andrea. "40% of Foreign Students in the US have No Close Friends on Campus: The Culture Shock of Loneliness." Posted at qz.com. November 28, 2012.

Vaughan, Diane. *Uncoupling: Turning Points in Intimate Relationships.* New York: Oxford University Press, 1986.

Vela-McConnell, James. "The Sociology of Friendship." In Part V, "The Sociology of the Self." In *The Cambridge Handbook of Sociology*. Edited by Kathleen Odell Korgen. Volume 2: *Specialty and Interdisciplinary Studies* (pages 229-236). Cambridge University Press, 2017.

Vernon, Mark. *The Meaning of Friendship*. New York: Palgrave Macmillan, 2010.

Villano, Matt. "Betrayed by a Colleague." (Career Couch) *The New York Times*, Sunday, May 14, 2006, page BU9.

_____. "When a Friend Is Also Your Boss." (Career Couch) *The New York Times*, Sunday, December 11, 2005, page BU11.

Volkrt, Beate. "Friendship." Posted at Oxfordbibliographies.com. Last modified on July 27, 2016.

Volpe, Allie. "How to Get Your Friends to Stop Treating You Like a Therapist." *The New York Times*, October 19, 2020.

Vozza, Stephanie. "Six Habits of People Who Make Friends Easily." *Fast Company*, June 22,2016.

Wallace, Jennifer Breheny. "Even Casual Ties to Others Can Better Your Health." *Washington Post*, Jully 9, 2018. Posted online and updated July 10, 2018.

Walton, Alice G. "New Study Links Facebook to Depression: But Now We Actually Understand Why" Published at Forbes.com, April 8, 2015.

Warner, Judith. "Friends for Life? Wait till Kids Enter the Picture." *The New York Times*, April 22, 2012.

Weihs, Karen, M.D.; S.J. Simmens; J. Mizrahi; T.M. Enright; M.E. Hunt; R.S. Siegel. "Dependable Social Relationships Predict Overall Survival in Stages II and III Breast Carcinoma Patients." *Journal of Psychosomatic Research*, November 2005, Volume 5, pages 299-306.

Weiss, Robert S., ed. *Loneliness: The Experience of Emotional and Social Isolation*. Forward by David Riesman. Cambridge, MA: MIT Press, 1973.

Weissman, Jordan. "Study: If You Want to Succeed, Don't Work with Your Friends." *The Atlantic*, June 18, 2012. Posted online.

Welty, Eudora, and Ronald A. Sharp, eds. *The Norton Book of Friendship*. New York: Norton, 1991.

Werking, Kathy. *We're Just Good Friends: Women and Men in Nonromantic Relationships*. New York: Guilford Press, 1997.

_____. Guest editor. "Cross-Sex Friendships." Special

issue of *Personal Relationship Issues (PRI)* newsletter, an official publication of the International Network on Personal Relationships, January 1994, Volume 2 (1).

Wheelis. Allen. *How People Change.* New York: Harper, 1975.

Wilkins, Emily A. "The Globalization of Friendship." *Skipping Stones*, March-April 2009.

Wilson, Michael and Janon Fisher, "Love Advice Led to Killing in the Bronx, Spouse Says," *New York Times*, March 19, 2005, page B3.

Wood, Janice. "Frequent Conflict with Family and Friends Can Double Risk of Death." Psychcentral.com, Posted on May 9, 2014.

Woolston, Chris. "Life After a Heart Attack: Don't Go It Alone." HealthDay®, 2017, updated January 20, 2018.

World Health Organization (WHO), "Global Health Observatory Data (GHO)," posted at the World Health Organization website.

_____. "Number of Road Deaths." 2013 statistics. Posted online at the WHO website.

Wrenn, Penny. "Friends in Business Together: 4 Success Stories." June 26, 2013, Forbes.com.

Yager, Fred and Jan Yager. *Just Your Everyday People.* Stamford, CT: Hannacroix Creek Books, Inc., 2001.

_____. *Untimely Death.* Stamford, CT: Hannacroix Creek Books, Inc., 1998.

Yager, Jan. "10 Friends That Every Woman Needs." Original article sponsored by Kimberly- Clark corporation and published in *Cosmopolitan* and other major magazines as an advertisement, August 2005.

_____. *Friendshifts: The Power of Friendship and How It Shapes Our Lives.* Stamford, CT: Hannacroix Creek Books, 1997, 2nd edition 1999. (E-book version, with a new introduction, 2010)

_____. *Friendship Thoughts, Famous Quotes, and a Journal.* Stamford, CT: Hannacroix Creek Books, Inc., 2014.

_____. *Grow Global.* Stamford, CT: Hannacroix Creek Books, Inc., 2011.

_____. "How to Make Friends After Fifty." April 8, 2017. Posted at https://www.drjanyager.com/how-to-make-friends-after-fifty/

_____. "Perspectives on Friendship." Special issue on Sociological Practice, edited by Ray Kirshak. *International Journal of Sociology and Social Policy.* Vol. 18, No. 1, 1998, pp. 27– 40.

_____. *Productive Relationships.* Stamford, CT: Hannacroix Creek Books, 2011.

_____. *So, What's Your Favorite Color? A Journal of Memories.* Stamford, CT: Hannacroix Creek Books, Inc., 2020.

_____. *When Friendship Hurts.* New York: Simon & Schuster, Inc./Touchstone, 2002. (E-book with new introduction, 2010)

_____.Who's That Sitting at My Desk? Workship, Friendship, or Foe? Stamford, CT: Hannacroix Creek Books, Inc., 2004.

Yager, Jeff. *Atom & Eve.* Stamford, CT: Hannacroix Creek Books, Inc., 2013.

_____. *Chuck & Alfonzo.* Illustrated by Nancy Batra. Stamford, CT: Hannacroix Creek Books, Inc., 2020.

_____ and Skye Bynes. *I Like God.* Stamford, CT: Hannacroix Creek Books, Inc., 2017.

Yalem, Marilyn with Theresa Donovan Brown. *The Social Sex: A History of Female Friendship.* NY: Harper Perennial, 2015.

Yang, Claire Yang; Courtney Boen; Karen Gerken; Ting Li; Kristen Schorpp; and Kathleen Mullan Harris. "Social Relationships and Physiological Determinants of Longevity Across the Human Life Span." *PNAS (Proceedings of the National Academy of Sciences),* January 19, 2016, Vol. 113, No. 3, pages 578-583.

Zajac, Robert and Willard W. Hartup. "Friends as Coworkers: Research Review and Classroom Implications." *The Elementary School Journal,* Vol. 98, September 1997, pages 3-13.

Zaslow, Alexandra. "Teen dies saving a life, completing bucket list." Published at Today.com on July 16, 2015.

Zwilling, Martin. "Make Your Competition Work for You." *Harvard Business Review,* April 29, 2011.

Movies, Documentaries, and TV Shows

Movies*

(*These were the ten most popular movies with a friendship theme chosen by the 178 men and women in my friendship snowball sample)

#1 – tied
Sex and the City (2008) Sara Jessica Parker, Kim Cattrall
The Shawshank Redemption (1994) Tim Robbins, Morgan Freeman

#2 – tied
Beaches (1988) Bette Midler, Barbara Hershey
The Big Chill (1983) Tom Berenger, Glenn Close, Jeff Goldblum

#3 *Bridesmaids* (2011) Kristen Wiig, Maya Rudolph

#4 *Stand by Me* (1986) Wil Wheaton, River Phoenix (Based on a Stephen King novella)

#5 *The Sisterhood of the Traveling Pants*

#6 *When Harry Met Sally* (1989) Billy Crystal, Meg Ryan

#7 *Toy Story* (1995) Tom Hanks, Tim Allen

#8 *The Avengers*

#9 – tied
The Hangover (2009) Starring Bradley Cooper.
Butch Cassidy and the Sundance Kid (1969) Paul Newman, Robert Redford
E.T.

#10 *Wayne's World*

Here are additional movies or documentaries with a friendship theme:

Bullies and Friends. Written and directed by Cassidy McMillan. (documentary)
My Own Private Idaho (1991) River Phoenix, Keanu Reeves
Now and Then (1995) Starring Christina Ricci and Gaby Hoffman
Palacios (2017). Libby Bibb, Olajuwon Davis.
Wonder (2017) Julia Roberts, Owen Wilson, Jacob Tremblay. Based on a YA novel by R.J. Palacio
Charlotte's Web (1973) Debbie Reynolds, Henry Gibson
Homeward Bound (1993) Pets played by Michael J. Fox, Sally Field, and Don Ameche
Gran Torino (2008) Starring Clint Eastwood

TV Shows

Beverly Hills 90210 (1990-2000)
Friends (1994-2004) Starring Jennifer Aniston
Girls (2012-2017)
The Golden Girls (1985-1992)
The O.C. (2003-2007)
Saved by the Bell (1989-1993)
Seinfeld (1989-1998) Starring Jerry Seinfeld and Julia Louis-Dreyfus
Sex and the City (1998-2004)
The Big Bang Theory (2007-)
Two Broke Girls (2011-2017)

Resources

In the pages that follow, you will find associations, organizations, and self-help groups that offer information or help on friendship-related issues, including website addresses. Inclusion in the list that follows does not imply an endorsement of any association, agency, or company by the author. Nor does omission of that association, agency, or company imply criticism.

The author and publisher specifically disclaim any responsibility for any liability, loss or risk, personal or otherwise, which is incurred as a consequence, directly or indirectly, of the use and application of any listings in this resource section.

Friendship-related Information Sites

Campaign to End Loneliness

http://www.campaigntoendloneliness.org.uk

Started in the United Kingdom in 2011, this organization seeks to identify and help those who are lonely, with a focus on the elderly.

drjanyager.com

https://www.drjanyager.com

whenfriendshiphurts.com

https://www.whenfriendshiphurts.com

These are two main websites related to my books and articles about friendship as well as providing information on the annual May International New Friends, Old Friends Week. You will also find videos of my TV appearances about friendship on the *Oprah Winfrey Show, The View,* CBS *Sunday Morning,* the *Today Show,* and *Good Morning, America,* among others.

Project BFF

https://project-bff.com/

Free information site co-founded in 2019 by Manya Chylinski and Terri Birkeland to share information about friendship through original blogs as well as sharing links to friendship-related articles that they recommend.

Selfgrowth.com

A free online resource with extensive articles and videos on friendship and other related relationship topics.

UCLA Parenting and Children's Friendship Program

https://www.semel.ucla.edu/socialskills/team
Founded in 1982 by friendship expert Fred Frankel, Ph.D., it offers several programs including a children's friendship program for first graders.

Social Media Sites including Apps and Sites for Making Friends

Bumble BFF

https://bumble.com/en-us/bff
This is the site and app that is part of Bumble but it is for connecting with potential friends rather than a romantic partner.

GirlfriendCircles

www.girlfriendcircles.com
Founded by Shasta Nelson, a membership friendship networking site to help women connect locally.

Girlfriendology

www.girlfriendology.com
Founded in 2006 by Debba Haupert, this site includes a blog, a podcast, and a community for fostering female friendships.

The Friendship Page

www.friendship.com.au
The Friendship Page, started in 1996 by Bronwyn Polson, an author

and lawyer from Australia, includes a friendship chat room, quotes on friendship, and a Find a Friend function. It also highlights the annual International Friendship Day celebrated on July 30 and August 3rd.

SKOUT

https://www.skout.com/

An app created in 2007 by Christian Wiklund and Niklas Lindstrom to help find people, including friends, around the world.

Facebook

https://www.facebook.com

The 2 billion+ free subscriber site that is usually more of a resource for keeping up with the friends you already have, through sharing of status updates, comments, and photos. However, there are certainly countless examples of new friendships that started on Facebook. (As with all social media platforms, post information about yourself and your loved ones with care.)

LinkedIn

https://www.linkedin.com

A popular free social media networking site with more than 500 million subscribers for business friendships and relationships. There is a completely free version as a well as a premium paid version.

Patook

https://patook.com/

A website and app that has the tagline "the strictly platonic friendship app." It also asks its users to have "Absolutely no flirting."

We3

https://www.we3app.com/

This is a website and app for meeting groups of friends of the same gender in your city. It boasts an algorithm with 150 factors for picking someone to connect to.

Friendship Force International

friendship-force.org

Description from the website: "Friendship Force International provides opportunities to explore new countries and cultures from the inside by bringing people together at the personal level.

Through the signature program of home hospitality, local hosts welcome international visitors into their culture, sharing with them meals, conversation, and the best sights and experiences of their region."

Established in 1977, Friendship Force now has chapters throughout the United States and in 45 countries. Its "citizen ambassadors" travel abroad to live with host families.

Road Scholar

roadscholar.org
Formerly known as Elderhostel, this is a not-for-profit travel organization that promotes international opportunities for education, travel, and friendship.

Stop Bullying Sites/Information

Bullies and Friends

bulliesandfriends.com/
Website for the documentary *Bullies and Friends*, made by Cassidy McMillan in response to the bullying-related suicide of a 14-year-old who had been threatened by three girls.

Cyberbullying Research Center

http://cyberbullying.org
Co-founded by Sameer Hinduja, Ph.D. (hinduja@cyberbullying.org) and Justin W. Patchin, Ph.D. (patchin@cyberbullying.org). Website has information on cyberbullying, including the researchers' studies and books, and resources for getting help.

Stop Bullying

www.stopbullying.gov
Website developed by the U.S. government with information on bullying and how to prevent it and deal with it when it happens.

Dealing with Caring for Someone Who is Seriously Ill Share the Care™

Share the Care™

http://www.sharethecare.org

Nonprofit organization started by Shelia Warnock to help those dealing with seriously ill people with advice about how to best handle their caregiving responsibilities. Warnock is also co-author, with the late Cappy Caposella, of *Share the Care: How to Organize a Group to Care for Someone Who Is Seriously Ill*, a self-book for caregivers. The book and the nonprofit are outgrowths of Warnock's first-hand experience in the late 1980s being part of a group of 12 women (10 friends plus her friend's two daughters) called Susan Farrow's Funny Family. After Susan was diagnosed with a brain tumor, they took care of their friend over the next $3^{1/2}$ years.

What Friends Do

https://whatfriendsdo.com

Founded by Aimee Kandrac and her mother Fran, this free site is an outgrowth of a site that Kandrac developed to coordinate information and help for her sister Stephanie's best friend Laura, who was being treated for a terminal brain tumor. The site helps thousands of friends work out ways to better help a friend in need.

Center for Loss and Life Transitions

http://www.centerforloss.com

Provides resources for grieving. Includes a free online searchable database of grief counselors.

HealGrief.org

Online and local groups for dealing with loss including the loss of a friend. Site offers articles and recommended books.

Police Athletic League (PAL)

http://www.palnyc.org/

Since 1914, this not-for-profit organization, together with the NYPD and the law enforcement community in New York City, has provided children and teens with positive role models and programs—such as after-school sports and arts activities—to help them acquire the skills to cope with life's challenges. Especially helpful for at risk teens who can find a way to avoid getting into trouble during unsupervised time. Offers a virtual classroom.

Three Doctors Foundation

http://threedoctors.com/

Co-authors of the bestseller *The Pact,* Samspon Davis, Rameck Hunt, and George Jenkins are African Americans who grew up in the projects in Newark, New Jersey. As teenagers they made a pact to help each other so they would avoid getting into drugs or crime. Two went on to become doctors and the third a dentist. They give back to the community through their Three Doctors Foundation.

Suicide Prevention

National Suicide Prevention Lifeline

https://suicidepreventionlifeline.org/

1-800-272-8255

Provides confidential help 24/7 if you or someone you know is depressed and threatening to commit suicide. Started in 2005 by the U.S. Substance Abuse and Mental Health Services Administration and The U.S. Substance Abuse and Mental Health Services Administration (SAMHSA) and Vibrant Emotional Health.

Therapists, Coaches, or Dispute Resolution Experts Dealing with Relationship Conflict Including Friendship or Associations That Could Make Referrals as well as Support Groups

Here are some associations or counseling services that offer in-person, phone, videoconferencing, or online help with a particular friendship, especially if there is conflict, or related friendship issues such as shyness, inferiority complex, fear of intimacy. *Disclaimer: Listings are not recommendations. Listings are just listings. You need to do your due diligence to check out the credentials and suitability for anyone or any resource listed below.*

American Psychiatric Association (APA)

http://finder.psychiatry.org/
This is the referral tool of this professional association of psychiatrists who could treat someone with friendship and related relationship issues.

American Psychological Association (APA)

https://www.apa.org/
Professional association of licensed psychologists available for counseling.

Association for Conflict Resolution (ACR)

https://acrnet.org/
Professional association that includes mediators, arbitrators, educators, and others offering conflict resolution services to those experiencing a conflict even a friendship-related dispute.

Danielle Bayard Jackson

https://www.daniellebayardjackson.com/
As noted at her website, this certified women's coach focuses on friendship and communication. Author of *Give it a Rest: The Case for Tough-Love Friendship* and Friend Forward subscription app.

Better Help

https://www.betterhelp.com/
Fee-based online private, individual counseling on relationships including friendship. Check out the website for how it works including fees.

BetterLYF Wellness Pvt Ltd

Delhi, India
Based in India, but with a global practice through online services. Counselors have a masters degree in psychology and additional supervision and training. For further information, go to: "Friendship" https://www.betterlyf.com/relationships/friendships.php

Coached Living

https://www.coachedliving.com/

Teresa Jones offers friendship coaching in addition to coaching for singles, couples, and ADD/ADHD.

MeetUp

https://www.meetup.com/topics/friendship-and-support/
Check out any friendship-related support groups available near you. Because of the increase in videoconferencing as a way to connect since the pandemic of 2020 started, there may be online or videoconferencing sites available from a more widespread area.

Psychology Today

https://www.psychologytoday.com/us/therapists
At the online site for *Psychology Today*, you will find this referral tool for locating a therapist to help you with relationship issues including friendship.

Relate

https://www.relate.org.uk/
Based in the UK and Wales, these trained and certified counselors are available for therapy sessions through a variety of in-person, phone, and Internet means.

TalkSpace

https://try.talkspace.com/
Online private counseling with a licensed therapist. Check out the website for details about how it works and fees.

Appendices

Appendix I
Friendship Over the Life Cycle

Appendix II
Applying Friendship Principles to Other Relationships:
Befriending Your Mother or Father

Appendix III
The Friendship Oath

Appendix IV
International New Friends, Old Friends Week: Day-by-Day Activities

Appendix V
College Courses That Might Want to Assign *Friendgevity*

Appendix VI
Applying the Four Sociological Theories to Friendship

Appendix VII
Critical Thinking Questions

Appendix I
Friendship Over the Life Cycle*

"We understand each other without words."

—49-year-old married Dutch woman with two
children, describing her best friend of 28 years.

Infancy

The goal of infancy is for a baby to get the emotional and physical nurturing that it needs from its mother or father so it can go to the next stage, toddlerhood, where there is greater self- sufficiency. Infants are totally dependent on their caregivers. Ironically, it is the strength of the parent-child bond during these first hours, days, weeks, and months that will enable the toddler and then the child, teen, and adult to successfully connect to his or her peers.

I am often surprised when a mother feels somewhat hurt when her one- or two-year-old shows an interest in other children. She is no longer the center of the infant's world, and that is a bit disappointing to some mothers who like being the total focus of their infant's life except for any other significant others, like a father, a sibling, grandparents, or close friends. The shifting of some of the attention away from the parent to a peer is a sign of the strength of the parent-child infant bonding. It means that there was enough nurturing and self-esteem building during those early months that the toddler feels emotionally strong enough to reach out to others.

Whether you are a 22-year-old who just arrived in a new city to start a new job and don't have any friends, or you're a 2-year-old reaching out to the other 2-year-olds in nursery school, the risk of rejection is very real. It takes self-confidence and the internalized belief that if for any reason this potential friend pushes you away, you'll always have your mother's love, or your father's love, to propel you forward. As I noted in *Friendshifts*, researchers have discovered that at as early as two or three months of age infants are oriented to the actions of other infants. By five months, they are concerned with other infants' cries.

Getting an infant into a play group or allowing him or her to be with other infants, is a positive experience for parents and their children. By 14 months, children have distinct playmate preferences. So, don't force your child to play with another kid at that age if he or she prefers someone else. It may not make sense to you, especially if this toddler was perfectly happy to play with anyone and everyone before. But individual inclinations are becoming stronger and it's important to honor those feelings.

Whether or not toddlers talk with each other while they play is not as important as the sharing and non-verbal communication of playing together that they are learning during school or playdates. How adults handle a child's disagreements, temper tantrums, and the occasional outburst of physical violence can set the stage for the child's ability to get along with his or her peers throughout the early years. "Use words" is a neutral way to steer the child who just hit a peer away from physical violence. You're showing that hitting is not acceptable and you're also suggesting another option.

Trying to sort through what happened that led to the negative outburst can take a lot of patience, but it will be worth it in the long run. Whether it's saying, or being the recipient of, words that are painful to hear, or the occasional push or shove, working things through is as instructive for the two-year-old as it will be for the older child, teen, or adult who has friendship challenges. Ignoring what happened, or sweeping it under the rug, is not the way to deal with a conflict, or to train your children how to deal with conflicts they have with other children.

You can read your toddler books about friendship, and discuss the concepts in the books, as a way of reinforcing the type of positive friendship skills that will help your child to be one of the most popular in the class instead of the one that few want to play with.

Here are a couple of available titles that you may find useful in teaching your children about friendship: *Being Friends* by Karen Beaumont and illustrated by Joy Allen, and *Making Friends Is an Art* by Julia Cook and illustrated by Bridget Barnes.

Psychologists Robert L. Selman and Dan Jacquette, as discussed in *Friendshifts*, put together stages of friendship starting with infancy through adulthood that help explain some of the ways friendships change as we age.

Selman/Jacquette Model of Friendship Stages from 3 to 15+

Stage 0	Ages 3-7	Momentary Playmatcship
Stage 1	Ages 4-9	One-Way Assistance
Stage 2	Ages 6-12	Two-Way Fair-Weather Cooperation
Stage 3	Ages 9-15	Intimate, Mutually Shared Relationships
Stage 4	Ages 12+	Autonomous Interdependent Friendships

Original art by Nancy Batra, represented, with permission, from 365 Daily Affirmations for Healthy and Nurturing Relationships by Dr. Jan Yager (Hannacroix Creek Books, Inc., 2016)

By age three and preschool, if a child is not getting along with other children, it may be time to consider getting outside help. There may be challenges going on at school or at home that a parent is too close to or unaware of, and professional intervention could make all the difference going forward. It is possible a child is not getting positive modeling at home. Perhaps siblings are picking on this child, or even being verbally or physically abusive in the name of "horsing around," and those negative behaviors are being brought into school and non-family play situations.

Working with a therapist might not be required, although you should not rule it out if there's a lot of anti-social behavior going on. You might want to observe your child at school, if it is permitted, or ask your child's teacher to watch what's going on for a day or two and take notes to see what the dynamics are. Is your child overly aggressive or, just the opposite, too shy to be included? Sitting down with a teacher or a guidance counselor and finding out what's going on with a child who's rarely asked to play could help move things in the right direction.

In most cases, children will naturally go in and out of friendships until they click with someone who might become a best friend for this month, this year, or for life. Five years old is when Betty made her best friendship, which has lasted 59 years. As Betty explains, "We've always lived within 10 miles of one another. Whenever we get together, it's as if no time has passed. We laugh and have a wonderful time. We never run out of things to talk about." That was true when they were five and it is still true all these years later.

Why is friendship so important, even in these early days? Studies show children with friends like school more than those who are friendless. Not surprisingly, they are more likely to get better grades and to be absent less often.

Do not be so quick to say "They're just kids" if a child is displaying overly aggressive behavior or even downright violence. There are enough examples of children as young as eight- or nine-years old committing murder, as well as those in their tween years, that being friendless and anti-social should not be ignored.

As a 62-year-old health care worker shared with me, "When I was 10 or 11, an older boy who lived up the block from me would threaten to beat me up. Another older boy did the same [thing] around the same time. I dealt with these bullies by taking a longer route home from school to avoid them." But one wonders what happened to those older bullies. Was their behavior just a phase, or was it a cry for help that the emotional problems behind their aggression was going to give them, and others, continual trouble?

In 2011, I provided my friendship expertise to a parent who was helping to develop a Friend Smart program with the PTA and school psychologist at an elementary school in Rockland County, New York. I was also a guest speaker on friendship two years in a row at the school when the program was introduced at night to the parents who would be helping to facilitate it in the classrooms. The concept behind the program was to help children become better friends and, through that proactive educational effort, to stop bullying before it starts.

The core concept of Friend Smart is the acronym BURP, which stands for:

Build – Use words that build someone up
Understand – What others may be feeling
Report – To get someone out of trouble
Practice – Try it over and over again!

Supported with training sessions for parents, as well as related games and giveaways, such as Friend Smart bracelets, the program was very popular with teachers, parents, and children alike to learn friendship skills that are not taught in school as consistently as they should.

I created a handout entitled "POWER: Developing Self-Esteem in Children," an anti- bullying strategy. Here is what the letters in POWER stand for.

P = Power and self-esteem start at home with a positive, loving family.
Help your child/children to feel loved and appreciated through realistic praise and positive reinforcement. Set limits and develop routines that inspire security and comfort.
O = Own your own positive self-esteem by being an example for your children. Stop adult bullying.
Have self-confidence yourself, but also admit that you are human and that you too sometimes make mistakes or revise what you think based on further consideration. Avoid intentionally or unintentionally bullying others through gossip, criticism, making fun of others, or stereotyping.
W = Watch and learn about self-esteem by reading books together, watching TV or movies, and discussing with your child what he or she is learning.
Read books, watch TV shows, and go to see movies that deal with self-esteem, overcoming adversity, and the triumph of the spirit. Self-esteem is something that needs to be developed.
Help your child to become more aware of self-esteem. Being strong enough to stand up to bullies is a skill that can be taught and learned.
E = Encourage your child to feel secure enough to ask for help.
Whether it's how to deal with a bully or how to do the math

homework, help your child to feel safe enough to ask for help from you, from other authority figures like teachers, or from others who are trustworthy. Depression in children is a warning sign that needs to be recognized. Learn to recognize the difference between being sad or blue or moody on occasion and experiencing short-term or chronic depression. If you child is clinically and chronically depressed, help him or her to get help.

R = Remind your child that he/she is able to stand up to anyone, including one or more bullies.

Help your child to have so much self-esteem that he or she will not let the bully win by becoming a victim. Empower your child to believe that there is no situation that cannot be handled. Being popular or having friends may seem like the most important thing in the world when you're young but being a friend to yourself is the most important friendship to have.

Teens

For most, the teen years are big "tests" because a child is eager to grow up and have all the privileges of an adult, but he or she still has a lot of emotional and even physical maturing to do. One of the ways teens often assert their independence is in their friendship choices. They may have chosen friends who lived nearby when they were younger because it was convenient, but living in a big city and taking public transportation, or riding a bicycle in the suburbs, or driving by age 16, it becomes easier to make and socialize with friends without as much parental scrutiny. This is when parents have to be especially aware of what's going on with their teens.

I am reminded of an interview I conducted in preparation for my friendship dissertation research. It was with a man who had his doctorate, and he was married and working at a university. He shared with me that when he was in junior high school—they called it junior high back then, not middle school—he had to give up his best friendship because that friend had started to shoplift when they went to the department store. He knew if he did not stop hanging out with his friend, it was just a matter of time before they both got apprehended for shoplifting. He would be arrested even if he had not done anything, just because he was with his friend when his friend committed the crime. Even if it all got sorted out later that he wasn't guilty, his parents would be devastated, and he feared what it would do to his reputation with his other friends and at school.

All these years later—he was in his mid-thirties when I interviewed him—he still felt bad about his decision, even though he knew it was the right one for him.

Unfortunately, too many teens do not make that kind of a painful but better choice for themselves. They go along with one wrong friend or a group of friends looking for trouble, and it can have disastrous consequences. A discussion of these types of situations, or those related to gang affiliation or activity, is outside the scope of this book. However, gangs and dysfunctional teen behavior have become a problem in most urban areas, and it has spread to the suburbs as well. For example, in Fairfield County, Connecticut, within the last few months, two teenagers, ages 17 and 18, were charged as accessories to murder because they were present when their 15- year-old friend shot and killed an 18-year-old former high school football captain whom they all confronted on the street. Even if it's not a formal gang that a teen is involved in, he or she can be in with a crowd that's into negative things, whether it's doing drugs, bullying, shoplifting, cutting school, or even committing violent crimes.

The opposite of that situation is the positive action that three African American teens growing up in the projects in Newark, New Jersey did. Fearing they would end up doing drugs or becoming criminals, like too many in their neighborhood, they decided to make a pact with each other to stay in school and pursue their career dreams of becoming health care professionals.

Sampson Davis and Rameck Hunt became doctors and George Jenkins became a dentist. They wrote a bestseller about their agreement and their achievements entitled *The Pact*. They also give back to the community through their Three Doctor Foundation; for example, they sponsor Healthy Body & Mind Charity Walkathons.

Although more and more families have two parents working even when children are young, it is by the teen years that both parents are likely to be at work. Whether it is for financial, professional, or even psychological reasons that a parent is no longer able to be home after school, that's okay. No one's saying one or both parents have to sacrifice their job or career because they have a teenager or two.

But you should make sure your teen is not just "hanging out" with friends and potentially getting into all kinds of trouble. If you and your spouse have to work, maybe your teen has a friend with a parent at home and he or she can go there to study after school. Another option is for your teen to have a part-time job for a couple of hours after school, where at least you'll know where he or she will be each day. After-school programs, whether those at school or those offered by other organizations—such as the Police Athletic League (PAL) in New York City—are positive environments where your teen can go to spend time with current friends or to make new friends.

Most teenagers can probably relate to what Justine, who is 16 and lives in Bruges, Belgium, shares about one of her three best friends, the one she's known the longest:

> *She has been my friend since we were little. She used to come over every day in the morning. We would go to school together, go to music class together, and stayed every evening until 8 p.m. or so. Even now [even though] we're both in different schools, we still see each other almost every day and just hang out. We do almost everything together, like studying sometimes or painting. We also go to parties or just sleep over every now and then. She lives two minutes away (with the bike), so that's handy, so we can just stay in each other's houses until 10 p.m. in the middle of the week. She's my age, and we met at primary school. We also just meet up sometimes randomly to go get hot chocolate.*

Young Adults Including Millennials

If you are lucky you can relate to the kind of best friendship that 16-year-old Justine described. But as you enter your 20s and beyond, it can become harder to have that kind of everyday best friendship unless you are roommates and live with each other, you live nearby, or you work together, especially once romantic partners and family obligations become more time-consuming.

Graduating from school and going off to college, joining the military, or starting a fulltime job are some of the first big adjustments to friendships from childhood, or *friendshifts*. For many, it is that dramatic change from the convenient everyday relationship that evolved so naturally from living nearby, going to school together, or hanging out at the local community center, that will determine if a friendship will go forward or wither and die.

Coupling off, and getting married, is another challenge to most friendships. Most friendships can absorb one of the friends getting married and the other staying single, and even one of the two having children, as long as the romantic partner does not voice too strong an objection to the friend. Similarly, the friendship can survive as long as the childless friend is comfortable in the difference in their priorities and lifestyles, and the friend with the baby, child, or teenager may have to learn to keep her bragging or complaining about her offspring to a minimum, reserving it for the child's parent or other friends who share her maternal challenges.

Choosing which friends to ask to be best man at the wedding, or maiden or matron of honor, or in the bridal party may, at the time, seem like an insurmountable challenge to even the closest of friends. Who does one pick for these honors? It can definitely require making clear decisions about who fits in what category of friendship. And if a friend fails to attend a wedding, even if she or he is not in the wedding party, there had better be a really good reason for it or it can become what I've referred to as a "crossing the line" situation that few friendships can recover from.

Thirty-five-year-old Elizabeth, who is single, has a friendship with both the husband and wife in a couple relationship, something Millennials and those who are now in their late teens through their twenties are more likely to do. So many of them attended, or are attending, colleges with coed dorms where having opposite-sex friendships is "no big deal" compared to their parents' or grandparents' generation. Opposite-sex friendships that are purely platonic have become "no big deal" for so many. Elizabeth, for example, shares how for her, the fact that her friend and his wife helped Elizabeth out by providing her with a place to stay is the nicest thing a friend has ever done for her:

> *Last year, I was in Seattle and my plans unexpectedly changed shortly after I arrived, and I needed a place to go. My friend and his wife, who is also my friend, opened their home to me without question and allowed me to stay with them for the remainder of my trip, and they included me in their Passover dinner, even though I wasn't Jewish. I can't express how thankful I am. I'm not sure what I would have done if they weren't there.*

Couples, Marriage, and Friendship

"In my happiest days, my wife is my best friend. In my saddest days, my wife is my best friend. She's the one I can share all my thoughts with."

—William Barkas, D.D.S. (1916-1996),
married to my mother for 54 years,
originally quoted in *Friendshifts*, Chapter 13,
"The Friendship Factor in Everyday Life"

The 20s through the 40s or 50s, when there are children at home, are often going to be a time for friends to really take a stand that their relationship matters despite all the other time constraints everyone is dealing with. There are the demands of children, romantic partners, extended family, jobs, and possibly even school or volunteer projects, but if friendship does not get the time and attention it needs, it will be hard to sustain it on past memories. Even social media posts to one's 1,500 "friends," including 10–20 actual friends and close or extended family members, cannot substitute for good old-fashioned "face time"—the kind where you sit across from your friend and smile and laugh or even cry, not the technological one that you can find on an Apple iPhone.

Being flexible and allowing yourself to have different ways of interacting and getting together with all the various friends in your life, from the range of experiences you've had by this point, will take you far. You do not have to include everyone you care about in your 10-year-old's birthday party. Maybe invite just one or two friends who also have 10-year-old children, or just have your family for dinner, and then your child could have a party with just his or her friends.

Making time for friends is actually the best way to ensure that the next phase of your life, the Empty Nester phase, won't be so lonely. Even if you haven't been keeping your friendships going because of how busy you are, you can try to reconnect. Hopefully you'll get your friendships back on track, or you can begin new friendships!

Empty Nesters

If you have raised one or more children, there may have been years when you thought this day would never come. And in the United States, for more and more families the Empty Nest phase is coming later and later as the high cost of rent and the challenging job market are leading more and more adults in their 20s and 30s to live at home, at least for a while. But for most, the day will arrive when your children are out of the house and it's just you or just you and your spouse. Now what?

Hopefully, you've kept your romance growing so you don't become one of those statistics: the couple that breaks up after a decade or two once the kids are grown. No, you and your spouse still love each other and you're excited that you now can date again and, yes, spend more time with your friends.

Some couples start to take trips with their friends, and that might even work out once, twice, or on a permanent basis. For others, traveling with friends is just not their idea of a good time.

But at least they're going out to dinner or even meeting at a fun destination so they can share the activity even if they don't share the whole trip.

If your friends have relocated or if you have found that your interests are just too different these days, it might be time to cultivate some new friends. It is actually not as easy for couples to find other couples to befriend as it is for single people to find other singles. But it is still possible by participating in trips that are organized to include others in your age group. Even just being friendly and active and going through the "getting to know you" process with a new couple that you would go through if you were a lot younger can help. You might also think about all those couples that you've liked over the years, but you never got around to inviting over or going out with because of the kids, or your aging parent who has since died. Perhaps by now you are comfortable enough in your work routine that you can put the time and energy into getting more social events on your calendar than you could handle in the past.

In Your 50s

Remember that everyone's 50s are different. Some 50-year-olds are empty nesters. Some have a second family in elementary school. Some are divorced and single. Don't make assumptions about your friends just based on a chronological number.

Nostalgia friendships are important to cherish and nurture just for the history that you share.

But that may not be enough. Without discarding or ending those friendships, if you have drifted apart from the good old days, look to strengthening your bonds with other friends or starting to make new ones.

After 50, even if you did not have to deal with it before, you will need to help your friends deal with death, particularly of their elderly parents. Going through this rite of passage can really become somewhat easier with the help of friends. Friends will also start to get ill and die as the years go by. Creating rituals and support systems for helping each other through these inevitable life passages is as important as enjoying the fun times that friendships can bring.

Having fun is as important to post-50 friendships as it was during the formative years. Try new activities together, travel, start a book club, explore sports or experiences you've always wanted to share with your friends.

Just because you feel as if you don't have as much time as you used to when you were young doesn't mean that starting a new friendship is going to happen quickly. The process is the same, whether you're 15 or 50. Although you have other concerns, such as family, work, or hobbies, you don't have to pressure your potential new friend, causing the friendship to end prematurely because of your neediness.

Just as each person may be at a very different place romantically at age 50 and in terms of their family situation, 50 can be quite different workwise. Some may already be thinking about retirement, some may be going back to school to start a new career, and some may be at the height of their careers. Find those who you are comfortable being around based on shared values and situations rather than just chronological age.

Just as you made time for friendship no matter how busy you were during your previous decades, make time for friendship in your 50s. Don't put it off till you have time, because you've just got to accept the reality that you're always going to be busy with multiple demands on your time.

In Your 60s

How much time you have for friendship in your 60s will have a lot to do with whether or not you and/or your spouse have retired or if you are working full time or part time. If you have retired, and you are not totally consumed with your hobbies or visits to your grandchildren, you could have more time for getting together with your friends. During this decade, it becomes more common for people to go on trips with their friends, especially if their adult children are unavailable for a family trip because of work or other commitments.

This is also the decade where, statistically, more friends are going to get sick and pass on than in previous decades. Disease or tragedy can strike at any age, but with the average life expectancy in the United States listed by the CDC (Centers for Disease Control and Prevention) for 2014 for both sexes and all races as 78.9 years, the closer you get to that average, the more common it is to have to deal with friends passing on.

In addition to friends dying, there is an increased number of relocations. Whether to get closer to the children and grandchildren after retirement, or to move away from states with harsh winters, or to downsize into a smaller home or a rental property, moving is going to impact friendships. Most of the time it means leaving behind the friends that you have made over many decades. But sometimes, it can actually mean reconnecting with old friends who never moved away or who, coincidentally, have chosen to move to the same community, state, or country that you have moved to.

In Your 70s, 80s, and beyond

Some of us are still working in our 70s—not as many in the 80s and beyond—while others have retired. What impact does what you are doing have on your friendships? Making new friends in your 70s, 80s, and beyond is usually a question of necessity rather than choice. For example, if someone divorces or becomes widowed, being the "third wheel" can be uncomfortable, so making new friends, or reconnecting with old friends who are in a similar single situation, may be the difference between having someone to do things with or being lonely.

The most important thing to remember is that it is a bunch of nonsense that making friends when you are older is impossible. Yes, for some it may be harder because they are more set in their ways and too demanding about what they want in a friend, or because they have physical or mental challenges caused by aging that make it more difficult to be mobile or even to interact with others. But if you have your health under control and you are open minded and positive about the possibility of friendship, it can actually be relatively easy to make a new friend, especially a casual one that may, in time, grow into a close or best friend.

After all, by the time you are in your 70s, and certainly by your 80s, your kids are probably grown. Even if you have grandchildren, unless you are taking care of them full time, your duties probably include just occasional babysitting or intermittent visits if you live far away. If you are still working, hopefully it's because you're doing the work you love. Even if you're working because you need the money, you're not a kid anymore so you won't take the angst or pressure of work to heart as much as you might have when you were a lot younger and possibly with children to raise.

Lynn Rosenberg and Pam Lane began a friendship that blossomed into a best connection when they were both in their early 70s. They are now both 76. When I asked Pam what she would say to someone if they wondered if it is hard to make a friend when you are older, she replied:

> *My response to that is, get out and participate in life because nobody is going to come knocking on my door and say, "Do you want to me my friend?" When I was much younger, I used to call myself a player. Today I would say, "Participate in life." I get out, go hear speeches. I go to lectures. I go to events. I'm not a wealthy woman but there are many things you can do for not a lot of money. Go where people gather*

together for a common interest. You will find like-minded people for cultivating new friendships. If you put yourself out there, and turn to your neighbor, and say, "My name's Pam. How did you come to be here tonight?" or something like that, you'll have to put it out, and opened the gateway to making a new friend.

Friendship in the 70s and beyond may be more of a question of health and mobility than it is the time and other relationship pulls that might have made friendship a more challenging pursuit in the earlier years. As noted in Chapter 1, however, and throughout *Friendgevity*, the way that friendship can increase your life span makes it a relationship worth pursuing especially as some friends die and others relocate to be closer to their adult children and grandchildren, or as family members pass away as well.

Appendix II
Applying Friendship Principles to Other Relationships:

Befriending Your Mother or Father*

The 173rd respondent to my confidential snowball friendship survey asked me in an e-mail if I could offer some advice on how to apply what I have learned about friendship to the family relationships in his life since, currently, he does not have any friends. Even if you are fortunate enough to have one or more close or best friends, you might find the friendship principles I have learned useful in how you get along with your relatives.

Having children, or adult children, who want to confide in you is a goal for most parents. But children and teens (and even parents) have to want that kind of relationship; as children become teens and young adults, they may prefer to share with their peers rather than their parents. Similarly, as parents deal with the realities of their children moving away and having a more independent life of their own, they may need some help learning to see their children-turned- adults more like a friend rather than a dependent child.

There are a wide range of possibilities in how you will interact with your own parents throughout your life; it can change dramatically. Even if you had a distant or less- than-ideal relationship during your formative years, you may be pleasantly surprised to have with one or both parents a much closer friendship relationship during your young adult or older years.

Address What Your Parent-Child Relationship Really is Today Rather than Living in a Dream World about How You Would like It to Be

*This section is an updated and edited version of what I wrote for the Kimberly Clark Corporation at their Kotex.com website. It is reprinted here to offer a wider distribution of the key ideas that are contained in this essay.

It is important to know what is really going on with your children (or parents) rather than what you wish to be true. For example, a mother I interviewed suggested I speak with her 13- year-old daughter because she believed they have the kind of relationship that other teens would envy; her daughter told her everything. But when I interviewed her daughter, she shared quite a different perspective. I asked her, "Would you go to your mother if you had a problem with a boy or something like that?" She quickly replied, "I think I'd go to my friend more. I think it would be easier to talk to a friend my age."

Shifting the Role, You Play With Your Parents May Change How You Relate

A modification in your parent-child relationship may also occur when you shift the role you play with your parents. This is what happened to Dorothy. She was so used to burdening her mother with the woes of her singleness that she never thought about what her mother, a 59-year-old office worker, might be worrying about.

Dorothy finally listened to her mother, instead of just talking and complaining about her own concerns. She was pleased to discover that her mother did reveal to her many of her own personal and business problems once she had the chance to do so.

As Dorothy says, "It was then that I saw my mother as a woman who also has problems. Maybe she could tell my father those same problems but, finally, after all those years of getting from my mother, I allowed myself to give to her as well. Somehow I felt like I would have to cope better on my own because my mother needed some advice [too]."

Suddenly You May Have a Greater Appreciation for Your Parent

Lil, whose best friendship faded after her friend's marriage—because her friend's husband made it difficult for Lil and her friend to maintain their friendship—now considers her mother to be her best friend. For instance, when Lil's two-year romantic relationship was ending, and all her friends were sick of hearing about Lil's emotional angst, she turned to her mother, who drove Lil back to her home in New Jersey. "Sit down and shut up for a few days," Lil says her mother told her, suggesting, albeit it in a rather harsh way, that Lil needed to digest what happened to her as she got a grip on herself as she learned to deal with the breakup. If she didn't, her friends had been making it pretty clear to her that they would stop taking her phone calls if the majority of what she was going to share about was her despair over her breakup.

Your Parents Are Ageing So You Find Yourself Motivated to Get to Know Them Better While You Still Have That Chance

As another woman I interviewed put it, "My mother gave me life. She was the closest person to me. She won't be around forever. I never want to feel that we failed to share our lives as completely as we could."

To Know Your Parents May Aid You in Getting Along with Your Other Relationships Including Friendships

Becoming closer with your mother or father may help you to become more comfortable with intimacy in all the other key relationships in your life.

Steps for Becoming Closer to Your Parents

How might you become closer to your adult children or to your own parents? For starters, try listening to your parent instead of just blurting out what is concerning you.

Ask questions and hear their answers, without judgment. You might even consider interviewing your mother or father, on audio tape or on videotape, recording for posterity what they say in response to your questions. Of course you may have heard lots of stories about or by your parents during your formative years, but it may be enlightening to ask those questions again, now that you are older or to ask different questions that the ones you used to ask. Consider buying a family history album and working together to fill in the questions that are asked as well as gathering old photographs together to complete the book.

Make time for each other. When you and your children were young, or when you were young, you and your parents might have taken a family trip every year or every other year. Once you left home, it could get harder to schedule trips like that because of everyone's school or work schedules. Then, as children have their own family obligations, just getting together with one's own family becomes a challenge.

Now is the time to make a commitment to an extended family reunion or vacation whether it's once every five years, once a decade, or, even better, once a year. Of course, it takes time and effort to plan such an event, as well as coordinating the schedule of numerous family members. But it will provide an opportunity to continue strengthening your relationship rather than relying on your previous memories of each other.

What Should You Do If You try to Befriend Your Adult children or Your Parents, but It Just is Not Working?

But what if all your efforts with your mother or father, or your adult children, see futile, or at least at this point in time, those attempts at more intimacy are not working? For example, Naomi tried and tried to be honest and to have a better relationship with her mother. She even asked her mother to attend a mother-daughter workshop with her, but her mother refused to go. So, what did Naomi do? "I could always talk frankly with my father, so I decided it was better to strengthen my relationship with him than to just keep fighting with my mother." She did not, however, give up her efforts to develop a closer relationship with her mother even though it was going to take much more effort and time to achieve that goal.

As Victoria Secunda writes in her chapter, "Rediscovering Our Fathers," in her book, *Women and Their Fathers: The Sexual and Romantic Impact of the First Man in Your Life*, the goal of that chapter "is to help daughters to find out what they missed with their fathers so that they can better understand their relationships with men outside the family, whether at work or in love."

Secunda writes that there are three steps to working through the father-daughter relationship: remembering, healing, and reconnecting. Notes Secunda: "The key is to really get to know the actual father—whether or not he is alive or even around—to pull him out of the shadows, apart from Mom, away from the newspaper, and really see him."

It is also useful to apply the same technique to getting to know one's mother: work at seeing her separately from your father or from the roles you were used to seeing her playing during your childhood and teen years as mother, wife, or worker.

The Social Media Factor

I initially signed up for Facebook so I could find out what was going on in the lives of my adult sons, Scott and Jeff, without being intrusive. I had to learn when to comment and when to just "like" a post so I would not be accused of being a helicopter Mom. So social media can be a way of staying more involved in your adult child's life by seeing the posts that he or she is sharing with his or her network of Facebook friends, which hopefully will include you.

You do have to be careful about what you say or do or don't say when you see posts by your adult children and even from your friends, extended family, and work-related connections.

Here is a prime example. When my older son Scott was 30, he shared on Facebook a picture of a concert venue in Colorado that he had always wanted to attend. The post announced that he finally got there so he could cross that off his bucket list.

What? Scott went to Colorado and did not tell his mother? I shared this information with my husband Fred who wisely said, "He's thirty years old. He doesn't have to tell you his every move," or words to that effect.

So, I did not say anything. I may have clicked on "like" to the post with the picture, but I did not overreact and risk getting defriended!

Social media can, if handled wisely, add a positive layer of communication with our children and, if your parents are on it, with parents. But be careful what you post. One of my friends did not realize initially that whatever she wrote in the comment section in Facebook could be seen by her hundreds of friends! It took her a while to learn to either send a private message on Facebook or a private e-mail rather than posting private comments that were being read by everyone, much to her embarrassment as well as the awkwardness of those she had commented to or about.

Is There Such a Thing as "Too Close?"

Twenty-seven-year-old Jane, who got married last year, had the opposite problem to Naomi's aloof mother-daughter relationship, described above. Jane's mother, who was divorced, shared with her daughter such personal details about her romantic relationships that it made her daughter uncomfortable. Says Naomi: "I finally had to tell my mother that I just didn't' want to hear about her various boyfriends and live-ins. I was handling the sexual aspects of my [own] marriage, and I thought my mother should be able to handle the intimacies of her own life."

If a married man or woman is too close to his/her mother, it may affect the intimacy of nuptial ties. But in Naomi's case, at least those close family connections did not prevent the marriage from taking place in the first place. As Nancy Friday notes in *My Mother/Myself*: "Very often the new mother-daughter friendship comes at the expense of what should be our prime union—with our husband."

Befriending Your Parents in an Appropriate Way May Be the Greatest Gift you Give Yourself

However, becoming a better friend with your mother or father, as well as with your adult children, as long as it is appropriate and not excessive and as long as it does not push other intimate relationships away, in a very basic way, is the beginning of becoming best friends with yourself. That is because if you are able to accept your mother, or your father, or your adult children, for who they are, despite their faults, and get to know them, and appreciate each one, you will be closer to gaining a better understanding of each of your parents, or children, as well as to achieving greater self-acceptance.

Appendix III
Friendship Oath*

Wʜen I was interviewed about friendship for the CBS News *Sunday Morning Show* for a series on friendship that they were producing, Russ Mitchell asked me what reasonable expectations for a friend and friendship are. I replied that it was an intriguing question since we do have very clear guidelines, even vows, that a husband and wife exchange when they marry, and there are expectations for a parent's duties. I thought about it and decided that a Friendship Oath might be useful to consider and even to share with friends. Afterwards, I composed the above friendship oath.**

Friendship Oath

By accepting the responsibility of being your friend, I promise to be honest and trustworthy. I will try to work out any differences or conflicts that we may have and will try to put the time and effort into our friendship that it requires. I know we both have work (or school), family, and personal obligations, and we will respect each other's other relationships and commitments, but I will also be committed to this friendship. I will try to only give advice if it's asked for, and I will also try to be your friend, unconditionally.

I will keep your confidences. However, I will also share with you if it is my policy to never keep anything from my spouse or any other primary relationship, with whom I entrust all my secrets. I will try to remember your birthday and be there for you when times are tough and when times are grand. Making time to talk, communicating by mail or email, or getting together is a priority. I will celebrate your achievements even though I know a tiny bit of envy or competitiveness is normal. I will bring fun and joy to your life as much as I am able to as I cherish our past, present, and future friendship.

The explanation of how this Friendship Oath evolved, as well as the oath itself, is reprinted, with permission, from Who's That Sitting at My Desk? *by Jan Yager, Ph.D. (Hannacroix Creek Books, Inc., 2004)*

Appendix IV
International New Friends, Old Friends Week

7 Days of Friendship Celebrations*

A version of this material appears as a blog at my website, https://www. drjanyager.com. Reprinted with permission.

I created the following seven friendship-related theme days to accompany National New Friends, Old Friends Week (renamed International New Friends, Old Friends Week), a week I started in 1997 to celebrate the new friends in our lives but also to take time and remember, and maybe even reconnect with, our old friends. These activities, as well as the information that is shared for each day, could be read on their own merits, separate from the formal celebration.

You could also decide to follow just one of the friendship-related themes on all the days.

(Sunday) Day 1:

Remembering and Finding Time for Your Old Friends - Friendshifts Day

In the midst of our busy lives it's important for us all to take the time to stop and remember our friends. At different times in our lives we may find we are more likely to take the time to remember the friendshifts—how our friendships may seem to be here today but gone tomorrow because we relocate, graduate from school, get another job, or leave camp.

Remember Your Old Friends/Friendshifts Day is a reminder that you might want to pick up the phone, send an email, write a letter, or send a card or a present to reconnect with an old friend. Say hello or set up a get-together now rather than tomorrow. Use International New Friends, Old Friends Week as another time, in addition to your birthdays and the holidays, to remember old friends, especially those who live far away now.

Activities for Remember Your Old Friends/Friendshifts Day:

On a piece of paper or on your computer, make a list of all the key periods in your life, including childhood, elementary school, middle school, high school, college, graduate school, professional school, the jobs you've held, volunteer activities, communities you've lived in, neighborhoods you've been part of, professional associations, or religious houses of worship. Leave enough room for filling in as many names as you can remember of those that mattered to you during those times in your life. Is there any name that emerges that makes you think, "I wonder where so-and-so is these days? I would like to catch up. I miss that friend."

(Monday) Day 2:

New Friend Celebration Day

What is the most recent friendship you have developed? Maybe you have actually started more than one friendship. That is great! Pick one of those new friends and plan a get-together on Day 2 of International New Friends, Old Friends Week. If you live or work in the same vicinity, try to get together in person. Have breakfast, lunch, tea, a drink at the end of the day, or dinner. Go out to a movie or concert.

If you do not live nearby, and you usually communicate through Facebook posts, email, or texts, and you can't get together in person, make the time for a phone call to catch up.

If you do not have a new friend, use today to try to cultivate one by going to an activity that interests you and introducing yourself to the people you meet, or by attending a professional meeting or business association networking event. Refer back to Chapter 3, "Making Friends," for additional suggestions on how to form new friendships.

(Tuesday) Day 3

Friendship and Work Appreciation Day

If you have a friend at work, go out to lunch together. Pick a nice place to eat. Make a promise that you'll talk about anything *but* work! Or get together after work and go out to dinner, take a cooking class together, go to a lecture or concert, or volunteer together. Depending on the weather, consider doing a team-building sports activity like going to a bowling alley or shooting some hoops or playing softball.

Day 4 (Wednesday)

Be Your Own Best Friend Day

One of my favorite self-help books from the 1970s is *How to Be Your Own Best Friend* by psychoanalysts Mildred Newman and Bernard Berkowitz. It is one of those books with a great title; just hearing the title makes you start to think a new way. So be your own best friend. The nicer you are to yourself, the nicer you will probably be to your friends as well as all the other people in your life. So, use Day 4 of International New Friends, Old Friends Week to Be Your Own Best Friend. That has to start from the inside out. You need to love and appreciate yourself, with all your faults as well as all your uniqueness.

Make a list of 10 things you like about yourself:

1. _____
2. _____
3. _____
4. _____
5. _____
6. _____
7. _____
8. _____
9. _____
10. _____

Now make a list of 10 things you would like to do that you do not usually make the time to do:

1. _____
2. _____
3. _____
4. _____
5. _____
6. _____
7. _____
8. _____
9. _____
10. _____

Pick something from this list to do on Be Your Own Best Friend Day.

Day 5 (Thursday)
When Friendship Hurts: A Day of Healing

In Alcoholics Anonymous (AA) one of their 12 steps, Step 9, is to make amends to those you have harmed. This is a similar idea but has nothing to do with AA or drinking—it has to do with friendship. Is there a former friend that you would like to reconnect with? Whether you ended the friendship or they are the one who ended it, use this day to reach out to your former friend and see if you can get your friendship back on track, or at least get a better understanding about what happened and why.

You can also use Day 5 to reach out to a current friend that you feel you are ignoring or not treating as well as you would like to be. Apologize, and vow to be a better friend.

Day 6 (Friday):
Defusing Bullies Day

Devote Day 6 of International New Friends, Old Friends Week to educating children and teens about how to deal with bullying. Approach it from both perspectives: how to deal with someone who might be bullying you, and how to avoid being considered a bully.

Bring in a guest speaker who is an expert on bullying. Watch a documentary about true life bullying and bullycide tragedies, such as *Rats & Bullies*, a film about 15-year-old Dawn-Marie Wesley of British Columbia who killed herself because three former friends were bullying her. Lead a discussion about how to prevent that from happening at your school or in your town or city.

You could also invite a guest speaker who was bullied as a child or teenager to discuss what it was like and why it's important to stop bullying and to not be a bully. Says Russell D. Bernstein, who also speaks to children and teens about bullying at schools and community centers:

"Access to social media sites at an earlier and earlier age coupled with the anonymity factor creates an environment ripe for cyberbullying and its subsequent detrimental effects on society. When I was bullied as a kid, unfortunately I didn't know that I could go to the adults at the camp where it occurred and ask them for help. With the Internet making the possibility of cyberbullying that much greater, it's even more important than ever that kids and teens know they don't have to deal with this alone. If someone is bullying them, whether offline or online, they need to tell a trusted adult (or even an older sibling or a friend they trust) so they can get help with the situation before it persists or escalates. Having that support network in place prior to the stress or bullying reaching an intolerable level is integral in coping effectively."

Day 7 (Saturday):

Online Friends Day

You know from reading *Friendgevity* that online friends can be friends that you make online and that stay online, and that's okay. But an online friend could also be someone that you would like to speak with on the phone or even make an in-person connection with, but you just haven't been able to do that yet.

Day 7 of International New Friends, Old Friends Week might be a good opportunity to make that happen. Pick up the phone and call your online friend. If you get his or her voice mail, no problem. Leave a message! At least you're making a step toward communicating in ways besides online.

If you and your friend have both decided that it is time to move your friendship toward the stage of meeting in person, and you're both comfortable doing that, use today to set up that meeting. To be safer, you should meet in a public place, and you could also bring one or two other friends along. You might also want to review the tips for safety and friendship that I shared in Chapter 4, "Making Friends," especially those related to online friendships. Even if you don't want to meet in person, for any reason, you could use today to put in a phone call and talk to each other by phone.

Appendix V
College Courses That Might Want to Assign Friendgevity

I have noticed that few textbooks assigned for the courses below have an extensive or detailed discussion about friendship, if at all. If you are taking or teaching sociology, psychology, or business, you therefore might find *Friendgevity* a useful required or recommended reference in the disciplines or courses listed below. Some of the courses, it should be noted, may not be widely available, but there might be administrative, faculty, or student interest in such a friendship-related course. After this Appendix, you will find two additional appendices that I created that might prove helpful including Appendix VI. "Applying the Four Sociological Theories to Friendship" and well as Appendix VII, chapter-by-chapter "Critical Thinking Questions."

Please note that at the very end of this book, you will also find a description of my two previous books on friendship, *When Friendship Hurts* (Simon & Schuster) and *Friendshifts* (Hannacroix Creek Books). Either of those titles might also be a useful required or recommended book on friendship for any of the courses below:

Sociology
Introduction to Sociology
Sociology of the Family
Sociology of the Family and Intimate Relationships
Relationships 101
Social Problems
Social Deviance
The Sociology of Friendship*
Gerontology

Criminology and *Criminal Justice*
Juvenile Delinquency
Peer Influences During Adolescence: Friends and Gangs

Psychology
The Psychology of Close Relationships
Social Development
Relationships 101
Child and Adolescent Development

Anthropology
Introduction to Anthropology
Friendship and Kin Structure

Business (undergraduate or MBA programs)
Work Relationships
The Essentials of Management
The Essentials of Entrepreneurship

Education
Child and Teenage Development

Philosophy
Introduction to Philosophy
(also see Chapter 3, "Perspectives on Friendship, in *Friendshifts*, for a discussion of The Great Friend and The Modern Friend approaches to friendship)

English
Themes in Literature Including Friendship

History
Great Friendships Throughout History

Appendix VI
Applying the Four Sociological Theories to Friendship

The Functionalist Perspective
(also referred to as Structural Functionalism)

Proposed by August Comte in the early 1830s, and expanded upon by Emile Durkheim, in the late 1890s, and Robert K. Merton, in the mid-1900s – he lived to 92, passing away in 2003, functionalism looks at the way that social actions or groups help society to operate smoothly. Friendship has a positive function in society in the following ways:

1. It provides early training for getting along with others outside of the family, including behaviors, such as sharing, being a good listener, and communicating thoughts and feelings, that can later be applied to romantic relationships.
2. If a romantic relationship does not work out, whether the couple breaks up or one of the pair ends it through divorce or death, friendship means that someone will have relationships to help them through the loss.
3. Friends can teach and share information and expertise with each other.
4. If someone was raised in a dysfunctional family, friends can offer a new, healthier perspective.

Friendship might also be dysfunctional:

1. The time that friendship takes for it to be intimate and important can take away from time that could be spent on romantic, familial, or work relationships.
2. Choosing the wrong friend can get someone into a temporary or prolonged negative state leading to academic, legal, or emotional troubles.

3. If a friend causes their friend to have self-doubt, it can harm, rather than aid, their social development.
4. As Mui, Sales, and Murphy point out in their scholarly article, "Everybody's Doing It: Initiation to Prescription Drug Misuse," besides getting exposed to prescriptions by family members, the 120 interviewees with a median age of 21 revealed that their misuse started because "peers often shared their legitimately prescribed drugs."

The Symbolic Interactionist Approach

(also known as the Interactionist Perspective)

First proposed by George Herbert Mead, and expanded upon by Erving Goffman, among others, the symbolic interactionist approach looks at the micro level and how it helps or hinders social group performance. Here are some ways that a symbolic interactionist might explain friendship:

1. If a friend treats someone well through positive communication including remembering their friend's birthday, answering their phone calls, texts, or e-mails promptly, it can enhance their self-esteem. These are all non-verbal and symbolic symbols of approval. The absence of these and other definite symbols, could be interpreted as rejection even if it is unintentional.
2. Friends can define someone's social world, limiting it or expanding it, as the case may be.
3. In a society where numbers count—votes determine who wins an election, grades in college are seen as a reflection of how much someone learned or whether or not someone is a good student, how many birthday greetings someone gets on Facebook might be seen as an indication of someone's popularity—these might be the wrong measures for friendships that are meaningful. In that regard, it might discount quality by over emphasizing quantity.

Conflict Theory

An outgrowth of the writings and theories of Karl Marx (1818-1883), the history of the world is seen as the chronicling of class struggle—between the haves and the have-nots. Individuals and groups are all out for themselves, trying to get the best situation. Those in power have more benefits, according to conflict theory, than those who are dominated and seen as the weaker class.

So how might conflict theorists view friendship?

1. Those at the top tend to have friendships with those who are also powerful and at the top. It is hard for those who lack that power to break into that elite group.
2. Conflict in friendship is normal since conflict theorists see social conflict as normal. Friendship conflict should be dealt with rather than avoided at all costs which could result in a more superficial relationship.
3. As individuals change their status throughout their lives, their friendships may change as well, what I referred to as *friendshifts* in my first book on friendship. These *friendshifts* are inevitable although some may resent and resist these inevitable changes.
4. The expression "birds of a feather flock together" epitomizes the conflict approach to friendship.

Feminist Theory

Feminist theory views social groups and actions through the lens of gender. Those who profess this theory see a gender gap in everything such as politics, economics, social issues, and relationships, including friendship. Here are some of the ways that a feminist theorist might view friendship:

1. Although there are exceptions, Dr. Shelley Taylor, and others, have determined that there is a "befriending" instinct which makes women more prone to nurturing and emotional connections in their friendships. This can put them at a disadvantage in business where friendships need to be more instrumental or goal-oriented and less emotive.
2. If women are perceived as being friendlier or needing friends more than men, a woman who deviates from that might be labeled unfriendly.
3. Males tend to have friendship that start with an activity, such as playing golf, or cards, and the friendship grows out of the activity. This can give them an advantage in business since they can be assessing during the activity whether or not they even want to develop a friendship. If women plunge in with talking and sharing because of their perceived need to connect, they

might trust too soon, hurting their career.

4. The "all boys clubs" that some men at the top turn to for advancement are so secretive and hard to break into that those clubs do not even have names, membership dues, or public personas. The formal clubs for women only may be seen as a step in the right direction but are those clubs really the way for women to advance?

5. If two women became friends at the job when they were at the same level and one is promoted, if you ask a woman if she had to choose between her new job and maintaining that friendship at the job, what would most women choose to do? Transfer their friend to another department? End the friendship? Turn down the promotion? Figure out a way to keep the friendship despite the change in status? What solution would most men choose if they found themselves in a similar situation?

Appendix VII
Critical Thinking Questions

If you are teaching or taking a college course that is requiring, or recommending, *Friendgevity*, here are critical thinking questions, related to each chapter, that might be helpful in getting the most out of this book for your course:

Introduction

1. Since we have now learned from the research of social scientists, epidemiologists, and medical doctors that loneliness is a preventable cause of reduced mortality, what should individuals or the government do, if anything, about decreasing loneliness in society?

2. The Introduction begins the case that friendship is a pivotal relationship that needs to be given the life-and-death consideration that it deserves. Do you agree or is friendship overrated as a relationship (compared to the importance of family or work relations)?

3. Do you agree that the pandemic of 2020 highlighted disparities in friendship? If yes, in what way? If no, why do you say that?

4. Did the pandemic of 2020 impact on your casual, close, or best friendships? If yes, how? If no, why not?

5. Do you spend any time on social media connecting with friends? If yes, how much time? Have you considered how that time on social media, as what as what you share, is impacting on your friendships? (Consider what the experts and average users of social media share about this in Chapter 2, "The Impact of Social Media on friendship.")

Chapter 1 – Friendship, Longevity, and Dementia

1. Of all the ways that you have learned that friendship helps to extend your life, which one resonated the most with you, and why?

2. Do you think friends or family are more important in extending your life? Is your answer based on scientific evidence or personal observation?
3. Why do you think having even one good friend can slow down or even stop the onset of dementia?

Chapter 2: The Impact of Social Media on Friendship

1. Do you think social media has hurt or helped the quality of friendships? Why? Why not?
2. What social media are you on, if any? Who introduced you to those social media? How big a part does your friendships play in how often, or what, you post on social media?
3. Do you think friends made online are the same, worse, or better than friends made through more traditional ways, such as taking a course together, living nearby, participating in a sport together?
4. Is it ever okay to "defriend" or "block" a friend on social media? Why? Why not?

Chapter 3: Assessing Your Friendship Skills and Current Network

1. Why is it important to assess your current friendship network?
2. Do you think friendship skills can be taught? Why? Why not?
3. What is your best friendship trait? What behaviors do you need to work on and why?
4. Are you pleased with your current friendship network? Why? Why not?
5. If you had to pick one skill that is the most important one to have in a friendship, what would that be, and why?
6. When is the last time you told a friend you'd love to get together, or call him or her, but you just don't have time, or some other excuse? Will you handle that situation differently since you read this chapter in *Friendgevity*?

Chapter 4: Making Friends

1. Do you think you can actively make an effort to make a friend or is it something that just "happens" like the way some people think falling in love romantically "just happens?" Why? Why not?
2. When is the last time you made a new friend? Who made the first overture? How long did it take for you to become tried-and-true friends?
3. Why do you think friendship seems to be less important once work and family responsibilities, such as taking care of young children, or even aging, dependent older parents, take up so much time?

Chapter 5: Healing Friends

1. What is your definition of a healing friend?
2. Have you ever had a healing friend? If yes, how did it start? Is it still ongoing? If it ended, what caused it to end?
3. Why do healing friends have such a high status in our lives and even in our society?
4. Name one of the traits you think is the most important one in a healing friendship. Why is that trait so pivotal?
5. If someone never had exposure to positive, nurturing, or healing friendships in his or her childhood, teen, or adult years, is it still possible to find, and cultivate, such a friendship? If yes, how would someone go about doing that?

Chapter 6: Frenemies and Fatal Friends

1. Why do you think people are so reluctant to admit that they have a *frenemy* or that they have been a *frenemy*, or a negative friend, to someone?
2. If your friend befriended someone that you thought might be what is referred to as a frenemy or a "fatal friend," what would you do about it?
3. Have you ever had a frenemy? What did you do about it?
4. Are frenemies ever salvageable or is it always a relationship to avoid or remove yourself from?
5. Fatal friends refers to those who cause their friend's death. But it also refers to friends who heroically lose their life while saving their friend's life. In addition to the examples shared in

Friendgevity, what examples from the news can you find that are examples of that?

Chapter 7: Dealing with Friendship Conflicts

1. Of all the suggestions about how to deal with friendship conflicts in Chapter 7, which one have you used in the past and did it work?
2. Do you think conflict in friendship is natural and normal? Why? Why not?
3. Is there a friend that you had a falling out with that you would like to reconnect with? If yes, what is stopping you from reaching out?
4. Consider your childhood experiences and how what happened to you as a child, including how your siblings treated you, or your very first friendship, was it positive or negative, and how those experiences may be helping or hindering your current friendship or attitudes about friendship.
5. What are some of the ways to break free from previous negative friendships or attitudes about friendship from your childhood socialization or previous friendships during your teen or adult years?

Chapter 8: 14 Tough Friendship Situations and How to Deal With Each One

1. What is the toughest friendship situation you ever found yourself in? How did you deal with it?
2. Pick one of the fourteen friendship situations and discuss a situation from either your life or someone close to you and how they handled it.
3. Why does it help to read about tough friendship situations, and possible situations, even if that circumstance has not yet happened to you?

Chapter 9: Making Meaningful Connections at Work and in Business

1. Do you think it is possible, or wise, to be friends with your boss? Why? Why not?
2. If you started out at the same level with someone, you became

friends, and then you got promoted, how do you think that would impact on your friendship at work and outside of work, or would it?

3. How important are friends in the workplace or in your business?
4. Is it opportunist to expect a friend to help you out if you are job hunting or looking to get ahead, or is that what friends do for each other? When is it appropriate and acceptable and when is it not just an imposition on the friendship but even an ethical breach?

Chapter 10: Coping with Illness, Dying, Death, and Grief

1. What would you do if a lifelong long distance friend cuts you out of her life because she has cancer and prefers to spend whatever time she has left with just her husband and the nearby friends she has made in the last decade?
2. If someone close to you is ill or dies and your friend does not come to the funeral, or memorial service, if there is one, can you ever forgive your friend? Why? Why not?
3. Where should someone turn to if their friend has died and they are having a hard time coping with their day-to-day responsibilities because of their overwhelming grief?

Chapter 11: Conclusion

1. Do you have any global friends? If yes, how do you deal with any differences in values or culture because of your different residences? If not, why might you benefit from reaching out to one or more friends around the world?
2. What is your #1 take away from *Friendgevity*?
3. Do you think friendship is overrated? Why? Why not?
4. Is it possible to have friends, a romantic partner, a job, a great relationship with your children, if you have children, or even with your pet, or must you choose which relationship you will invest most of your time in? Explain your answer.

Appendix I – Friendship Over the Life Cycle

1. How early can a boy or girl start a friendship?
2. What are some of the skills that children learn that can be applied

to friendship even before a genuine friendship has formed?

3. Why is it so important for children to get together with other children even if they have a big family with lots of siblings and cousins?

4. What are the biggest life changes that can take a toll on friendship? What can you do to minimize the negative impact of those *friendshifts*?

Acknowledgments

There are so many people to thank for making *Friendgevity* possible. First and foremost are all the men and women, and teens, who shared with me about their friendships through interviews or surveys. I especially want to thank everyone who I interviewed or corresponded with whose quotes are in *Friendgevity*. But whether someone is named or anonymous in the book, I appreciate every single person who took the time to share with me about friendship.

Second, I want to thank my two sons, Scott and Jeffrey, Scott's wife Lindsay, my husband Fred, and even my grandson Bradley, who cheered me on throughout the years that it took to research and write this new book. Thanks also to Jeff's significant other, Justyna, her son Aidan, and a shout out to my grandson Brock who already has many friends. My best friend, Joyce Guy Patton, has been there for me, as usual, even letting me interview her about friendship just a few weeks after her beloved husband of 45 years, David Patton, had passed away. Our 50-year friendship has only grown in importance to me over the years; Joyce has never let me down and I hope she would say the same thing about me.

I have other close friends who are near and dear to me: Robyn Fuchs Goldstein, Mary Tierney, Gail Tuchman, Sharon Fisher, Marcia Hoffenberg, Jennifer Ash, and Judy Copeland. There are also many friends who might not be my closest or best friends, but they are friends who are near and dear to me, namely Nona Aguilar, Betsy Turner, Elia Schneider, Ginny Mugavero, Nance L. Schick, Monica Meehan, Adrianna Navarro, Joseph Novoa, Paula Fins, Pramila Poddar, Ed and Candy Craven, Dara Tyson, Jane Ubell-Meyer, Abra Wilkin, Linda Marsa, Elizabeth Loving, Linda Chiarelli, Russell Bernstein, Joyce Nova, Eileen Clancy, Esther Kreider-Verhalle, Shawn Post, Eileen Clancy, Linda Larsen, Aruna Gracias Rathod, Linda Swindling, Stacie Goosman and so many others. (If I left out anyone, I hope you will "cut me some slack" and forgive me for that oversight!)

I am also blessed that I consider many extended family members to be my friends, especially my sister, Eileen B. Hoffman, who is an amazing person in addition to being my sister. I am so fortunate to have such a wonderful sister, through thick and thin. Also, my sisters-in-law Karen Lobovits and Becky Shadeed; my mother-in-law Mary Yager; cousins Stu

Silver, Phyllis Henkel, Holly Cosby, Suzanne Posner, Leila Posner, Carol Ann Finkelstein Shoretz, "Happy" Klein, and Daryl Shulman, and their families; my niece Vanessa Hoffman and her husband Dave, nephew Sky Lobovits, his girlfriend Kerry; my great niece Coral Lobovitz; my nephew Ariel Lobovits and his wife Trish and their children, Lilly and Seth; and so many others including more nephews, nieces, and cousins. Even though they have passed away, I still want to thank my parents and my brother. I miss them very much but their spirits are still with me along with many positive memories: the late Gladys Barkas, William Barkas, D.D.S., and my brother, Seth Alan Barkas.

Richard Quinney, professor emeritus, Northern Illinois University, has been a mentor to me since we first communicated when my book, *Victims*, was published by Scribner's back in 1978. I am extremely fortunate that over the years Dr. Quinney and I have become friends as well as mentor and mentee. Other colleagues who have been especially supportive over the years are Robert Garot, Jayne Mooney, Vicky Cannon, Greg Snyder, Jacob Felson, Sheetal Ranjan, Vince Parillo, Marcus Aldredge, Julia Nevarez, Mike Brown, Duffy Spencer, Dan Perlman, J. Barry Gurdin, Rebecca Adams, David Friedrichs, Henry Pontell, Robert Garot, Alisa Thomas, Theresa Rockett, David Green, Carla Bellamy, Steve Glazer, Jacob Felson, Amy Adamczyk, Andrea Siegel, Laurence J. Stybel, Jane Pollak, Steve Duck, Nella Barkley, and the late Jeffrey Zaslow, James M. Shuart, Bill Daniels, Albert Ellis, among others. Thanks to the staff members at colleges where I teach including Alisa Thomas, Theresa Rockett, Francine Troisi, Keisha Griffin, and Ruth Tekle. I also want to thank all my students over the years, undergraduate and graduate, as well as attendees at my workshops and seminars.

I am appreciative of SurveyMonkey, an online site that I subscribe to that enables me to send surveys through the Internet and also compiles statistics according to certain characteristics, including gender, age, income level, and other variables. I have used SurveyMonkey to analyze the results of surveys I created and distributed to a snowball sample, and I have also used the SurveyMonkey Audience program, which allowed me to buy anonymous respondents from throughout the United States and from the United Kingdom and Australia. (More recently, Survey Monkey Audience has added other countries that you can purchase respondents from, such as India.)

Selected cartoons by the talented Cathy Wilcox were provided by Finch Books, who originally commissioned a series of cartoons, one per chapter, from this renowned Australian cartoonist for the Australian edition of *When Friendship Hurts*. Hannacroix Creek Books, Inc. purchased the rights to those cartoons. (Her website is located at https://www.cathywilcox.com.au/)

Thanks to Andres Alvez, who did the original artwork showing two women communicating via videoconferencing because of the COVID-19 pandemic. I also want to thank Nancy Batra, who designed the cover for Friendgevity as well as the art in the Appendix in the Friendship Over the Life Cycle section. It was reprinted from the 365 Daily Affirmations for Healthy and Nurturing Relationships which had many additional line drawings by Nancy in that book. (Lindsay Arber did the narration for the audiobook version.)

I want to thank the Opinion Research Corporation, and Janet Ulrich, formerly Vice President of CARAVAN® Services, which conducted several randomly selected telephone surveys for me on various topics over the years, including my 2007 survey of 1,009 men and women on friendship.

Thanks to the for-credit interns for Hannacroix Creek Books, Inc. who read and provided feedback on *Friendgevity*: Ashley Hazan, Iyana Baskerville, Emily Flint, Rebecca Justiniano, Jillian Zieger, and Carson Bailey.

Reading Group Guide

FRIENDGEVITY
Making and Keeping the Friends
Who Enhance and Even Extend Your Life
Jan Yager, Ph.D.
Author, *When Friendship Hurts* and *Friendshifts*

Friendgevity
Making and Keeping the Friends Who Enhance and Even Extend Your Life
by Dr. Jan Yager

1.   Here are some questions posed by the author that you might find useful in your book club discussions of *Friendgevity*:

2.   What does the title, *Friendgevity*, mean?

3.   Why is it important to look at how social media is impacting our friendships, whether we are personally online or not?

4.   What key research findings does Dr. Yager point to that confirm that friendship is tied to longevity?

5.   Frequent arguments with a friend—or with a spouse or child, for that matter—can shorten your life. If you or someone you care about is prone to recurrent fights, what can be done about it? Name at least three ways that you might improve this tendency.

6.   Dr. Yager has rules for fighting fair. What are three of those rules? Do you have any additional rules of your own to contribute?

7.   Let's share about our current close or best friends. How did you meet? What was it about your friend that made you want to start a relationship? Is there anything about your friend you find annoying? If there is, how do you deal with it?

8.   Have you ever had a friendship end? If you wish it hadn't ended, what are some of the suggestions that Dr. Yager offers in *Friendgevity* that you might have applied to that friendship to try

to salvage it? Would you consider trying to reconnect with this former friend? Why? Why not?

9. How are online friendships the same or different from friendships you developed or maintain off the Internet? Are there any pluses to online friendships? What are some of the minuses, if any? How can you work around any of those negatives?

10. What is your favorite chapter in *Friendgevity*? Why? Share with the group about what you learned in that chapter, including any anecdotes or examples that you want to point out to the rest of us.

11. As discussed in Chapter 7, Tom and Jared had a crisis in their friendship. What was it? Do you have any suggestions for how they could have handled things so the situation went differently? But they got their friendship back on track, and Tom thinks it's even stronger because of the conflict that they overcame. Has that ever happened to you with one of your friendships? Please share about that. If you tend to end friendships because of conflict, do you think Tom and Jared's example can help you try to deal more effectively with conflict in your own friendships?

12. In the Bibliography section of *Friendgevity*, Dr. Yager shares the top 10 movies about friendship that her snowball international sample of 178 men and women revealed to her. How many of those movies have you seen? Which one is your favorite? If your favorite movie about friendship is not listed, please share what your choice would be and why?

13. Reread the suggestions for each of the seven days of Dr. Yager's annual International New Friends, Old Friends Week. Will you celebrate the week this year? If you do, will you try to follow Dr. Yager's suggestions for every day, addressing a unique friendship issue and using the week to reconnect with your old and new friends?

14. What is a healing friend?

15. What is a frenemy?

16. What is a fatal friend?

Reading Group Activity

Turn to the part of the book where Dr Yager shares the "How Well Do You Know Your Friend?" quiz. If you are friends with anyone in your book club, partner up now. Then take the next 5 minutes to answer as many questions as you can about each other. At the end of 5 minutes, let's share about what you knew about each other and how many questions you now need your friend to help you answer. Isn't this fun! Try it out with one or more of your other friends, in the book club or outside of it. You may be amazed at how much, or how little, you know about your closest or best friends! The good news is that you can learn about them, and they can learn about you. All it takes is time, interest, and asking the right questions and listening to your friend's answers, as she or he listens when you share.

A Note About *Friendgevity: Making and Keeping the Friends Who Enhance and Even Extend Your Life*

This book has been more than a decade in the making. But way back in 2002, almost twenty years ago, I already knew that the Internet was having an impact on our friendships and included a section on Internet friendships in *When Friendship Hurts*, my second major popular prescriptive book on friendship. "Internet friendships" is what they were called back then. Now we call them "online friendships" or, as I call them, Facebook friends (FBFs) or SMFs (Social media friends), because they are friendships that we develop or maintain through Facebook or other social media including Twitter, LinkedIn, Pinterest, Instagram, and other sites.

Scientific research has proven that friendship can extend your life. I wanted to get the word out about that. I share the cutting-edge research from neuroscientists, psychologists, epidemiologists, and sociologists which shows that friendship can not only extend your life but can delay the onset of dementia.

It's also important to emphasize that loneliness kills and loneliness usually means lacking friends. Fortunately, loneliness, and lacking friends, are preventable conditions. *Friendgevity* helps dispute the myth that it's harder to make friends as you get older. Seventy-three-year-old Lynn Rosenberg and her new best friend, Pam Lane, whom she met only nine months ago, are just two of the many examples of older women and men making friends—and strong, positive, close and best ones or, as I say in *Friendgevity*, healing friends.

Thank you for reading *Friendgevity* and for discussing it in your book club! I welcome hearing from you about *Friendgevity*, and encourage you to share not just your reaction to the book but your own friendship stories as well: the good, the bad, and the ugly, as they say, and, most of all, the wonderful! Happy reading and discussing! Dr. Jan Yager https://www.drjanyager.com

https://www.whenfriendshiphurts.com
e-mail: jyager@aol.com

About the Author

Jan Yager, Ph.D. is a sociologist and a friendship, relationship, and business coach, workshop leader, and author who has been studying friendship for decades. Her award-winning books, translated into 33 languages, include *Friendshifts; When Friendship Hurts; Who's That Sitting at My Desk?, 365 Daily Affirmations for Healthy and Nurturing Relationships; Friendship Thoughts, Famous Quotes, and a Journal;* and others. She has been interviewed on the *Today Show, Good Morning America, CBS This Morning,* and NPR. For more on the author, visit

https://www.drjanyager.com

or

https://www.whenfriendshiphurts.com

Index

About the Author

Dr. Jan Yager has been researching, speaking, writing, and coaching about friendship for several decades including her acclaimed book, Single in America, her sociology dissertation for her Ph.D. at the Graduate Center of the City University of New York (1983), and her follow-up books including a scholarly book on the topic, *Friendship: A Selected, Annotated Bibliography*, and such popular books as *Friendshifts*; *When Friendship Hurts*; and *Who's That Sitting at My Desk? Workship, Friendship, or Foe?*; and *365 Daily Affirmations for Friendship*. Dr. Yager's books have been translated into 33 languages, with two more languages in preparation.

The author has taught at the college level since her mid-twenties, including, since August 2014, as an Adjunct Assistant Professor at John Jay College of Criminal Justice, part of City University of New York (CUNY), in New York City, among other colleges and universities.

In addition to her Ph.D. in sociology, Dr. Yager has an M.A. in criminal justice from the Goddard College Graduate Program and she did a year of graduate work in art therapy at Hahnemann Medical College.

For more on Dr. Yager's background and credentials, including clips from some of her major TV appearances, such as the *Today Show, Oprah,* and *Good Morning America*, go to https://www.drjanyager.com and https://whenfriendshiphurts.com.

For speaking engagements, contact your favorite speaker bureau or the author directly at jyager@aol.com.

Confidential Dr. Jan Yager Friendship Survey URLs

If you would like to complete the author's comprehensive confidential friendship survey, here is the URL/link to that questionnaire:

https://www.surveymonkey.com/r/3JR63JG

If you want to complete the author's shorter 12-question confidential friendship survey, focused on friendship and social media, here is the link to that survey:

https://www.surveymonkey.com/r/3TJRHD2

FYI: You are able to keep either of these confidential surveys completely anonymous or you may provide your contact e-mail information for possible follow-up. Please note that if you do provide your contact information, it will not be shared.

Other Friendship or Relationship Books or Journals by Dr. Jan Yager That You Might Find of Interest

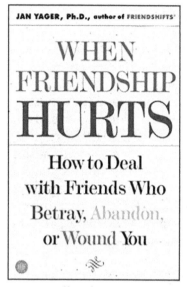

When Friendship Hurts
(Simon & Schuster, U.S. and Canada—Hannacroix Creek Books, Inc., all other countries)
In 29 translations
Available in e-book, print, and audiobook versions

We have all had friendships that have gone bad. Whether it takes the form of a simple yet painful and even inexplicable estrangement or a devastating betrayal, a failed friendship can make your life miserable, threaten your success at work or school, and even undermine your romantic relationships.

Finally, there is help. *When Friendship Hurts* explores what causes friendships to falter and explains how to mend them—or end them. In this straightforward, illuminating book filled with dozens of quizzes and real-life examples, Yager covers all the bases, including:

- The 21 types of potentially negative
- Identifying damaging friends and how to find ideal ones
- The email effect - how it is changing friendships
- The potential complications of friendship at work
- How to stop obsessing about a failed friendship
- and much more

Reviews:

"This valuable book will be a rescuer to all readers struggling to deal with an ailing friendship."

—*Publishers Weekly*

Featured in *The New York Times, Good Morning America.*

The Power of Friendship
and How It Shapes Our Lives

2nd edition/e-book version
(with new cover, introduction,
bibliography, resources,
and Appendix)

Jan Yager, Ph.D.

Friendship coach and author of
When Friendship Hurts

Friendshifts:
The Power of Friendship and How It
Shapes Our Lives
Hannacroix Creek Books, Inc.
Available in e-book, print, and audiobook
versions

Based on the author's doctoral thesis and additional surveys and interviews. "Friendshifts" is a word Dr. Yager coined to denote how sometimes our friendships may shift throughout our lives, and even how we define a friend. Fortunately, in some instances, lifelong friendship does happen. FRIENDSHIFTS explores what you can do to help a friendship to last. Even with the most enduring friendships, there may be an ending because of death, The examples, anecdotes, quotes, and studies cited throughout *Friendshifts* reinforce that the right friends will help you to get ahead or to be happy, and the wrong friends can sabotage you or even get you hurt or killed.

> "Yager ably demonstrates how friends can improve the quality of our lives, enhance our self-esteem, provide encouragement, and compensate for family defects."
>
> *—Library Journal*

> "Rewarding, sensible self-help manual for making, keeping and improving friendships sociologist Yager's how-to takes its title from a word she coined, which refers to the way friendships change as we move through life's stages...."
>
> *—Publishers Weekly*

Featured on *The View, Oprah, Today Show, Sunday Morning,* etc.

365 Daily Affirmations for Friendship
Hannacroix Creek Books, Inc.
Available in e-book, print, and audiobook versions

Friendship coach, expert, and sociologist Dr. Jan Yager shares positive and upbeat statements about friendship as well as a selection of famous quotes on this key relationship topic. The introduction covers the value of friendship, the key ingredients to a great friendship, identifying when a friendship needs help, making friends in your adult years, how can you tell if you're a good friend yourself, a list of ten friends that everyone needs, and ten truths about friendship to make it easier to find, keep, and grow our friendships. Part 1 covers 365 affirmations. Part 2 includes Activities to improve friendship in your personal life as well as at work or in business. The book ends with a bibliography and resources related to friendship.

Sample affirmations:

#1 "I am worthy of a positive friendship."
#18 "Everyday, there are potential new friends with whom I might meet and connect. The world is full of friendship possibilities."
#123 "I 'agree to disagree' with my friends."
#249 "I am open and honest while still being tactful."

Friendship Thoughts, Famous Quotes, and a Journal
Available as a hardcover or trade paperback edition

A unique 176-page friendship journal that includes an introduction about friendship and journal keeping by friendship coach and sociologist Jan Yager, Ph.D., followed by 140 quotes on friendship written by philosophers, essayists, poets, playwrights, celebrities, psychologists, sociologists, authors, and leaders that she's been gathering for decades. Each quote is reprinted at the top of a blank lined page where you can journal. After the quotes/lined blank pages, there are 4 more pages to add your own or other friendship quotes plus 2 blank pages for drawings or photos. There are even excerpts follow from several of Dr. Yager's books on friendship and work relationships including the seven top ways to make time for your friends. This journal also has a contact directory to fill in as well as Resources for online friendship sites and a Bibliography. Use this friendship journal for yourself or give it to a friend..

Sample Friendship Thoughts/Quotes:

"There is a curious fact about friendship that we have always known but rarely acknowledge. By understanding others, we also come closer to understanding ourselves."

—Bradley Trevor Greive, *Friends to the End*

"In research at our clinic, my colleagues and I have discovered that friendship is the springboard to the other important relationships of life."

—psychotherapist Alan Loy McGinnis, *The Friendship Factor*

"I had three chairs in my house, one for solitude, two for friendship, three for society."

—Henry David Thoreau, *Walden* (1854)

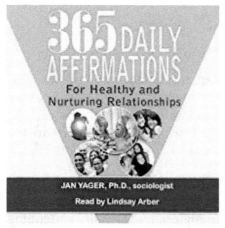

365 Daily Affirmations for Healthy and Nurturing Relationships

Available in e-book, print, and audiobook versions, narrated by Lindsay Arber

In this unique affirmation books, there are 365 positive statements related to key relationships including parent-child, sibling, extended family, friend, romantic partner, neighbors, co-workers, or service providers. Includes an introduction by relationship and business coach and author/sociologist, Dr. Jan Yager as well as activities in the back of the book on how to improve your relationships at work and in your personal life. The print and e-book version are illustrated with original line drawings by illustrator Nancy Batra.

Sample affirmations:

Friendship affirmations
#226 "I am a devoted friend."
#246 "I deal with our conflicts."

Neighbor affirmations
#162 "I am learning my neighbor's names."
#166 "I am friendly with my neighbors without having to be their friends unless I want to be."

Parent-child affirmations
#10 "I am respecting my child's uniqueness."
#16 "I am sharing a meal or taking a trip with my child."

Between Friends
A Play in Three Acts
(forthcoming)

This unproduced play covers a ten-year span and delves into the way that friendships are made and tested by the main character and several of her best friends. When the play begins, they are in their early thirties.

Out of 103 submissions, "Between Friends" was a finalist in the New American Playwrights Project (NAPP) that is part of the Utah Shakespeare Festival.

Jan Yager is a member of the Dramatists Guild. For seven years, she was a theatre critic for *Back Stage* newspaper. Jan studied acting at the American Academy of Dramatic Arts in high school as well as attending the Gene Frankel Theatre Workshop for six months. She also studied mime with Paul Curtis.

> *Please send an e-mail to jyager@aol.com if you would like to be notified when this play is available for sale (or sign up for the mailing list at https://www.drjanyager.com and you will be added to the mailing list to be notified of upcoming new books, blogs, articles, seminars, or webinars by Dr. Yager.*

Productive Relationships:
57 Strategies for Building Stronger Business Connections
Hannacroix Creek Books, Inc.
Translated into Portuguese, Spanish, Vietnamese, Russian, and Czech
Available as an e-book, print, or audiobook

Productive Relationships is a practical guide to developing productive business relationships to hasten your success, whether you work for a major corporation, or are a self-employed entrepreneur or freelancer. Dr. Yager covers everything from dealing with workplace bullies as well as negative and positive types you may encounter at work and how to cope with each one, workplace violence, and using social media effectively for more productive relationships.

Sociologist and business coach Yager did extensive original research throughout the United States and internationally. Over the years, her bosses have included legendary publisher Barney Rosset, Norman Mailer, academic chairs, and many executives.

Business Protocol
How to Survive & Succeed in Business
(The first edition was published by John Wiley & Sons)
Third edition
Narrated by Sandy Orkin
Business Protocol has been translated into Spanish, Russian, Vietnamese, and Chinese.
Also available as a print book
An award-winning book on how to use business etiquette as a strategy for success by international speaker Jan Yager who is also a sociologist and workplace consultant. Here she explains her six business protocol principles developed from an extensive survey of more than 200 human resource professionals. Business Protocol also covers image, gift-giving, ethics, international etiquette and communication skills. Chosen as a main selection of the Executive Book Club.

Grow Global
Using International Protocol to Expand Your Business Worldwide
Hannacroix Creek Books, Inc.
Available as an audiobook, print, or e-book

A practical guide to more effectively doing business globally whether you work for a corporation or are a self-employed entrepreneur or consultant, and whether you do your global outreach by traveling to distant places, over the phone, or just over the Internet. Based on extensive original research, sociologist, business and relationship consultant, coach, and speaker Dr. Jan Yager covers the 15 international protocol concerns that readers need to be aware of as well as tips on foreign business travel, making your website more global, faux pas to avoid, negotiating styles, contracts and getting paid, gift-giving, legal considerations, and ethics. There is a chapter that provides a country by country etiquette guide and another chapter on how to build a global relationship so that the business will follow.

What They Are Saying About *Grow Global*:

"Making a deal happen through business protocol is more important than ever. This very helpful book is a guide for all willing to go global."

—Kanak kr Jain, CEO, Suskan Consultants
Private Ltd, Kolkata, India

WHO'S THAT SITTING AT MY DESK?

How to succeed by mastering work relationships

Jan Yager

"This book shows you how to work well with others to supercharge your career."
—Brian Tracy, best-selling author and speaker

Who's That Sitting at My Desk?
Workship, Friendship, or Foe?
Hannacroix Creek Books, Inc.
Available as an e-book, print, or audiobook

Building on two decades of original research into workplace issues and friendship patterns, sociologist and consultant Dr. Jan Yager offers insights into how to succeed by mastering workplace relationships. Based on an international survey of 400 men and women and over 100 interviews, Yager discovered a relationship unique to the workplace and business. Dr. Yager calls it a workship - more connected than an acquaintance but not as intimate as a friendship. However, workships, especially positive ones, help work to be more productive and more fun and are the "safest" and least complicated connections at work and in business.

What They Are Saying About *Who's That Sitting At My Desk?*:

"An informative, well-written, and entertaining commentary on social relationships in the contemporary world of work,"

—Jay Weinstein, Ph.D., Professor of Sociology

"An invaluable guide for maintaining your workplace relationships in a genuinely rewarding and balanced manner. Bravo!"

—Nella Barkley, President, Crystal-Barkley Corporation

"A much-needed book about an important subject that is often discussed but rarely understood."

—Mark Sanborn, President, Sanborn & Associates, Inc.

So, What's Your Favorite Color?
A Journal of Memories
Hannacroix Creek Books, Inc.

A journal filled with lots of questions that you might want to ask your friends and your family members so you can have a permanent record of their answers. Questions such as "Dad, what's your favorite color?" or "Mom, what was your favorite book when you were growing up?" or "Sis, what's your favorite childhood memory?" In this journal, you will find a place to write down answers from one or more of your friends to share with you, through an interview or by writing down their answers, about their favorite movie, book, what their three wishes would be, and lots more.

Recipients of the journal can share their answers with you, over the phone, in person, through videoconferencing, or via e-mail, or, if they prefer, they can write in the journal on their own.

In the back of the journal is a place to include selected pictures about all the people who are important to you who will become part of this legacy journal.

Birthday Tracker and Journal
Hannacroix Creek Books, Inc.
Available in hardcover or paperback formats

This a special place to record important birthdays for family, friends, and others, month by month. It includes an informative introduction on birthday celebration traditions and lists birthday birthstones and flowers by month for gift-giving considerations. There is also a place to keep track of birthday cards or presents that you send, or receive, lined blank pages for your birthday reflections, and a place for birthday photos.

Color illustrations by author/artist Jan Yager appear throughout. This unique book is a perfect gift or for one's own use to organize this special birthday (and even anniversary or other special occasion!) information.

CPSIA information can be obtained
at www.ICGtesting.com
Printed in the USA
BVHW041259081221
623555BV00013B/383